Words of Praise for Diary of a Psychic

"I love Sonia Choquette. She's a beautiful, sweet soul
with a Divine connection. Her book **Diary of a Psychic**
shows how you, too, can connect with your own
psychic abilities. In my world, Sonia is tops!"
— **Louise L. Hay,** best-selling author of *You Can Heal Your Life*

"Sonia Choquette is the most authentic person in psychic phenomena
I have ever encountered. Her readings are incredibly accurate."
— **Dr. Wayne W. Dyer,** best-selling author of
10 Secrets for Success and Inner Peace

"It is a pleasure to endorse the work of Sonia Choquette.
She is a highly talented psychic with a gift for
helping people understand their life path."
— **Caroline M. Myss,** best-selling author of *Sacred Contracts*

"Sonia is the unfettered heart, a gifted seer who offers the spiritual
truths like so many apples from the tree. She opened up doors
for me that were nailed shut, and I encourage anyone who
seeks to open their heart to her special brand of sunshine."
— **Billy Corgan,** singer, songwriter, and founder of
the Smashing Pumpkins and Zwan

"Sonia Choquette deserves the old-fashioned term 'oracle.'
She is both a seer and a guide. She not only illuminates
the path but the obstacles that may bar our progress.
Her help is invaluable and deeply grounded."
— **Julia Cameron,** best-selling author of *The Artist's Way*

DIARY OF A
PSYCHIC

Also by Sonia Choquette

Ask Your Guides

The Psychic Pathway

The Psychic Pathway to New Beginnings

The Psychic Pathway to Joy

True Balance

Trust Your Vibes

Trust Your Vibes at Work

The Wise Child

Your Heart's Desire

DIARY OF A
PSYCHIC

SHATTERING
THE MYTHS

SONIA CHOQUETTE

HAY HOUSE, INC.
Carlsbad, California
London • Sydney • Johannesburg
Vancouver • Hong Kong • New Delhi

Published and distributed in the United States by: Hay House, Inc.: www.hayhouse.com
• **Published and distributed in Australia by:** Hay House Australia Pty. Ltd.: www.hay
house.com.au • **Published and distributed in the United Kingdom by:** Hay House UK,
Ltd.: www.hayhouse.co.uk • **Published and distributed in the Republic of South Africa
by:** Hay House SA (Pty), Ltd.: orders@psdprom.co.za • **Distributed in Canada by: Raincoast:** www.raincoast.com • **Published in India by:** Hay House Publications (India) Pvt.
Ltd.: www.hayhouseindia.co.in • **Distributed in India by:** Media Star: booksdivision@
mediastar.co.in

Editorial supervision: Jill Kramer   *Design:* Tricia Breidenthal

Library of Congress Cataloging-in-Publication Data

Choquette, Sonia.
  Diary of a psychic : shattering the myths / Sonia Choquette.
    p. cm.
ISBN 1-4019-0192-1 (tradepaper)
        1. Choquette, Sonia. 2. Psychics—Colorado—Biography. I. Title.
      BF1027.C48A3 2003
      133.8'092—dc21

                2002152323

              ISBN 13: 978-1-4019-0192-9
              ISBN 10: 1-4019-0192-1

            09 08 07 06   8 7 6 5
              1st printing, July 2003
              5th printing, May 2006

    Printed in the United States of America

This book is dedicated to my daughters, Sonia and Sabrina. Thank you for the gift of your delightful spirits; your wise insights; your endless sense of humor; your honesty; and your profoundly generous, forgiving, and loving hearts. It is my greatest joy to be your mother and to witness your psychic voices as they emerge into the world. You are my light.

And to my mother, who taught me to see what is true in life, I shall be forever grateful for the gifts you have given me.

Contents

Every story in this diary is true, but most names have been changed to protect the privacy of those concerned.

Preface

When I was in the sixth grade, my family lived in Denver, Colorado, and it was a time of great change for us. Our neighbor, Dorothy, had a stroke and went to the hospital. My grandfather, Albert, who lived upstairs, had a gallbladder attack and fell down in his apartment. My oldest sister, Cuky, finished college, got a job as a flight attendant, and moved to Kansas City. My older brother, Stefan, moved into his own apartment and left for school in Golden, Colorado.

My mother became very moody and emotional with all these changes, and my father seemed to be around less and less, as he worked seven days a week at Montgomery Ward. The atmosphere in our home was tense and dark. Most of the time I was afraid. I wasn't sure of what. Life just felt so heavy and sad.

I don't know if my brothers and sisters felt the same. If they did, they certainly didn't let on. My mother spent a lot of time in the basement where she had a photography studio and darkroom that my father had built for her. She was either developing or hand-coloring photos, sometimes selling them to clients, sometimes giving them away. Either way, she was mostly in her own world.

Not being able to name the source of my unease and anxiety, I was on psychic high alert. It was as if I were patrolling the borders, watching out for enemy invaders—which meant, ultimately, anything that made my mom upset. More and more she was prone to spontaneous outbursts of sorrow, and the slightest upset elicited a huge dramatic reaction. She was troubled and miserable, and felt raw and fragile. I was terrified by her and for her and only wanted to do everything in my power to cheer her up.

I quickly learned that the best way to do this was to talk to her about my "vibes" and tell her I was psychic, just like she was. This seemed to be genuinely uplifting to her. Because her world was so completely involved with psychic matters, having me follow in her footsteps gave her a friend and confidante.

We witnessed each other's psychic experiences and acted as each other's sounding board. When my mother would try to tell my father or my brothers and sisters about her vibes or her psychic impressions, they'd roll their eyes or stare at her, not knowing how to respond. "Okay," they'd say, listening, but not knowing what to do. They didn't seem to notice that she dreamed about her own mother whom she hadn't seen since she was 12, but *I* was definitely aware. I could see how it made her happy; how it relieved her of a deep pain.

They didn't pay attention when my mother would stop us in the middle of a sentence and say, "Someone's in trouble. I feel it." I think it's because her vibes during this time were most often the bearers of bad news. A vibe from her meant trouble, so who needed it? But I was interested. I wanted to know and to be like her.

During this time, my mother also started doing psychic readings for people in our dining room after dinner. These people were mostly her friends, other women who got married during World War II and came over from Europe as she had.

There was Charlotte, her Austrian friend, who lived next door; Rita, a Mexican woman, who married another photographer; and Evelyn, my mom's best friend and my godmother—a Spanish woman from Barcelona who married a man named Fred, had five kids, and lived on the west side of Denver near the mountains.

All the while, my own psychic abilities continued to flourish. Every cell in my body became a psychic receptor, and I picked up on all sorts of things from everyone. Quite frankly, most of it was extremely uncomfortable.

One of the first people I distinctly remember tuning in to was Evelyn. Like my mother, she was extremely glamorous and exotic looking. She was taller than my mother at 5'5", slim with a large, black bouffant hairdo over milky white skin. She wore dark, heavy eyeliner, with green eye shadow up to the brow and pointed on the side—giving her a sleek, panther-like appearance. She had a dark mole on her left cheek and wore heavy, bright orange lipstick. She dressed in tight, leopard-print dresses, which she accessorized with thin stiletto heels with pointed toes.

Evelyn looked a lot like Sophia Loren, which complemented my mother's own exotic style. She had a peculiar, high-pitched, nasal voice, as if she had a clothespin on her nose, and spoke into the air rather than look you straight in the eye.

Fred, a somber, dark-faced man, was much taller than Evelyn and taller than anyone else I knew. Fred wore a beige overcoat and a hat over his balding head, and every time I saw him, he looked stern, impatient, and humorless.

They rarely visited our home together; Evelyn visited alone from time to time, but she and my mother mostly talked on the phone. When Evelyn did come by, she and my mom would disappear for hours into the dining room so my mom could read for her and they could talk.

The first thing I ever became psychically aware of was that Evelyn was desperately unhappy, even though she always put on a cheerful face in front of us.

Whenever she came over, I felt overwhelmed with fear and worry and thought that she was in trouble. She gave me bad vibes—not because she was a bad person, but because something bleak or bad was lurking around her. I was afraid she might bring it upon my mother, too. All I could do was worry and watch, while they sat in the dining room for hours with the door closed. Sometimes I quietly lay outside the "reading room," as the dining room was now referred to, hoping I could hear what was going on. I couldn't hear their voices, but I *could* "hear" their pain, and it frightened me.

The mood in the house continued to darken. My grandfather got worse, and on Christmas day we received a call that he had to be moved from the hospital to a nursing home. My dad and his family struggled over what to do next, and my mother was overcome with grief and despair. Each day was more tense and fragile than the next, and all I could do was ask my spirit guide, Rose, to help me, help *us,* and show me what to do to keep my mother from further sorrow.

One day I came home from school, and just as I walked through the front door, I was overwhelmed with nausea and the desire to pass out. I barely made it to the stairway, where I swooned from dizziness and a dark cloud of anxiety. I remember gasping for air as if I couldn't breathe. And all I could think of was Evelyn.

My mother rushed to the hallway and saw me. Frightened, she shook me and shouted, "What's the matter with you? What's going on?"

"I don't know," I said, feeling weak and confused. "I can't breathe." I laid down on the stairway and shut my eyes. Fifteen seconds later, it passed. I suddenly felt perfectly alert and back to normal, as if nothing had ever happened. I sat up and said, "I'm okay now. But I keep thinking of Evelyn."

"Evelyn? How strange!" she said, as confused as I was over what had just happened. "Go to the kitchen and get something to eat. You probably didn't have enough for lunch today."

My mother sounded impatient, which I came to learn was how she sounded when she was really afraid. I got up and headed toward the kitchen, certain that what had just happened had nothing to do with lunch. It had to do with Evelyn. It had to do with all my bad vibes about her and my fear. I prayed for my angels to come. I didn't know why, but I needed them.

Three hours later the phone rang, and after answering, my mother became nearly hysterical. It was Evelyn's daughter, Sharon. At exactly the same time that I had become sick, Evelyn had committed suicide by getting in her car in the garage and letting it run. She was dead.

That day was a turning point for me. Once Evelyn was gone, my mother became very depressed. There were too many losses in her life, too many awful experiences. With the loss of her family, the loss of her childhood, and now, the loss of her dearest friend, I knew I had to do something to help her.

I started coming home every day after school, half dreading what I'd find. I'd do a psychic reading for my mom, using a regular deck of playing cards, searching, praying, for things to tell her to cheer her up and catch her interest.

I'd listen for my vibes; I'd ask my guides to tell me anything that would keep her looking forward instead of backward to keep her attention and interest on the future, not the past. I knew with every cell of my being that if I didn't, if I couldn't, the dark cloud my mother had escaped from would suck her back in, just as it had sucked in Evelyn, and her fate would be the same.

My mother was in trouble. Her energy was like a frantic, turbulent ocean with no bottom and no anchor, with nothing to grab onto to find her ground. My father seemed a million miles away because he worked morning, noon, and night to pay the bills. My siblings were clearly consumed by their world. My older sister and brother were gone, and so was Grandma, and now Grandpa. My mother needed help, and my guide, Rose, told me that I came into her life to be that help.

With the help of the cards, my vibes, and Rose, day by day I began to see the future. At least enough to let my mother know there was a day to look forward to.

My four o'clock readings became a ritual. First we'd sit at the table with a cup of Constant Comment tea with sugar. Then I'd light a small, white votive candle. Next I'd ask my mother to shuffle the cards, cut them into three piles, and put them back together any way she wanted. Then I'd take the deck and randomly pull out cards one at a time and lay them down in intricate, whimsical patterns. I'd place a card on the table and gaze at it for a long time, wondering what it meant, what it was trying to tell me. I'd stare at the cards for a long and serious time, wondering what they meant, what they wanted to tell me. I wanted them to talk to me, to tell me how to heal my mother's heavy heart. I wanted them to give me information that would make her laugh, praying they would tell me how to navigate through this cloud hanging over our home, to give me clues to keep us going.

And to my utter relief and amazement, they did. They started to talk.

I followed them like a detective. I felt as if I were on a treasure hunt, and each card, or each cluster of cards, was another gem. Some clues were ridiculous. But to me, each was meaningful, and as long as it kept my mother going, that was all that mattered.

During these readings, I led and she followed. Although I was just a child, I felt as if I really wasn't one anymore. I was a scout. I knew in my heart that I was in charge. And although I had no idea what all this would lead to, I had to trust in, and simply forge into, the unknown.

The amazing thing was that my mother *did* follow, at least in the reading room. I remember some of our very first readings. In one, I laid out a card, the three of hearts. I stared at it and listened for direction. Sometimes I sat for many minutes before speaking, while my mom waited patiently.

"You will get some new shoes," the card told me. "They will be beautiful. A gift."

She listened, delighted at the news I shared with her. "Really?" she said, like a child hearing she'd won a prize.

"Yes."

"When?"

"Soon, very soon."

"Good. I'll write that down." And she did.

She wrote down everything I saw or heard in my readings, no matter how trivial.

We worked as a team. I wanted her to keep looking forward. She wanted me to keep looking inward. We both grew.

So did my abilities. Soon I went from seeing new shoes to hearing news from Romania and the family she'd lost, to knowing that my father would get a raise. She wrote down every word. And some of it actually began to happen.

Even though half the time I suspected I was just making everything up, I believed that it all mattered. And the great and profound thing that set the course of my entire future is that my mother also believed that what I saw mattered completely.

Inch by inch, day by day, detail by detail, I saw and heard and felt more from my tattered deck of cards. The cards were my grid, my template, my psychic point of reference. Through them I began to tap in to the other side.

xvi

Acknowledgments

I'd like to thank my parents, Sonia and Paul Choquette. You've shown me the wisdom of following my heart and listening to my spirit. You'll never know how much I love and appreciate you both.

To my husband, Patrick Tully—thank you for believing in me and supporting me even when it was difficult to do so. And for allowing me to go so far away and trust that I would return.

To my dear friend, Julia Cameron—thank you for acting as my midwife and catcher's mitt for this important work, and for safely guiding it into the world. I am eternally grateful for your interest, mastery, patience, and friendship.

To my older sister and best friend, Cuky—thank you for being my greatest champion and for always believing in me.

To my brother-in-law, Bud, who has always welcomed me into his heart and home, without questioning my psychic gifts.

To my dear friends and soul sisters, LuAnn Glatzmaier and Joan Smith—thank you for holding my hand, charting my course, advising me through life, and being my true soul supporters and friends throughout my journey. Without your direction, encouragement, guidance, and kinship, I'm certain I would have lost my way.

To my neighbor Sara Wilcox—thank you for walking with me every morning as I coaxed this book into the world. You were my sounding board and confidante, and with your help I found my voice.

To my freelance content editor, Linda Kahn—thank you for working so diligently on my behalf, shaping a mountain of papers into a readable manuscript while never once making me feel guilty.

To my freelance copy editor and new friend, Bruce Clorfene—thank you for your patience and mastery in polishing this very rough draft into a finished work . . . twice. I am deeply grateful for your generosity and affection throughout this process.

To Erica Clorfene Trojan—thank you for being the bridge across the water. Your spirit and enthusiasm gave me courage to share my heart when I was in doubt.

To Louise Hay, Reid Tracy, and Danny Levin at Hay House—thank you for believing in this project and taking it into the world without hesitation, and especially for providing it such a wonderful home. I am deeply grateful.

To Jill Kramer, Shannon Littrell, Christy Salinas, and all the behind-the-scenes support people at Hay House who work with such love and dedication to help raise the vibration of this planet—and especially for believing in the project, the most dear to my heart.

To David Smith, without whose help this project would not have happened.

To my teachers, Charlie Goodman and Dr. Trenton Tully, who continue to guide me from the other side—thank you for providing me the education and training I needed to fulfill my karma and purpose and my heart's desire to serve the world in this lifetime. You were an essential part of my path and at times my greatest source of love and comfort.

And a special prayer of gratitude to my guides Rose, The Three Bishops, Joseph, The Pleiadean Sisters, and Dot. Thank you for being my shining stars and helping me fulfill my mission. I love you all.

And most of all, to my clients—you have been my greatest teachers over the years. It has been a privilege to serve you, and I humbly thank and honor you all.

PART I

Natural Gifts

(1956–1969)

Chapter 1

A SPIRITED FAMILY

The emblem of my early childhood was our two-story, redbrick Victorian house near Fourth Avenue and Bannock Street on the west side of Denver very close to downtown. Solid and immovable, it had a large front porch ringed by four big lilac bushes. Our house contained my world: my Romanian-born mother and American-born French-Canadian father; my six brothers and sisters; my grandmother and grandfather on my father's side; and a house full of angels, spirit guides, and out-of-body helpers—some of whom stayed, and some of whom were just passing through from the other side.

My parents moved to Denver from Sioux City, Iowa—along with my grandparents, Albert and Antonia Choquette—nine years before I was born, eager to make a fresh start after World War II. They bought a house, which was originally designed as two separate apartments, and began a new life. My father, Paul, a very handsome man, was 21 when he married my mother in Dingolfing, Germany, where he'd been stationed in the Army as part of the American liberation after the war.

My mom had been a newly liberated prisoner of war (POW) when he met her, only 15 at the time and living with several other displaced persons who were all just trying to survive after the war's devastation. As destiny would have it, they met, fell in love, married, and soon after returned to America, expecting their first child.

My mother, Sonia, after whom I was named, was quite petite, only 5'1". She was the second to youngest in a family of ten children, born to a religious mother and a sophisticated, intellectual father who owned vineyards and cultivated grapes for wine. When she was 12, she and her family were forced to evacuate their home with an hour's notice to avoid clashes between the Germans and the Russians. In the chaos, she became separated from her family.

As night fell, so did the bombs, and she found herself among other terrified strangers in the middle of an air raid, forced to run for safety and hide in the fields near the Hungarian border. The next morning, German soldiers swept through the fields, flushing out all those who were hiding, my mother included, and declared them POWs. She, along with the others, was placed into a prison camp where she spent the next three years.

During the march to the camp, my mother said the prisoners were threatened with being shot if they said a single word to one another. So instead of speaking, my mother prayed, and in answer to her prayers, her psychic abilities opened up, born out of necessity and survival.

She told me on one of those very rare occasions when she was willing to speak about those painful and horrific years, "I prayed to Heaven, and Heaven answered. By the time we got to that camp, I heard my inner voice and discovered my spirit guides, and through their constant counsel and companionship, my inner voice kept me alive."

My mother's psychic voice became her lifeline to survival. She called her psychic gift—her inner voice—her "vibes," and she brought that gift with her to America, to our family and our home. During her imprisonment, my mother suffered many injuries, indignities, and illnesses, such as rheumatic fever and tuberculosis. She recovered, but not without scars. Her eardrums were permanently damaged, eventually robbing her of most of her hearing. By the time I was born, my mother could lip-read, but she was profoundly hard-of-hearing.

Ours was a strict Roman Catholic family, following the example of my father's parents, but my mother was raised Romanian Orthodox. In her spiritual tradition, church guidance and personal guidance were not in conflict—they were two sides of the same coin, so having personal contact with Heaven by means of psychic ability was considered natural, and spirit guides were even part of her religious practice. Therefore, even though I was raised in a Catholic environment and went to St. Joseph's Catholic

School from the first to the ninth grade, I never perceived any conflict between being psychic and being a good Catholic girl. Talking to Heaven and getting personal answers through my vibes, like my mom, was not only normal, it was expected.

My parents had seven children. The oldest was Cuky, named after the daughter of a German woman who had been extremely kind to my mother when she was newly freed from prison. The very next year Stefan was born, named after my mother's father. Cuky and Stefan made up the first phase of our family because there were no other children for the next six years.

After Cuky and Stefan came the rest of us, seven in a row, until the family was complete. The second phase started with Neil, two years older than I; then Bruce, a year older. Next came yours truly, Sonia, named after my mother (but nicknamed "Sam" by Stefan when I was five for no particular reason and called that by everyone except my teachers until I left home when I was 19). Then came Noelle, one year later; twins, who were born prematurely and died, and whom my mother never talked about; and finally the baby, Soraya, six years younger than I.

Most of my siblings spent their time and energy being American, doing their best to fit in. I, on the other hand, resonated most with my mother and was drawn to my roots, my Romanian background, the world she came from. I wanted so much to be like her.

Until they died, my grandparents lived on the second floor of our house, and their apartment consisted of the front two rooms of the second floor, a combined living room/bedroom with a big picture window overlooking the street, and a small kitchen. I remember them somewhat, but not nearly as well as I'd like. (In fact, one of my very first psychic experiences was about my grandmother. I recall coming home from kindergarten and entering the house only to feel a great sense of dread, of sadness, and worrying that something was terribly wrong. Even though there were no signs of trouble, I knew something wasn't quite right. That evening my grandmother had a stroke in the backyard.)

The first floor was laid out in a square, split down the middle with equal rooms on either side. On the right side of the house was our huge living room and double parlor with a rounded archway between, with the dining room just behind it separated by slatted folding doors from the parlor on one side and the kitchen in the back. On the left side was a large entryway and hall with a stairway leading to the second floor and a long corridor leading to the kitchen in the back. Just behind the kitchen was a back porch leading to the basement, where my father had built my mother (who was an artist, among other things) a photographic studio and darkroom where she spent many long and creative hours.

The second floor, except for my grandparents' rooms, was converted into bedrooms for all of us children. I shared a bedroom with Cuky from the time I was out of a crib until she went away to college when I was ten. Our bedroom was in the back right corner of the house, separated by an open archway from Neil and Bruce's bedroom. My room, the old kitchen, used to have linoleum walls, but when I was three or four, my parents covered the walls in beautiful, textured white wallpaper that looked like a field of flowers; and placed large, orange throw rugs on the floor to cover the linoleum. To the left of our bed, against the wall where the old kitchen sink used to be, was a large built-in closet that my dad made for us, with a two-foot space between the top of the closet and the ceiling.

Neil and Bruce shared their room with Noelle. They had twin oak bunk beds pushed against the far wall opposite the archway, and she had a very little kid's bed just around the door. If I positioned myself just so at the end of my bed, I could see her from my room.

Next to their room in the middle of the hallway was a very small room that belonged to Stefan. He didn't have to share it with anyone and was the only one of us with a door that locked. At first my parents' bedroom was downstairs in the dining room, but after my grandparents died, they moved upstairs and put Soraya and Noelle in what used to be Grandma's kitchen.

It was tight quarters, but we didn't mind. This was before the days when everyone talked about "personal space and boundaries," so we never dreamed of complaining.

My mother was an artist, seamstress, painter, and photographer, and my dad was a salesman who worked in the farm-equipment department at Montgomery Ward. He was also a master carpenter, electrician, painter, plumber, and all-purpose handyman. Between my mother's aesthetic requirements and creative impulses and my father's practical skills in implementing them, the two of them were constantly reinventing our decor. They worked as a team—wallpapering, carpeting, refinishing the basement, the kitchen, even the backyard—so we lived in a simple, but beautiful, ever-changing home.

My mother was also very glamorous. She wore her black hair in a French twist, exotic cat's-eye makeup, and sexy dresses with shoes that had stiletto heels and pointed toes. I thought she was the most beautiful woman in the world. Despite our limited means, my mother strove to create the best for all of us, and it showed in our home and in our clothes.

My mother sewed everything she wore, as well as beautiful outfits for all of us, which were hand-tailored, elegant, and made of fine fabrics and beautiful textures. She introduced us to beauty, sensuality, and sophistication that had no doubt been passed down from her own childhood. We all spent huge amounts of time in her sewing room, taking turns helping her, depending upon which one of us she was sewing for.

We lived in a changing neighborhood comprised of aging people and many Hispanics. The entire area was made up of large Victorian homes with little lawns, big porches, and no fences.

In the outside world, Nixon was President, and the Vietnam War was at its height, which bothered a lot of people, but not me. No one in our family was going to Vietnam, and Nixon had just normalized relations with Romania. My mother could now travel home, something prohibited up until then, so as far as I was concerned, he was a good President.

Also living in our home was a whole group of angels and spirit guides. Most were from Heaven, but some were dead relatives from Romania who spoke to Mom. They watched over us, protected us, helped us do our work, and sat with us when we were sick. Most important, they brought messages to my mom about her relatives back home because she had a very difficult time receiving news about them. They also made sure my mother knew whenever we were in trouble or did something rotten. Like extended family members without bodies, they camped out in every nook and cranny of our house, feeling quite at home while keeping an eye on us at all times.

The spirit guides mostly talked to my mother and were known to regularly interrupt any conversation we had with her, dropping in with sort of a psychic *hot-off-the-press* news flash about my dad being home late from work, a friend preparing to call, or some other vibe they were getting.

Normally, the spirits spoke as a group, and although I didn't know exactly how many there were, I knew there had to be a lot of them because they covered a lot of territory—from walking us home after school, to helping my father's sales at work, to showing us where we should drive in the mountains for the perfect picnic spot, to what to do for a sore throat in the middle of the night. All-purpose, multitalented, and practical helpers, they worked for us day and night. All we had to do was call on them and they were there.

My mother mostly referred to these out-of-body helpers as her "spirits," but there were some she knew on a first-name basis. For example, there was Michael, the family angel, gofer, and good sport, whom we summoned for everything from finding things to sitting by our beds when we had the croup and went to the hospital. Then there was Jolly Joe, the family clown, who popped in unexpectedly, usually when things were tense in our home, or whenever one of us was having a bad moment. He helped my mother develop a tremendous sense of humor in difficult times and emphasized the "when life gives you lemons, make lemonade" philosophy of life.

Then there was Henry, the large African chief, who sat at our door at night and was our version of a burglar alarm. A little later, there was my mom's mother after she passed, who kept my mother from missing her.

For me, having spirits run the house was perfectly natural, but sometimes I had to admit they were annoying and definitely cramped my style. They said *no* more than *yes,* and tattled on us to my mother whenever we were up to no good—so we never got away with anything. I remember the time when Bruce and I stole two sodas off the truck in front of Mr. Prays's grocery store right across the street from our house, sneaked into the alley, and chugged them so fast I thought I'd burst from all the warm carbonation. Burping all the way home, and feeling bloated with guilt, we were met by my mom at the door. She displayed an "I know who you are and I saw what you did" look and said sternly, "Do you have something to tell me, or shall I tell you what my spirits say? Here's your chance to confess before your father comes home!"

It was useless to try to get anything past her, because she *did know* everything we did. Those darn spirits were spying on us and reporting back to her no matter how hard we tried to outsmart them. The spirits were also extremely strict and made all the final decisions in our home.

I distinctly remember, for example, being five years old when my first best friend, Vickie, the brown-haired, blue-eyed girl I'd just met who lived only three blocks from us, asked me if I could sleep over at her house on Friday night. It was an exciting and novel proposition and something I really, *really* wanted to do.

I thought about it all week, preparing for the exact right moment to ask my mother, because not only were the spirits strict, but my parents were, too, and they kept all of us on a very short leash. I knew it would be a hard sell, but I was determined to try. Only I needed a plan.

I had Vickie come home with me every day after school that week just so my mother could see what a nice girl she was. I sang her praises at the top of my lungs at dinner and even got my mother to agree that she was the "nicest friend" I could ever have. I carefully laid the groundwork for Friday, deciding that it would be best if Vickie and I asked her together, convinced that my mother wouldn't have the heart to say no directly to Vickie's bright blue, pleading eyes.

Right after school at 12:45, we skipped home hand-in-hand, positive that our carefully laid-out plan would work. When we got to my house, still holding hands, we tiptoed right up to my mom, giggling with nervous anticipation. After a few moments of hemming and hawing, I posed the question: "Could I sleep over at Vickie's?"

My mother listened, then shifted her attention to her guides. I could tell by the way she turned her eyes up and to the left that they were having a conference about this. She was quiet for a moment, shook her head, took a breath, and then said, with an apologetic tone, "If it were up to me, I'd say yes, because I know how much you want this. But my spirits say no for some reason, so the word [always *their* word] is no. Sorry."

Devastated and really disgusted with the spirits, I threw myself at Mom's mercy, launching into my best rendition of "Please! Please! Please! or I'll suffer forever." With this, she turned to me with utter detachment, completely unmoved by my performance, and very coolly repeated herself. "I don't think you heard me," she said. "The spirits said no."

We were crushed. When I pleaded for a reason, she didn't have one to offer, nor did she feel she had to give one.

"I don't know why," she said. "They didn't tell me. Vickie can stay here tonight, though. We'd love to have her join us." So she did, although that was not nearly as delicious as the privacy I had looked forward to at her house. (*Especially privacy from the spirits,* I thought angrily, as we gave up.)

Years later, Vickie told me that her mother frequently left the house at night after she went to sleep and went to the local bar to meet her friends. Vickie spent a lot of nights home alone. When she told me this, I remembered my mom's spirits refusing to let me spend the night. I wondered if this was why.

Having the spirits around was mostly a good thing, and I took great comfort in knowing they were there. They seemed to wield so much executive power in our house, though, that it soon got to the point where we didn't speak directly to my mother at all. We asked to speak to her spirits instead, thereby saving a step. I remember one time when our family was planning to go on a Fourth of July picnic the next day, but rain threatened to cancel our plans. Worried sick that we'd miss out on the fun, and watching the rain continue to pour down on us, I couldn't take the stress anymore. "Mom," I said, "ask your spirits if we're going to the picnic, because I'm worried that the rain will ruin it."

She paused, looked up to the left, listened, and then smiled. "Don't worry," she said, "we're going."

Hearing a huge crack of thunder at just that moment, I asked, "Are they sure?"

She gave me a look as if I had just committed a huge faux pas. "The word is yes," she said, "so relax."

Oops! I thought, embarrassed that I had questioned the spirits. *Sorry,* I apologized to them. The next day the sun was blazing in the sky, and we had a glorious time at the picnic.

In addition to spirit guides, my mother also had *vibes,* a running psychic commentary on the unseen side of life. She had vibes about who was calling on the phone, where we should park the car, what to have for dinner, whether someone would visit, if the neighbors were feeling good (because so many were older), and a million other things. They were feelings turned inside out about how the world affected her and what she thought about it all. They were her uncensored impressions of coming attractions and hidden events.

Following in her footsteps, I, too, paid attention to my vibes. That part was easy because everyone in our family did that. If we had a feeling, we said so without thinking about it, and many of them were about things to come. But that wasn't enough for me. I wanted more.

When I was about six years old, I was sitting at the foot of my mom's sewing machine, helping her remove a seam from some lime-green velveteen fabric that she was using to make me a winter pantsuit. I was holding it for her as she split the threads apart, and I asked her if only *she* was able to talk to the family spirits.

"Of course not. *You* can, too, if you make the effort," she said, continuing to split the seam.

I thought about her answer for several moments with intense curiosity. Although the spirits annoyed me at times, especially when they said no to things I wanted to do, they were mostly comforting and good to have around. Just knowing they were there, I never felt lonely or alone. But I did want to talk to them personally rather than having to always go through her.

"How do I do that? How can I hear them like you do?" I said. "I want to talk to them myself."

She kept sewing, pondering my question, listening for the best answer. She was silent for so long that I wondered if she'd heard me. After all, she was nearly deaf. But she had definitely heard. She was just waiting to hear how the spirits would answer instead of giving me her *personal* opinion. A very big difference.

Then she said, "First of all, you can't hear the spirits unless you agree to listen. If they tell you something and you don't listen, then they know you aren't sincere and don't appreciate their help. So they'll go away. That's the first thing they say." She fell silent again, obviously listening for more.

"Don't ask anything of the spirits you don't want to know," she resumed. "You can't ask, then wish you hadn't. If your spirits give you direction, you have to follow it." All the while, she was sewing.

Mom paused again, stopped sewing, and said, "And finally, you must turn your attention completely inward, absolutely stop talking in your mind, and listen. Just listen. And that's it. You will hear them."

I sat quietly, thinking about what she had said.

Mom continued. "Just one more thing, Sam, and this is now just *my* opinion. Everything you hear from your spirits is far, far more accurate than what you'll ever hear from the outside world." She went back to sewing, nodding her head as if agreeing with herself.

She looked up. "I may be deaf, Sam, but I hear what matters."

Even though I was young, I knew that what I was asking for was serious and that it would deeply impact my life. After all, having spirits tell me what to do meant that I'd have to cooperate, and already I had moments when I didn't like that. Because this was such a big challenge and would require discipline on my part, I knew I shouldn't rush into anything. I realized that I should probably think about it first. So I did, for all of about one minute.

"I want to talk to the spirits myself," I announced. "I'm going to do what you said and hope I can hear them, too."

My mother was thrilled. "Good," she said. "That's a very wise decision, Sam. I don't think you'll regret it. So go on. Give it a try."

I summoned my courage, desperately wanting to succeed, when suddenly my favorite Saturday morning cartoon, *Rocky and His Friends,* popped into my head. There was a sequence where Bullwinkle the moose sat with a turban on his head at a table with a crystal ball, and Rocky the flying squirrel was by his side. Then Bullwinkle said, staring into the crystal ball, "Eenie-beenie, chili-weenie, the spirits are about to speak."

Rocky, excited and anxious, asked, "Spirits? But Bullwinkle, are they *friendly* spirits?"

To which Bullwinkle replied, "Friendly? Just listen . . ." Then it cut to a commercial break.

For some reason, as I got ready to dial in to the spirits, I said to myself, *Eenie-Beenie, chili-weenie* . . . then on a more serious note, *Anyone there?*

11

Then I stopped talking in my head. Just to be sure, I even stopped breathing. I listened with my whole heart and soul, my entire being. I waited. There was silence. I held my breath. Suddenly, I heard them in my head just like my mother said I would. They didn't sound like human voices; they sounded like the most beautiful, deep chorus of resonant voices, definitely not my own, saying, "We are here. And we love you."

My back straightened, my eyes popped open, and I burst out laughing, astonished that my psychic call had actually been answered.

"I heard them!" I cried excitedly, now laughing out of control from the surprise and making my mom laugh, too. A mixture of delight, excitement, accomplishment, and new possibility engulfed me. I knew I couldn't talk to them anymore at that moment. Not until I calmed down.

"I did it!" I shrieked to my mom. "I . . . me . . . Sam . . . heard the spirits!" Wanting to be absolutely certain she'd witnessed this, I repeated, "I did it. Did you see that? I did it. Now I have spirits, too. Like you."

Laughing with me, she said, "I see that. It will take practice, but eventually you'll hear them like you hear me. It takes time to do this regularly. Just keep practicing, and be sure you listen. That's the important thing."

My mom rolled up her sewing and sat face-to-face with me. "Always listen to your spirits, Sam. They're closer to God than you or I, so they know better than we do what's best for us. Besides, you'll soon see that they're good company."

Chapter 2

MEETING ROSE

Once I heard my spirits, I talked to them all the time. I knew they could hear me. It was just a matter of practice for me to tune in to them on a regular basis.

I had no trouble following the rules my mother passed along. I was completely willing to listen, follow the spirits' guidance without question, and stop talking in my head. The first two were easy. The third took more practice and was something I did in my room every night just after the lights went out.

As I said, my bedroom used to be the kitchen in the original second-floor apartment. At night, the space above the closet my dad had built became a mysterious black hole, and in my imagination, it was the place where my spirits lived. I'd lie in bed, focusing on the void, and talk to it as if I were talking to Heaven.

First, I'd pour my heart and soul out about what had happened that day. Then I'd wait to hear the reply. It took a while, but eventually my spirits' voices came through, an inner chorus speaking not in my head but in my heart. I especially heard them when I was almost asleep, mostly whispering, "We love you."

After hearing this night after night, I finally summoned the courage to ask my spirits their names. Mom knew hers by name, and I wanted to know mine in that way as well. Just before falling asleep, I said, "I sure wish you'd tell me your names and what you look like. Will you?"

To my surprise, I heard the most soothing, sweet, feminine voice answer me. "I am Rose, and I love you."

"Rose," I repeated. "Rose. What a beautiful name. Thank you for being here, for watching over me." I woke up the next day wondering if I'd dreamed the whole thing.

After several weeks of talking to Rose, I wanted to know what she looked like, so I asked her. In that void above the closet, or in my imagination—I couldn't tell the difference—I saw a beautiful light. In the center emerged a very small woman who looked like a nun. She wore a brown and beige habit, different from the sisters at school. She had a very kind, sweet face and appeared to be about 20 years old. She smiled at me and held her arms open, and when she did, I felt warm energy flow through me. She looked like the picture of St. Thérèse, "The Little Flower," that I'd seen at school.

"Are you St. Thérèse?" I asked her as I looked at the light. But all I heard in my heart was "Rose," so I wasn't sure if she was or wasn't. Either way, talking to Rose became my bedtime ritual. It was the same every night. Once I was in bed; the lights were out; and the voices of Neil, Bruce, and Noelle faded as they fell asleep; I made myself stay up and wait to talk to Rose. She became my confidante and confessor. We'd have long, telepathic conversations—me in my bed, she in the black space above the closet. Sometimes I'd see her in my imagination, and sometimes I'd just hear her or feel her, but I knew when she was there by the warm, loving feeling that came over me. That was Rose.

One night I asked Rose what to do about a girl in my class named Lillian who was tormenting me. She had short brown hair, freckles, and a gap between her teeth; and although she was almost as tall as I was, she was larger and probably weighed 15 pounds more. She had a younger brother and an older sister, but there was a big age difference between them, so she was like an only child.

Lillian was a lousy student who mouthed off to the nuns and had to stay after school a lot. She was the class bully and scared everyone, boy and girl alike. I did everything in my power to avoid her, which wasn't easy because she was always literally in my face.

Lillian was mean and threatened to beat people up all the time at the slightest provocation, and sometimes she did. One day I made the fatal error of hitting her with a dodge ball, putting her out of the game. The other kids laughed, embarrassing her, and making her furious with me. She came up to me after school with five or six other girls behind her, shaking her hairbrush in my face, gritting her teeth, and snarling like a pit bull. "I'm gonna get you!" she threatened ferociously, scaring me to no end. I wasn't exactly sure what the hairbrush was about, but judging by the look in her eye as she waved it at me, I knew it didn't mean she wanted to play beauty parlor.

I was scared and asked Rose what to do that night. Lying in the dark waiting for the answer, I heard in my heart, *Invite her to go swimming with you.* I knew this meant inviting her to Celebrity Lanes Indoor Olympic Indoor Sports Center, where I went with my family on Sunday afternoons.

Rose's suggestion seemed outrageous. The thought of spending my swim afternoon—the highlight of my week and my special day with my father—with Lillian appalled me. I wanted to get away from her, not invite her to something I'd only invite my best friend to. Besides, she hated me. Why would she want to come swimming with me? Confused and unhappy with the answer, I wondered if Rose had heard my question correctly.

But then I remembered the rules. I had to listen and do what she said without question, or she'd go away.

Okay, I thought, trying to hide my overwhelming resistance, *I will.* The next day, Sister Mary Ellen lined us up at school for picture day, and sure enough, Lillian was as menacing as ever. She took her place in front of me, hairbrush in hand, and growled, "I'm going to get you!" She raised the brush, bristles pointed my way, and stuck it right in my face.

I was silent, feeling trapped because the line toward the photographer was moving at such a snail's pace. This gave me time, however, to think about Rose's assignment and muster up my courage to do what she said.

Five minutes later, Lillian turned to me again, narrowing her eyes to be sure I got her threat. I took a breath; it was now or never. *Here goes,* I mentally told Rose, *but you have to help me.* Then to Lillian, I said, "Hey, Lillian. Pssst." Shocked that I'd even dare to address her, she spun around, raising both fists, one still holding the brush, and lunged at me, ready to duke it out. I jumped back, ducked, winced, and closed my eyes in case she hit me. Still, I managed to say, "Do you want to go swimming with us at Celebrity Lanes on Sunday?"

Utterly disarmed by my invitation, she stopped in her tracks, dropped her arms to her sides, appeared confused for a moment, and then took a long look at me. "I'll have to ask my mom," she said, then turned around and looked forward, as if nothing were wrong between us.

We got our pictures taken, returned to our seats, and finished the school day. When the bell rang, Lillian was waiting for me outside our classroom, and said, "What time?"

"Four," I replied. "We leave at four, and we come home at eight."

"Do I need any money?" she asked flatly, but not meanly.

"Seventy-five cents," I said, "and candy money for after."

"I'll tell you tomorrow," she said as she turned and left.

I felt Rose's vibration sweep over me, and I relaxed. I hoped I could stay calm and enjoy myself if Lillian joined us. I was confused because I didn't really know whether I wanted her to come along or not.

The next morning she met me on the front steps of the school. "My mom said yes. She'll bring me to your house," she said. Her tone was lifeless and cool. Without another word, she walked in. That was on Tuesday. She didn't speak to me for the rest of the week. On Sunday she showed up at 3:50 P.M. and piled into my dad's Cadillac with the rest of us, absolutely silent. She looked stoic, yet fragile. I actually felt sorry for her.

We went swimming and, surprisingly, had fun. I can't say I was totally at ease, but it worked. My dad drove her home afterward. She never spoke to me or threatened me again the entire time we were at school.

This was the first of an endless stream of suggestions that Rose offered when I needed help. Ours was an ongoing telepathic exchange. I took it for granted that she was always around. Eventually, I didn't even have to ask her for help; she just gave it. She was to become my closest companion, confidante, and advisor; and it was she, not me, who made all decisions for me. As my life naturally grew more complicated, it simplified things a lot.

Chapter 3

FINDING SANTA

When I entered the first grade at St. Joseph's, I was already completely at ease with my vibes and had no second thoughts about sharing them with my family. I constantly shouted out who was on the phone before picking it up, only to be right. I announced what was in letters before they were opened. I was particularly good at finding parking spaces, as well as my mom's keys every time she misplaced them.

It didn't take long to figure out another good use for my vibes. When Christmas came around the following winter, I was so excited I could hardly wait. That is, until that one day when I was walking home from school with my advent calendar in hand, telling my brother Bruce how excited I was for Santa to come. He turned to me as if I were some kind of idiot and said, "Santa? Santa's not coming. Don't you know that Santa's not real?"

Stunned to hear such a blasphemous statement, I retorted, "Of course he's real. How else do you get your Christmas presents?"

"Mom and Dad give us our presents," he said quite matter-of-factly. "Dad gets them from work." Completely shocked by this information, and holding on to my beloved Santa for dear life, I adamantly rejected what he said.

"That can't be true. They have no money to buy us presents. Mom tells us that all the time. So they couldn't do that."

True, we didn't have much money, but still, every Christmas the tree was loaded with every new toy, doll, or game we could ever want, piled high with more goodies than we ever thought possible. Christmas at our house was truly magical.

"Yeah, I thought about that, too." he said. "But I heard Mom talking to Charlotte [our next-door neighbor] on the phone last week, and she told her that our toys came from Ward's because Dad gets a discount."

I had to admit it made sense. I'd wondered how Santa knew to bring the exact same doll carriage that I'd seen on display at Ward's last Christmas. Normally, my father sold tractors, trailers, lawn mowers, and saddles in the farm department, but every year from Thanksgiving to Christmas, his department was transformed into Santa Land and filled with toys. My vibes said that Bruce was right, but still I didn't want to believe it. "What about Santa? Does he come at all?" I asked, not wanting to give up on him immediately.

Bruce stopped right in the middle of the sidewalk and said, "Hey, we don't even have a fireplace, so figure it out."

It was another bothersome detail that I'd chosen to overlook. "I guess you're right," I said, having to accept his theory. "But I'm really disappointed."

"Don't be, because I need your help."

"What do you mean?"

"I want you to help me find the presents before Christmas. I want to make sure they got what I want. That way, if they didn't get them, I can give them more hints."

That was forward thinking. "Wow! Do you think they have presents hidden in the house now?"

"They have to. But I've been looking, and so far I haven't had any luck. I know they're around somewhere, but I can't figure out where. So why don't you find them, okay?"

"Maybe they didn't get them yet," I offered.

"No, they did. That's what Mom was talking to Charlotte about. So do you think you can use your vibes for something useful and find them?"

"Sure," I said, excited by the assignment. "I think so."

"Good. Start looking when we get home."

So that's what I did from the minute we walked in the door. Using my radar, I went from room to room, scanning for toys. But it didn't work.

I didn't pick up a thing. I couldn't tell if it was because there weren't any presents or because I couldn't find the toy vibe. Like a Geiger counter sweeping the terrain, I left no corner unscrutinized. Still I had no luck. No matter where I focused, or actually looked, I came up empty.

At first I didn't worry, figuring that I had time to work on my project because Christmas was still four days away. But as time went by and nothing turned up, I started to get nervous. To add to my anxiety, my mom carried on something terrible about how once again we had no money, and how we shouldn't expect the kind of Christmas we had last year. It didn't make sense, because Bruce had heard her spill the beans to Charlotte about Dad getting cheap toys from Ward's. So where were they?

We searched the furnace room in the basement, in every closet, under every bed, behind every chair and sofa, and even in the drawers. Nothing. And it was now only the day before Christmas.

I kept asking my guides where the toys were, and all I heard was "in the trunk." My mom had an old trunk that she kept in the furnace room, but I searched it and found nothing, not even a single candy cane. Still, the only vibe I got was "in the trunk." Perhaps that meant that they'd eventually put our stuff in the trunk, so I kept going back, but nothing changed.

Following me, Bruce said, "Are you sure you heard that they're in the trunk?"

Defensive and equally frustrated, I said, "Yes. I'm sure," secretly wondering if I was wrong. Maybe we couldn't find anything because there wasn't anything to find. What if there really wasn't any money and what Bruce heard Mom saying to Charlotte was wrong. Maybe there *was* no trunk full of presents. But even then, my guide insisted, "In the trunk."

"But, it's sure as heck not *this* trunk," I shot back at the black hole.

"Then what stupid trunk are they talking about?" Bruce snapped, exasperated. "It's Christmas Eve, and we've looked everywhere. And Mom and Dad are certainly not going shopping tonight."

He was right. My mom was up to her ears baking strudel and Christmas cookies with Charlotte. They were getting ready for our traditional Christmas Eve party and sure weren't going anywhere.

"I don't know," I said. "All I know is they're in some trunk."

Just then my dad pulled up in his chartreuse, fin-tailed beast of a 1957 Cadillac and parked. The minute he did, I knew.

"*That* trunk!" I said, pointing to the car. "Of course. I'm sure they're in there."

I knew I was right. *But how do we get Dad's keys to open the trunk and look?* I wondered.

19

Bruce read my mind. "Leave it to me," he said. "I'll get the keys. Don't say anything."

As Dad walked up to the porch, we tried to act as if nothing was up. We both smiled stiffly and said "Hi." It was hard. We burst out laughing. Dad completely missed it, however. He was too much in a hurry to notice. He had a lot to do before the party.

Several hours later the house filled up with guests. The tree was lit, and the grown-ups were drinking rum and eggnog and doing the polka.

In no time we were completely forgotten. As I was savoring the very last drop of eggnog, knowing I was only allowed one because it was for our guests, Bruce came up behind me and tapped me on the shoulder. With an ever-so-slight nod toward his right hand, his eyes directed me to look in his fist. He slowly turned it over and barely opened his fingers so I could see what he was holding. There were Dad's keys.

"I snatched them from his coat pocket," he whispered. Neil and Noelle were standing right behind him.

"What are they doing here?" I asked, thinking that this was only between Bruce and me.

"I told them they could come along because I needed them to be lookouts for me when I got into Dad's coat. Don't worry. They won't tell. Let's go."

Like four undercover agents on a mission, we waited until everyone ended up in the kitchen like they usually did when our parties really got going. Then we snuck out the front door one at a time, leaving it slightly ajar so we could get back in without ringing the bell.

Dashing down the front porch to the car, freezing to death because it was snowing really hard by now, we kept saying, "Hurry up," as Bruce tried several keys before one finally clicked. We held our breath as the heavy trunk lid slowly rose. A magnificent bounty of toys and games of every kind fairly exploded. There was Chatty Cathy, the talking doll I'd begged for since September; a *Monopoly* game; and, oh my God, *Clue*. There were five Barbie dolls, a Ken doll, Skipper, three GI Joes, and two electric race cars. And that was just what was on top.

Covered with snow, but squealing with delight and squabbling like fiends, we poked carefully through the stash, not wanting to disturb anything lest we get busted. Then Bruce became executive director and said, "That's enough," and slammed the trunk shut.

We all agreed that this was going to be the best Christmas yet. We slithered back into the house and ran upstairs to get the snow out of our hair so we wouldn't get caught.

I was terribly excited, but I couldn't tell if it was over finding the toys or knowing where they were. As I dried my hair with a towel, I heard my inner voice say, "I told you in the trunk." "You were right," I answered back. "Thanks."

That proved to be a great Christmas for me—not only because it was fun to find the toys (and I even got what I wanted), but because both Bruce and Neil were impressed that I'd successfully located the stash. From that Christmas on, they respected my vibes. And that was the best present of all.

PSYCHIC RADAR

It soon became apparent (at least to me) that I had a real knack for picking up vibes. I often played psychic games, first with my mom, then by myself—not only for entertainment, but also to exercise and strengthen my psychic muscles so that mine would be as strong as my mother's. We playfully called these "psychic sit-ups," and like calisthenics, we did them every day.

For example, whenever the phone would ring, I'd shout out who was calling before someone answered it. Whenever we went to the grocery store, I'd announce the daily special before we arrived. And when we visited my Aunt Emma and Uncle Rudy on Saturday afternoons, I'd describe in advance what they were wearing, or what my aunt had made us for dinner.

Sometimes Neil, Bruce, or Noelle played these psychic games with us, competing for who could answer correctly, but it was soon obvious that psychic vibes weren't as important or as interesting to them as they were to my mother and me. The more I did my psychic sit-ups, the stronger my psychic radar got, especially when it came to knowing who was calling on the phone—so much so that I started to perceive when someone was going to call before the phone actually rang.

I did this for the first time when I was about five. I walked in the front door and was headed for the kitchen to get something to eat, when suddenly I found myself next to Charlotte as she picked up her telephone and dialed our number. Somewhere between the front door and the kitchen, I'd left our house and was suddenly in hers. I could see that she was excited to tell my mother something, wanting her to be the first to know. As she dialed the first number on her rotary phone, I snapped back into my own body and was once again on my way to the kitchen, only now I was heading for the phone. A split second before the first ring, not missing a beat, I said, "Mom, Charlotte's calling you." Before I even could finish my sentence, the phone rang. I picked it up and said, "Hi, Charlotte! It's me, Sam."

24

Not expecting to hear me say her name before she announced herself (because, of course, this was long before caller ID), Charlotte was at a loss for words. "How on earth did you know it was me?" she finally asked.

"I don't know," I said. "I was on my way to the kitchen when suddenly there I was in *your* kitchen instead, and I saw you dialing our number. So I knew it was you."

"That's incredible," she said. "I can see you've got your mother's talents."

"I know," I replied, thrilled to hear her say this, my goal realized. I handed the phone over to my mother. It turned out that Charlotte was calling to tell my mom that she was pregnant, which was very exciting because my mom was pregnant, too.

My psychic radar continued to scan my world, motivated largely by the attention and approval I got from my mother, and, of course, the fun factor involved. It was always very amusing to entertain myself and everyone else in the family with my psychic pronouncements, and I wasn't above admitting how much I loved being noticed.

Being in the middle of seven kids and pretty shy, highly sensitive, and easily overwhelmed by my two older, aggressive, and loud brothers, it came as a delightful surprise that I could distinguish myself in such a positive and entertaining way and actually get approval for my psychic feats. I became quite the psychic show-off, challenging my siblings to use their psychic senses like I did mine and see whose was the best. I challenged them to name who was calling on the phone, or see what was in the mailbox, or other trivial psychic pursuits I invented. With each contest, I consistently proved to be the champ.

Not taking my coveted position in the pecking order for granted, I secretly kept up my daily psychic calisthenics to further push my newly sprouting psychic sensors out into the world.

One of my favorite ways to do this was to play a game I'd invented called "I wonder. . . ." I played this game as I walked home from school with my friend Vickie. We had to walk six blocks straight east on Sixth Avenue from Galapagos Street to Bannock Street, then left three more blocks to our respective houses. On the way were two traffic lights, one at Delaware and Sixth, and one on Bannock and Sixth.

In my game, in order to win we had to correctly name the color of the next car to stop at the red light. I'd predict, for example, that the next one would be blue, and then we'd wait and see if I was right. If I was, I'd get another turn. If I was wrong, I'd lose. The penalty for losing was that I had to stay at the light and predict the next three colors correctly before we could continue walking home. Because we got out of school at 3:00 and had to be home by 3:30, the stakes were high, which made the game all the more exciting.

If I won two times in a row, I entered the championship level and then had to describe other details of the car, such as whether it was a station wagon, and whether it had four doors or wood paneling. Coming up with these details correctly gave me up to 5 extra points, and once I totaled 30, I was officially state champion. The ultimate goal of this game was to get 100 points and become *world* champion.

Either way I played the game, I made sure that Vickie never got a turn, no matter what. At first she didn't notice because I was so good at play-ing that it distracted her from her own try. Eventually she caught on and protested. I managed to convince her that her turn was coming and to just wait. But I lied. I never intended to let her have a turn. I know this was selfish, but the truth was I didn't want her to be able to be psychic like me. It was *my* thing that we did in *my* family, and I didn't want to share it with her. I just wanted her to be a witness to prove how good I was.

Not surprisingly, this little game ceased to be of any interest to her pretty fast, and when I'd earned 27 or 28 points, she stopped walking home with me, saying she quit. But I didn't care. I was in a world of my own, and she had served her purpose. I was far enough along in the game to be a contender for world champion, so I could happily proceed by myself. It was a great way to amuse myself, and it didn't cost a thing, which was very important, because we never had any money to call our own.

My psychic monopoly didn't stop with Vickie, though. Not only did I want to be the *best* psychic kid in my family, I wanted to be the *only* psy-chic kid in my family. As such, I didn't share my game with my brothers and sisters either.

My vibes were so sensitive that when my mother or one of my brothers or sisters was in pain, in trouble, or having a problem, it brought me to tears. I didn't just worry about them, I *physically* felt their pain in my body, absorbing it like a sponge. When someone was angry, I felt as if I were getting electrocuted. When someone was sad, I felt as though I were suffocating and couldn't breathe. When someone was extremely happy, I felt high, as if my feet didn't touch the ground. So in the name of self-preservation, I used my vibes to anticipate and intercept trouble so I wouldn't have to feel the fallout.

Bruce was particularly prone to getting into trouble for one reason or another, and often got into conflicts with people who didn't understand him. Needless to say, this frightened me a lot, which meant that he warranted my constant surveillance. Watching him became my self-imposed assignment. My radar told me that he needed me to protect him.

One day I got an intense, panicky psychic feeling about him on the way home from school, and I knew he was either in trouble or *causing* trouble. This feeling of dread and danger came over me like a fast-approaching cloud, and I felt as if I couldn't move in any direction. On red alert, I had to find him. He wasn't in the schoolyard, so I figured that he'd set off on the seven-block walk home. I usually walked home on Sixth to Bannock and then turned left toward our house because it was the safest way to go. Scanning the area, however, my vibes told me that Bruce was on Fifth behind Baker Junior High, the huge public school across the street from our Catholic school, and official enemy territory. It was a well-known fact among us St. Joseph's students that public-school kids were bad and that we should avoid them at all costs. No wonder I had bad vibes.

Scared to go that way, but certain that Bruce was in trouble, I overcame my fears and walked—no, I ran, in that direction anyway. Sure enough, when I reached Fifth I could see him, and it didn't look good. There he was, about a half a block away, completely surrounded by a gang of public-school kids, both boys and girls, yelling at him and threatening him. To my horror, there he stood and, Oh my God, he was yelling back!

Terrified for him and incredulous that he was blind to the fact that he was facing a death squad, I burst out crying, dropped to my knees, and began to furiously pray for my guides and angels to come and rescue him *now*.

My heart was pounding through my chest so hard that it hurt. I summoned every guide, every saint and angel, and even God Himself (whom I rarely thought to bother) to step in and save him. Looking up, I could see that the crowd had multiplied, and I couldn't even see Bruce anymore.

"Please help him!" I screamed, demanding that my guides do something immediately.

Just then, my prayers must have been miraculously answered, because as the crowd got louder and my brother appeared to be dead meat for sure, out of nowhere, the saints and angels came marching in. Before my astonished eyes, Dad, of all people, who always worked morning, noon, and night at Montgomery Ward and never, ever came home in the afternoon, turned the corner of Delaware and Fifth in his car. Seeing the crowd and his son in the middle of it, he pulled over and got out.

Although he wasn't a large man, he was a former Army boxer and packed quite a punch. He had a quiet, low-key essence, but he nevertheless exuded a powerful vibe of his own that made it absolutely clear to anyone that if you messed with him, he'd pulverize you. So no one did.

At first the gang didn't see him because they were so busy taunting my brother. The obvious leader—a short, stout Hispanic kid with a gray sweatshirt and buckteeth—was ready to mash my brother into smithereens, until he heard my dad shout, "Hey! What the devil is going on here?" The gang turned to look at him and instantly clammed up. He took one step toward them, and that was the end of that. They scattered like mice when the cat shows up, leaving Bruce standing alone, like the cheese.

I was so astounded to see my dad that I couldn't speak. Wondering if he was a mirage, and not my father at all, I ran over to him and threw my arms around him just to make sure he was real, something I didn't often do. Shoving us into the car, he gruffly asked Bruce what was going on. Bruce very nonchalantly explained that as he was walking home, minding his own business, he accidentally bumped into the gang leader and pushed him off the sidewalk. The angry kid jumped back on and yelled at him to get off the sidewalk, which Bruce refused to do. Things deteriorated from there. They got into a standoff, and the crowd began to gather, rallying the gang leader to beat Bruce up. That must have been just about the time I felt my bad vibes. "That's about it," Bruce said, as if reporting on the weather.

Unfazed by his (in my estimation) near-death experience, and acting as though nothing serious had happened, Bruce then calmly asked my father, "By the way, why did *you* show up? I thought you were at work."

Slowly turning the car onto Bannock, Dad said, "I was home for a late lunch because I was asked to work this evening. When I got into the car, for no particular reason I decided to drive this way instead to see if any of you kids were walking home. It's a good thing I did, judging by what I found."

"But you never drive this way," I gushed, still astonished that some-one up there had heard my prayer and then had sent a knight on a white horse to save my brother's life, or at least save him from a black eye.

"That's true," he said. "Just lucky, I guess."

We arrived home and Dad let us out, warning us to go inside and stay out of trouble. Feeling completely drained by the ordeal, I wondered if I could even make it to the front door. I just wanted to collapse right there on the sidewalk.

Bruce, on the other hand, leaped out of the car and skipped up the steps in no time, and Dad drove off in his usual steady manner. I was so con-fused by their reaction versus mine that I didn't know *what* to think. I had just witnessed an incredible miracle, and neither one of them had even acknowledged that anything out of the ordinary had happened. I sat for a minute and tried to make sense out of it all, because neither of them seemed to comprehend the miraculous synchronicity of what had happened. It was as if they had both fallen asleep. I said a prayer of thanksgiving to my angels and guides for hearing my prayer and coming to our aid. Then I went inside, wondering if only *I* knew what had really just happened.

Chapter 5

EAVESDROPPING

Life went on as usual, or as *unusual*, on Bannock Street. Because of my psychic interests, I began to gradually and subtly separate myself from my brothers and sisters and move further into my own psychic domain. While they busied themselves with ordinary kid things, like bike riding, playing in the yard, or fighting with each other, I spent my time and creative energy stretching my psychic radar farther and farther to see how far it would go.

At nine years old, I was moving past phone calls and cars at red lights. My new psychic horizon, and one that spontaneously opened up in me, was tuning in to other people's thoughts. I found that I was cognizant of what other people were thinking and details of their private lives, sometimes getting more information than I was prepared to know.

For example, I knew that my best friend Vickie's dad didn't really live at her house, even though she insisted he did, saying that he "only worked a lot." I also knew that one of my teachers wasn't happy being a nun, although everyone agreed that she was the best nun in the school because she was so kind.

I also began to notice that people didn't act the way they felt, and the way they felt was mostly unhappy. It sometimes made me feel embarrassed and uncomfortable that I could tune in to secrets I shouldn't know—like the fact that the secretary in our church rectory had a big crush on one of the priests, and she dressed so nicely and fixed her hair before she went to work because she wanted him to notice her and think that she was pretty.

I didn't even want to *think* that thought. A priest, at least as far as I was taught, was an agent of God and completely off-limits as a love interest. It simply didn't make sense. Consequently, I often found myself giving her a mental scolding, trying to get her to snap out of her ridiculous and impossible flirtation—that is, until I was in the rectory one afternoon delivering something from Sister Mary Canisius. When I saw the priest standing at the secretary's desk, I knew, much to my horror, that he liked her, too!

30

That was way too much to get my brain to understand, and it sent me reeling. Although the two weren't doing anything inappropriate, their vibe was completely flirtatious and, as far as I was concerned, totally gross. *How could they?* I thought, gasping. I couldn't even look the secretary in the eye, even though she was the one I was sent to see.

Fixing my gaze on the wallpaper behind her head, I handed over the manila folder, quickly told her it was for Father Norbert, and then turned to leave. Oblivious to how I felt, she stopped me from bolting, saying, "Hi, Sam. How are you today?" She was happy as a clam because she had Father's attention. "Do you know Father? Say hello to him, and mind your manners."

Of course I knew him and even liked him up until now. "Hello," I said flatly, throwing him a dirty look. "I gotta go back now."

I ran out of there as fast as I could. Seeing their flirtation distorted my entire view of priests, nuns, life, church—and everything I loved. *What were they doing?* I wondered all the way across the street and back to the classroom. *Don't they know they shouldn't be doing that?* Then I considered that maybe they *didn't* know.

At any rate, the whole thing was too much to absorb, so by the time I returned to my seat in my third-grade classroom, I'd decided not to think about it anymore. However, I did decide that I wouldn't go to the rectory again. It gave me bad vibes.

I was also aware of things about people in my neighborhood. I knew that Art—the chain-smoking old man who lived by himself in the spooky, yellow stucco house with cracking walls and a large rickety porch just around the corner from us on Fourth Avenue—drank a lot and cried sometimes when he was alone because he had a very sore leg, no money to get medicine, and nobody to help him. Later I learned that he had diabetes, and both of his legs were suffering terribly from circulation problems. I'm ashamed to say that knowing this about Art grossed me out a little.

I knew that the husband of the lady down the block was lying about going to work, and that he went to a bar instead and drank vodka and Squirt.

I knew that the man who lived in the next block in the large, three-story mansion was not as rich as the kids in the neighborhood insisted he was.

I knew these things by a sort of psychic osmosis. When I was near people, these tidbits of information just popped into my head as if they had leapfrogged from their brain to mine. I didn't *think* them or *hear* them like I would do later when my guides started to appear. I just *knew* them like eyes see them or ears hear them. I simply *knew* I was right. Sometimes I worried that all this would get me into trouble, but I never doubted what I knew

I did have enough smarts, however, to know that I shouldn't share these private bits of information with anyone except my mom, and not even her sometimes—especially if the information I knew was embarrassing to someone. I did not ever, *ever* want to embarrass anyone. Besides, it wasn't as though I wanted to know any of this. I'd much rather have known the answers to tests, or how to make some money, or whether Vickie was really my best friend like she said she was, or if she was starting to be Darlene's best friend like I felt she was. Those were the things I wanted to know. I mostly ignored the stuff about people that popped into my head.

When I felt something sad about someone, like when I knew Art's legs gave him a lot of pain, I tried to be extra nice. I would never admit this to anyone for fear that the other kids, even my own brothers or sisters, would think I was crazy because he was so creepy, so skinny and dirty, and smelled like he hadn't taken a bath in a long time. I prayed for him a lot.

I also felt bad that I couldn't tell people I knew someone was misleading them or lying to them. This was too risky and dangerous, and there was always a strong inner voice inside of me that said the things I knew about people were not to be talked about. I was taught never to gossip, and sharing what I psychically knew about others would definitely qualify as gossip. That was a sin, and I refused to do it.

Knowing as much as I did about people spoiled some of the fun of being a kid. It was even depressing at times. But it just was what it was. I suppose I could have talked about all this to my mother, but I didn't want to burden her already heavy heart with more sad or depressing news so I didn't. It just felt as though I had a lot to carry around. And as for

31

confiding in someone else, I was fast learning that it was too difficult to explain psychic things to nonpsychic people. It would be like telling a blind man what the sky looks like, or explaining a symphony to a deaf person. In my mind, it was the other people, not me, who should be self-conscious. If they didn't have a vibe sensor of their own, how on earth would they understand mine? I mostly just kept my mouth shut and took most insights in stride.

The other interesting thing about my psychic childhood was that I never considered it weird that I knew what I did about people—uncomfortable maybe, but natural, not something to be suspicious of or apologize for. I could clearly see that people who weren't psychic behaved in strange ways—saying what they didn't mean, lying to the people they supposedly loved, loving people they weren't supposed to love, being sick and not asking for help, and feeling confused and scared while putting on a false face and acting as though everything was just fine. I felt as if there was an elephant in the room that other people pretended wasn't there.

I marveled at the fact that I knew things about people that they didn't know themselves, because, as far as I was concerned, some of it was so incredibly obvious. How could they miss it? But they did. I wondered if they weren't psychic because they didn't have the ability, or because they didn't *want* to have it. Maybe to some it was better not to know.

I may have been psychic and been able to pick up more than most people about the world and the strange characters in it, but at the same time, I couldn't help but notice that many people were just the opposite, sticking their heads firmly in the sand, preferring not to see even the things that were in plain view, wanting instead to know nothing at all. Later I'd come to understand how negative behavior and thought patterns block people from their psychic sense.

But at this age, I just thought that there was a boulder in their road and wondered why they didn't see it, or if they did, why they didn't move it. I actually felt sorry for them because my psychic sense was so fundamental to my life.

Chapter 6

MIND READING

When I was still in the third grade, I experienced another dramatic shift in my psychic sensibilities. I didn't just *feel* what people thought, I actually began to hear it in my head, which was disconcerting and exciting at the same time.

One day as I was more or less daydreaming at my desk, I heard my teacher Sister Mary Margaret's voice say, "I'm going to give these kids a surprise spelling bee tomorrow. That will keep them on their toes."

Astounded to hear her voice so clearly, I snapped straight up in my chair, wondering if she'd spoken out loud and I'd just missed it. She noticed my abrupt jolt and the surprised expression on my face and studied me for a moment, frowning and suspicious. "Sonia, what are you up to?"

"Nothing," I said, feeling guilty at eavesdropping on her thoughts and fearful she'd know, because Sister Mary Margaret was an irritable nun prone to hitting you on the head whenever she felt like it, which was often.

She continued to eye me suspiciously while I concentrated on my desk. Then she said crossly, "Quit daydreaming and get back to work."

Her harsh tone made me shudder and surprised the other kids, who stared at me, wondering what was going on. I was normally Miss Goody Two-Shoes, who never, ever got reprimanded. Excited at hearing my teacher's voice in my head, and even more excited about what I'd heard,

I couldn't help but want to tell someone; it was too big to keep to myself. So I told my friend Diane when we were on the playground at recess.

"Guess what?" I said. "Tomorrow we're going to have a surprise spelling bee."

"No way," she said. "It's Wednesday, and we only have spelling bees on Friday."

"Maybe so, but I heard Sister Mary Margaret say we are, so we are."

"Say it to who?"

"Never mind," I said, knowing she'd never believe me. "She just said it."

Even then, I was smart enough to know that telling Diane I'd heard her say it in my head was dangerous. The kids at school already didn't think much of me because I was such a "good girl," so telling them that I could hear someone think out loud wasn't a good idea and would do nothing for my already-suffering reputation.

"But don't tell anyone else, okay? It's a secret," I said.

"I won't," she promised.

By the end of recess, the entire class knew.

Sure enough, the next morning Sister Mary Margaret blew the whistle she wore around her neck and announced, "All right, students. Let's see who did their spelling homework last night. Everyone line up across the wall. We're going to have a spelling bee."

My eyes and everyone else's in the class fairly popped out of our heads. Everyone quickly exchanged glances, and some kids smirked and laughed because, little did Sister know, it was no surprise. It was a big deal to me, however. This was perhaps the first public confirmation I'd had that my vibes were reliable. The kids jumped up and ran for the blackboard, unlike the usual dread that accompanied Sister's frequent ambushes. Because of what I'd told Diane yesterday, this time they were ready.

One by one, each student rattled off the spelling words flawlessly. After three rounds, only one kid (Robert Barcelona, who always went down anyway) missed a word. Not Teddy Alvarez, who was a terrible speller. Not Bobby Castillo, who never even got the first one right. Not even Darlene Glaubitz, who intentionally missed words just to make the boys laugh. That day we all spelled like champs.

Amazed and pleasantly surprised, Sister pushed the glasses she usually wore at the tip of her nose against her face and slowly closed the spelling book. Eyeballing us one at a time, she said, "Well, well, well. It seems we have a miracle happening today. You've all done very well."

My heart was pounding so hard as she spoke that I thought it would fly through my chest. Astounded that what I'd heard yesterday was correct, and moved that the kids had believed me when the word spread across the playground, I nearly burst into tears. I was always on the brink of tears because I was so sensitive. But today I desperately tried to control my emotions because I didn't want to embarrass myself. Every time I did start crying for no reason, everyone laughed at me and I hated it. I could feel all eyes on me, and it took everything in me not to lose it.

Just as we were about to be dismissed, a girl named Debbie ruined everything by saying, "Sonia told us we were going to have a spelling bee today."

She was such a jerk. I never did like that girl.

"Excuse me?" said Sister Mary Margaret. "What did you say?"

"Sonia told us, Sister. On the playground at recess yesterday." She spoke with a sharp nod of the head, looking very smug and quite pleased with herself for tattling on me.

"Yeah," piped up the other kids, wanting to be in on the bust. Even Vickie, my best friend, ganged up with the rest. It was too painful to hear. *Those dirty rats,* I thought. *How ungrateful!*

The entire class began shouting in a chorus, enjoying letting Sister in on the secret. "Sonia told us you were going to give us a spelling bee. So we knew." I sat there, my eyes now hot with tears, gripped with fear and a feeling of total abandonment. I flashed on how Jesus must have felt when he was taken to see Pontius Pilate—total betrayal.

Furious and confused, Sister stared menacingly at me, her eyes burrowing right into the center of my chest. "Is this true, Sonia? Did you tell the students about the spelling bee?"

Terrified, I couldn't speak. I could only nod yes as the tears poured down my face.

The lunch bell rang. Sister slammed her hand onto her desk and commanded, "Everyone, out. And stay in single file. Now march." The class glanced over at me with a combination of malice and pity in their eyes as I started to fall in line.

"Not you, Sonia!" Sister shrieked. "I want to speak with you at my desk."

Everyone burst out laughing.

"Silence!" Sister boomed. "Unless, of course, you want to join her."

It became so quiet you could hear a pin drop. Shaking and crying and afraid for my life, I approached her desk, watching my classmates merrily skip off to lunch. Even Vickie didn't look at me. I'd often had fantasies of being left for dead or betrayed like this.

Sister, not happy to have been outsmarted, glowered at me. "You have some explaining to do, young lady, and it better be good."

I opened my mouth, but no words came. I was unable to find my voice. I didn't even know how to begin.

She tried again. "Did you tell the other children we were going to have a spelling bee today?"

Summoning all my courage, I managed to squeak out an almost inaudible, "Yes."

"When?"

"Yesterday."

"Yesterday?"

36

"Yes," I said, looking down to avoid her mean expression.

She stared at me with a laserlike intensity and asked in a quiet, yet menacing, tone, "How did you know?"

"I don't know," I answered. "I just heard you say it."

"What do you mean, you heard me say it? I did *not* tell you."

"I didn't hear you say it to me. I heard you say it in my head."

Sister was silent, furious at my answer. "What do you mean, in your head?"

"I don't know," I said. "I just sat at my desk yesterday before recess and heard you say it. Just like that. I heard you say, 'I'm going to give these kids a surprise spelling bee tomorrow.' You were thinking it, and I heard you say it."

Not knowing how to handle my revelation, she resorted to her all-too-familiar assault tactic: "Don't you ever lie to me like this again. If you do, I will give you 50 whacks with my paddle." She was referring to the well-known and well-worn 18" by 4" wooden board she kept on her desk with the words "Heat for the Seat" emblazoned in red across it. It had a picture in one corner of a crying boy bending over rubbing the seat of his pants. She raised the paddle over my head and whacked me very hard. Then she whacked me again.

Holding my hands over my head to protect myself, I scrunched down and winced, my ears ringing from the pain, wondering if I should tell her I wasn't lying.

A voice popped into my head the moment I thought this. "Don't."

"And be glad it was a lie," she snarled, as she whacked me again, "because if you aren't lying and what you're saying is true—that you heard me think—then Lord have mercy on your soul, young lady, because that's not right."

Now that's a concept I've never heard before, I thought, as I hunched over to protect myself from further insult and injury.

"Don't you ever, ever, *ever* talk like that again," she said. "And because you *are* lying, you will stay after school for a one-hour detention and go to confession when that's over. Now, shame on you is all I have to say. I'm so disappointed that you, of all people, would stoop so low. Just march yourself to lunch, and never let it happen again."

Tears pouring down my cheeks, my heart doing a Mexican hat dance, and confusion distorting my view, I ran out of there so fast that I ran straight into a wall.

The entire episode threw me for a loop. I always knew that Sister Mary Margaret was a grouch, and I knew she didn't think much of any of us, but I'd managed to protect myself from her bad temper by being absolutely certain to do things the way she wanted. I was even scornfully called "teacher's pet" by the class, an unenviable position, but the safest one under the circumstances. Now, for reasons I didn't understand, I was being treated as though I'd done something terribly wrong, and I hadn't. And worse, it was public knowledge.

Up until now, my psychic experiences were reserved for my family—extremely private, and held in highest regard by my mother, and by me as well. The idea that having a psychic thought or awareness, quietly or out loud, would be anything other than cause for great self-congratulation and personal satisfaction was inconceivable.

What did she mean, "shame" on me? She should have said, "Good job. You helped everyone win the spelling bee." How unfair.

After my initial wave of terror passed, rather than feeling ashamed and full of remorse, I became angry—furious, in fact. And defiant. She wasn't going to take away my best talent, the one that already at such a young age I was intensely proud of and had been cultivating for some time. Sister was stupid for saying those things.

I sat in the lunchroom alone, the other kids having finished and gone back to the playground. Frantically trying to sort out the entire episode before I had to go back to class stamped with Sister's version of *The Scarlet Letter,* I desperately asked God, "Why did this happen?"

Chewing on the last bite of my cold Spam-and-cheese sandwich, I suddenly heard a voice, loud and clear just like the day before, only this time it was the voice of a beautiful woman soothing my injured and traumatized sensibilities like a balm. "Forgive her, Sonia. She doesn't understand you. Just be quiet for now. We love you."

It was my guide, Rose—the one I'd spoken to in my heart every night since I was five. The one I heard in my head at night just before I went to sleep. I recognized her by the feeling that came over me, as though my shredded aura had been instantly rewoven. It was absolute love.

I was so excited at being able to hear her voice as clearly as any person's that I stopped thinking about Sister Mary Margaret. In my heart, I knew that my guide, Rose, was bigger than she was and would protect me.

This was the first time I actually heard Rose speak out loud directly to me, and not just silently in my heart. I was as startled as I was yesterday when I'd heard Sister Mary Margaret thinking to herself. I started to cry, only this time in utter relief. Just then the bell rang and I had to go back to class. I composed myself because I didn't want my face to look tearstained and blotchy.

"Thank you, Rose," I said. I knew I'd be okay.

In class, Sister acted calm and neutral toward me, and I no longer felt threatened. Little did I know that she'd had just as disturbing a lunch hour as I had because she'd been forced to think about what I'd said and started to wonder about other things, too.

I didn't realize it at that very moment, but in the past 24 hours I'd opened my *clairaudient channel*. It was to become my main psychic artery for doing my life's work. I had unknowingly opened my telepathic circuit, giving me the ability to hear my guides and psychically tune in to other people on an even deeper level than before. I'd eventually use this channel in my work as both a psychic teacher and healer. It was to become my psychic switchboard, simultaneously allowing me to tune in to others, tune in to my guides, and eventually into the matrix of the soul. At the time, however, all it meant to me was: *Thank goodness I can hear you, whoever you are, because I need help down here.*

My reality and perspective changed deeply that morning. I'd never been challenged by anyone about listening to my inner voice, nor had anyone suggested that it was a *bad* thing to do. I withstood the challenge and became more fiercely committed than ever to listening to my vibes, realizing that what I knew was important and that I'd have to defend it when I was tested.

That day I also became aware that not everyone felt the same way about vibes as I did, and that I could be attacked anytime along the way. And because of that new realization, I had to start being very careful.

Chapter 7

SECRET AGENT

In spite of my run-in with Sister Mary Margaret, I was thoroughly enthralled with my newly uncovered ability to tune in to others and actually *hear* what they were thinking—and even better, to hear the *voice* of my guide, Rose.

I paid close attention to both my vibes and what Rose and any other guides said, and in retrospect, I can see that without knowing it I was actually beginning to do psychic readings *on* people, not *for* them.

At this time, when I was around ten or so, there were several popular TV series that featured international spies, which totally fascinated me. My favorite show was *The Man from U.N.C.L.E.*, although I liked *Get Smart* and *Mission: Impossible* almost as much. All three shows had central characters that infiltrated enemy territory and elicited information without being noticed or caught. Intrigued by their dangerous and glamorous lives, I imagined myself to be an international psychic spy whose job it was to get as much information as I could without being discovered.

My first assignment was to spy on our next-door neighbor, Lawrence. He lived with his older sister, Dorothy, in the brown brick Victorian house north of us.

Lawrence divided his time between this house and another one where his mother lived, so he was only around part of the time—which part we never knew. Dorothy stayed in the house and rarely came out. Rumor had it (among my brothers, sisters, and me) that she was sick and maybe crazy, too. She had pale white skin, dyed coal-black wavy hair, and black marble dots for eyes. She wore bright red lipstick that she painted into a heart where there were supposed to be lips, completely ignoring the outline of her mouth; and drew a very thin line of wobbly, black eyeliner across her upper eyelids. To top it off, she deposited two circles of red blush on her cheeks, all under a thin cloud of white face powder that crinkled in the corners around her eyes and the ridge of her nose and was splotchy along the edge of her chin. To me, she looked like she was 100, although I recall hearing my mother once say that she was 77.

Lawrence was short and roly-poly, but very distinguished looking. He stood about 5'4", had a friendly, wrinkled face; wore three-piece black suits and a black fedora; had a pocket watch; and carried a briefcase. Whenever we met him in front of the house, he gave us shiny half-dollars, which to me were nothing short of a small fortune and bought more candy at Mr. Prays's across the street than I could eat. The trick to getting the 50 cents was to be in front of his house exactly when he arrived, otherwise you'd lose your chance.

It frustrated me to no end when Noelle or Bruce got 50 cents because they happened to be out front of his house when he arrived and he was long gone before I could show up. Seeing their newly purchased treats, I wanted money, too, in a big way. I decided to get practical and use my psychic abilities to spy on him so that I could tell in advance when he was coming and then be strategically placed to intercept the cash.

Using my inner radar, I'd stand in front of his house and try to locate him. I did this by closing my eyes and visualizing what he looked like. The best way to describe how this felt is like being a radio tuner scanning for a particular station. Like everyone, Lawrence had a particular rhythm or vibe that he broadcast, and it sounded to me, for lack of a more accurate description, like music. His music was solid, determined, intentional, and peppy, like a march. In fact, the more I paid attention to people's energy and vibrations, the more I experienced them as a particular kind of music. Some people had a vibration that felt like a cha-cha. Some felt like a waltz. Some felt like a church hymn. Some even felt like a funeral march.

When I began my spy mission, I simply stopped in front of Lawrence's steps every day after school and psychically listened for a few minutes, checking to see if he was in the vicinity. I searched days at a time for his energy, mostly to no avail. I wondered where he might be traveling, and when he'd return.

Then one day after school, I felt it. I could actually determine his vibration in the air. His music, like a one-man band, was marching toward the house. Just as I turned the corner of Fourth and Bannock, I focused my inner attention, and eureka! I could sense that the vibration was getting louder. He was close. I was sure of it. Ever the spy, I nonchalantly cast my eyes in every direction as I scanned, without moving a muscle in my head so that no one would could tell I was looking around.

I stood perfectly still, intensely focusing as I psychically cased the joint, looking and searching for him in every nook and cranny. As I listened for him, I suddenly heard his voice, even though he was nowhere to be seen. But he wasn't talking to me. He was talking to Dorothy, sounding upset, saying, "Oh my, Dorothy, what's happened to you? You don't look well."

I heard him, I said silently to myself. *He's coming.*

Sure enough, before I could even complete my thought, his large black car turned the corner and parked in front of his house.

Thrilled that I was right, I all but squealed, "Hello, Lawrence! How are you today?" nearly shoving my palm in his face in want of my 50 cents, the earned reward for my psychic feat.

"Well, well, lucky me," he said, smiling down at me. "I'm just fine, young lady, and even better now that I see you."

Then, plunging his hand into his pocket, jiggling his coins slowly and methodically, looking me right in the eye, he said rather seriously, "Tell me, are you getting good grades?"

"Straight A's," I said, chomping at the bit for him to give me the hard, cold cash.

"Is that right?" he said, looking very pleased with me. "Then you won't mind if I give you . . ." He pulled out a shiny silver half dollar and held it up to my face. ". . . this, will you?" And he passed the money to me on the back of his hand.

Intensely pleased with my successful interception of him, and feeling like the greatest international psychic spy on the block, I snatched the money as fast as it appeared and said, "Thank you, Lawrence. You are soooo nice."

We chatted for a few seconds, then as if reminded of why he was there, he said, "Excuse me, now. I must go in and see Dorothy."

Without thinking, I said, "Oh, yes, you must get going. She's really not looking well today. Something may have happened."

Startled by my comment, his face darkened. "Why? Have you seen her?"

"No, not really," I said, knowing he wouldn't understand why I said this. "I just have a feeling."

He paused, looked confused, and not quite knowing what to say in response to my comment, quickly went into the house. Afraid that I'd done something wrong and was going to get into trouble for it, I ran home, stayed in my room, and didn't tell anyone about the 50 cents.

42

At dinner that night, Mom said to Dad, "Did you hear, Paul? Dorothy had a stroke today. Lawrence had to take her to the hospital."

CHAPTER 8

REWRITING THE RULES

The year I turned 11, my childhood effectively ended. My sister Cuky moved away, my brother Stefan left for college, and Grandpa went to a nursing home. With all of them out of our home, the house felt dark and empty.

I missed Cuky as much as Mom did, and I was just as depressed. Cuky was so much fun to be around. She seemed like a second mother to me, and now that she was gone, I felt that her light was definitely missing. I knew in my heart that *I* had to become that light now, especially for Mom, who seemed so sad and overwhelmed. The best way for me to shine and brighten the mood was to do readings. It gave her something to look forward to . . . and I looked forward to them, too.

The more I stared at those ragged-edged cards, the more I looked deeply *into* life. But I soon discovered that the clues to the future weren't just in the cards. The clues to the future, to the unseen and unknown, were evident everywhere around me if I only paid attention.

My orientation to the world changed, too. Driven originally by a deep desire to help my mother through a sad period, I realized that my abilities and interests weren't exclusive to her. Like ripples on a lake, I slowly expanded my focus and attention to other things. My realm of curiosity also expanded. I didn't just want to know things for my mom. I started to want to know things for *me*.

Everything and everybody, not just the cards, invited me to "read." I started paying close attention and studying the energy of people around me, asking my guides to tell me everything about them. I became an incredible voyeur.

I was fascinated by the priests and nuns at school. I wanted to see behind their black habits and ropes of rosary beads and into their hearts. I wanted to get into their cloistered world, their elite and mysterious sect, and peer into their private affairs. I wanted to know everything about them, especially their personal relationship with God and with the saints and angels.

I'd been closely aware of these higher forces ever since I was very young. In our home, the saints and angels didn't just exist in heaven—they lived with us, and we were on a first-name basis. Michael, my mother's primary angel, had now been adopted by me and accompanied me wherever I went, and I often wondered if Rose was not really The Little Flower, St. Thérèse. Once a friend asked me how I reconciled the guides I listened to with being such a good Catholic, but I never saw a conflict. The guides were just another division of heavenly helpers, maybe a department the church might have missed or didn't know about. But they never worked in contradiction to the church; they simply provided more of the same.

I was in the seventh grade and was getting quite tall, already 5'6" of the 5'8" I'd eventually grow to be. I was very skinny, with long, spindly legs; shoulder-length, wavy brown hair that I tried to iron on the ironing board to make it straight; and much to my great dismay, a newly acquired, very thick pair of glasses.

Until the time I started reading cards for my mom, I had 20-20 vision, maybe even better. But as my focus changed, so did my vision. The more I developed my psychic sight and began to look for the unseen world, the more my physical eyes weakened. In a few short months, my eyesight had so deteriorated that I was nearly blind. Or at least that's what my optometrist, Dr. Reed, told me when I had my first eye exam after being unable to see the clock three feet from my bed to get up in the morning, or the blackboard in class from the first row. Now outfitted with two spheres mounted in what the eyeglass salesman called "fashionable tortoise frames" (for a 75-year-old woman, maybe!), I looked and felt the part of the vintage junior high school nerd.

I was already fairly unpopular at school because I was so smart. At St. Joseph's, in a predominantly working-class, blue-collar community, being smart wasn't held in particularly high esteem. Having boyfriends and girl-friends, getting married, and having babies were life's ultimate goals—not going to college or having a career. It just wasn't part of the culture at the time. So, as the class brain, I was already not cool, but now with the thick glasses hanging off my face, my social life was doomed. In addition, I was a giant compared to the other kids in my class and in the school. I was always the last kid in line, since the nuns always insisted we line up from shortest to tallest, and I felt alone because of it.

I did finally manage to carve out a niche of respect for myself that felt good. Because of my height and sharp instincts, I was a great volleyball player and gained some social status among my classmates because we began to win games.

Consequently, I began to play volleyball after school, and I loved every minute of it. I was especially fond of one of my two coaches, whom I affec-tionately called "Sister Mary Volleyball."

Around 5'5", stocky, with short black bangs that sprouted from beneath her habit and framed her face, she was fun, inspiring, and on a mission to win. She made the team run 30 laps around the gym and do 50 push-ups before we even got to serve the ball. She was tough, and most of the girls didn't like her because she demanded so much. But I was dis-ciplined by nature, so what she required was easy, and I excelled at it.

One day after putting away the volleyball net, I left the gym and started walking down the alley toward the street, when all of a sudden I heard my guide, Rose, say, "Go back to the gym. Now."

Startled, I turned and stared back at the gym. There were no kids around, and the alley was deserted. I had just said good-bye to Sister and had left her in the gym alone, so I wondered why I was being told to return.

"All right," I said. I walked back to the gym, opened the door, and went in. Not seeing a soul, I headed for the locker room, surmising that maybe I was sent back because I had left something, although I had all my books with me, so that didn't make sense.

Still following my guide's orders like a detective following a trail of clues, I caught something out of the corner of my eye in the locker room. Stand-ing near the sinks were Sister Mary Volleyball and "Mr. Gym," the boy's gym helper, kissing. Stunned, I jumped back, afraid they'd see me. Appar-ently Sister saw something, if not me, and yelped with surprise. I moved farther away from the locker-room foyer trying to hide. As Sister raced out of the locker room, I was still backing into the gym and hesitating, not knowing which way to go, so we nearly slammed into one another.

"What are you doing here?" she asked, surprised and embarrassed.

"Uh, I left my book," I lied, feeling just as discombobulated as she was.

Blocking me with her arm, no doubt to prevent me from entering the locker room, she said in her stern nun's voice, "No need to go. I'll look for you. Wait here." Having no intention of going in there, and relieved that she offered to do it for me, I gladly waited.

She disappeared into the locker room, and I knew she was panicked, and I actually felt bad for her. The amazing thing was that in the short time she was gone, my psychic sense told me that this is why I had to come back.

"To see *this*?" I asked Rose incredulously, hardly believing that I had been led into a terribly embarrassing situation that I had absolutely no business seeing. "Yes," Rose said. Then my psychic sense flooded me with an entirely different picture than my first impression. I knew that no matter how it might appear to the world for the two of them to be kissing, it wasn't wrong. I knew without a doubt that Sister Mary Volleyball absolutely loved Mr. Gym. Even though it mortified me to no end, despite my busting them, I felt no desire to judge them. Quite the opposite—now I wanted to protect them.

I flashed on Mr. Gym crouched in the toilet stall, terrified that he might be discovered, exposed, and humiliated, and I felt compassion for him. However, the thought of him in there with his feet up on the toilet seat and Sister scrambling to find a nonexistent book, simultaneously trying to hide him and recover her own dignity, made me laugh out loud. I didn't want either one of them to worry about my discovering them, so I walked even farther away from the locker-room door.

Sister darted out of the locker room, but by now I was in the middle of the gym, giving her a lot of space, signaling to her that I wasn't about to pursue.

She was flushed, her eyes darting in all directions, and said, "I don't see anything in there. Have you tried your locker?"

I looked her right in the eye, and said, "Don't worry, Sister. It's okay."

Then we both fell silent and just looked at one another. I couldn't help smiling as I looked into her eyes and heart. I really wanted to laugh again, but mostly out of nervousness. I knew she knew that I knew, and we both didn't know what to do about it.

"Like I said, don't worry," I declared. Then I was seized with the incredible insight that I was actually supposed to find her and give her that message. "I just want you to know it's okay, and I love you. It's good to be loved, you know."

That part just flew out of my mouth, as if Rose were saying those words through me. Even though Rose said it, I knew that I, too, needed to hear it.

Sister Mary Volleyball's eyes filled with tears, and she gave me a hug. I left the gym and walked slowly home, confused and embarrassed, but completely at peace.

I never told anyone what happened.

I heard later that Sister Volleyball left the convent, and Mr. Gym left the church. I wondered if it was true.

47

Chapter 9

SEEING PAST
APPEARANCES

As I continued to do psychic readings for my mother, the word slowly began to spread, driven mostly by her unrestrained enthusiasm for me. First, she told her best friends—Gen, Sarah, Charlotte, and Kathy Duncan—the women whom she talked to all the time. Then she mentioned it to the neighbors, at least the ones who seemed to understand.

Trusting her rave reviews, people grew curious, and before long, one by one I started seeing them as clients. I was becoming known as the neighborhood kid psychic. They showed up because my mother told them that if they had a problem, they should have a reading "just to see."

As much as I appreciated my mother's belief in me, her public display of enthusiasm was quite intimidating. It was one thing to read for *her*, because after all, she was my mom, and I didn't really feel the need to make sense to her, be right, or make a good impression. I knew that I was safe with her because she listened to everything I said and didn't question it.

But when it came to other people, I didn't get that same reaction. They questioned me on why I said or felt something; and when they asked me what I meant or told me they didn't get it, it made all of this much more difficult to do. With strangers, I faced a whole new level of expectation and risk. Not only that, but my mom, in her enthusiasm, made it even more difficult for me by bragging so much about my abilities that she made it sound as if I had x-ray vision.

The very first person I didn't know who Mom suggested I read for was a woman named Theresa. She had originally come to see my mom for a reading, and they had just finished when I walked in after school.

Theresa was tall with a medium build, a deep furrowed brow, squinty brown eyes, and olive skin that was bumpy and pitted as if she'd had acne earlier in life. Her medium-short hair was dyed red with black roots peeking through, looking quite messy, as if she hadn't taken the time to comb it when she'd gotten out of bed that morning. She had an overbite over thick, puffy, dry lips; and a weak, somewhat pointy, double chin. She looked confused or out of it when listening to Mom and made her repeat everything. Between my mother being hard of hearing and Theresa not really listening, it actually made for a funny exchange, I'm sorry to say.

50

Theresa was a study in opposites. In contrast to her unattractive face and disheveled hair, her clothes were chic and lovely. She was wearing a beautiful black cashmere sweater, which fell to her hips; a silk, multicolored scarf wrapped around her shoulders and fastened with a delicate gold and red antique-looking pin, a tweed burgundy and black skirt, and black leather knee boots with platform soles, which I noticed because her chair was turned sideways as she sat at the table. She wore large diamond earrings, a ring on every finger, and a pair of frameless glasses dangling on a chain around her neck and resting on her rather buxom chest.

As I looked at her, I thought that she didn't match, and I had the immediate feeling that she was playing dress-up in that outfit—that those weren't her *real* clothes. She may have worn them, but it didn't look like she *owned* them.

Theresa sat at the end of the dining room table. She had both a cup of cold coffee and my deck of cards spread out in front of her (which my mom had used to do the reading), with the red handkerchief I kept them in carelessly cast to the side. That they'd used my cards without my permission made me angry at both of them, so I immediately disliked Theresa and was not too fond of my mom at the moment, either.

The vanilla-scented votive candle (we both agreed scented was better for the vibes) that my mother always lit when we did readings was still flickering, but it had nearly all melted, so I knew they must have spent all afternoon there. A large, bronze-framed mirror against the back dining-room wall reflected the entire scene, including the look on my face as I saw them. It was definitely not my usual happy-camper expression. Seeing my blatant feelings staring back at me, I immediately forced a smile.

"Oh, great, you're home," my mom said, genuinely delighted to see me. Come on in," she insisted, holding out her hand as if giving me permission to enter. She excitedly introduced me to Theresa. Holding my hand and squeezing it, she said, "This is my daughter Sonia, but we call her Sam. She's the one I told you about. You won't believe it, but she's a fabulous psychic. She's absolutely extraordinary."

Intrigued, Theresa said to me, "Really? Is that right?"

I didn't know how to answer. Only 11 years old, I certainly didn't consider myself to be that great, and having my mother bragging in such unabashed terms was embarrassing, even stressful. I'd only been doing readings for a short while, and mostly just for her. I had 10, maybe 15 readings outside of the family under my belt, and at least half were for people I knew well and felt comfortable with. Reading for friends and family was one thing, but for a stranger?

Before I could qualify my capabilities and put them in a more accurate perspective, my mom continued her runaway train of compliments: "See for yourself. Have her do a quick reading for you right now if you have the time. Go on, she's great."

Before I had a chance to consider the idea, she said, "You don't mind, do you, Sam?" giving my hand, which she was still holding, a gentle but deliberate little squeeze, as if to say, "If you *do* mind, get over it."

At this moment, I realized what too much of a good thing meant. Even though I deeply appreciated Mom's enthusiasm for my psychic abilities and the way in which she respected every reading I'd ever given her, it felt as though she was setting me up to meet impossible expectations from her friend, and I wanted her to stop.

Turning back to Theresa, who sat there looking like a mop in fancy clothes, she was clearly interested in receiving as much attention as she could. Happy to have me be the next one to give it to her, my mother persisted. "Honestly, Theresa, if you have the time, you shouldn't pass this up. You won't regret it. Sam can read for you right now. Won't you, Sam?" She gave me her "We have company, so whatever you do look happy" smile that silently meant "Don't you dare embarrass me, or even think to say no."

I found myself sitting in the reading chair at the head of the table, my cards quickly gathered up and thrust in my hands. My mom was now sitting opposite Theresa at the other end of the table, shuffling my deck. I felt like I was on autopilot. I hadn't even taken my backpack off my shoulders.

51

Silently pleading with my mom to back off proved futile; she was much too focused on Theresa. So I prayed to my guides for help. They must have heard me, because suddenly Mom realized how trapped I was feeling. She started backpedaling a bit, trying to reign in the expectation she'd set in motion.

"Only ten minutes!" she exclaimed, nodding at me to let me know that she'd picked up on my feeling and was working on it by letting Theresa know there was a limit to the reading (unlike the three-hour reading she'd just received). But Mom wasn't able to contain her enthusiasm entirely; I couldn't tell who I was doing it for, Theresa or her.

Knowing that the only way *out* was *through* it, I slowly removed my backpack and set it on the floor, gathered my cards, and arranged them face-front in the same direction, as though to reclaim them for myself. I shuffled them a bit and handed them to Theresa, and with a heavy sigh and a great deal of resentment, I flatly told her to shuffle, looking as bored as possible—adolescent hormones and attitude had taken over completely.

Theresa took the deck, and ignoring my misery gave the deck three swift shuffles, slammed it down in front of me, and said in a loud and definite voice, "Here! Is that enough?" not meaning it as a question, but as a statement. She was so impatient to get on with the subject of "all about me" that she couldn't even be bothered with an adequate shuffle.

Well, that was hardly a shuffle, I thought as I picked them up. "I don't know, " I said sarcastically. "I'll have to see if I can feel your vibration. If not, you'll have to do it some more," all the while thinking, *How on earth do you expect me to get anything from such a wimpy shuffle like that?* I was hoping that she might be a wee bit psychic herself and feel my irritation. Judging from her blank face, I could see that this wasn't going to happen.

As I picked up the cards, wondering why in the world she didn't comb her hair, I wasn't prepared for the energy that came over me. The minute I fully held the cards, I stopped thinking about my feelings and began feeling Theresa's energy as though I were inside her body, her heart, and her emotions. I became overwhelmed by a strong, almost overpowering sense of compassion for her and wanted to comfort her.

Then I was hit with a second wave of feeling, one of absolute fear— *her* fear. She was afraid of something, and I wasn't sure of what. *So afraid,* I thought, *no wonder she didn't comb her hair. She's too scared to remember to.* Wanting to know what was behind her fear, I changed the channel in my head. I no longer felt any desire to criticize her. I experienced some of her fear as if it were my own. It felt crippling and debilitating, and I thought, *Wow, she looks pretty good for someone so scared, but no one should have to feel this way.*

She smiled at me, waiting, and for the first time I saw her spirit, the energy inside her, and not just her appearance. She looked sweet and terribly wounded. This was the first time I consciously experienced shifting my viewfinder from my head to my psychic channel so dramatically. Without realizing it, I'd opened up another door to my eventual mission in life. I found out exactly where my vibes came from: *my heart.*

My heart had been closed to Theresa when I'd first met her, but now with her sitting in front of my cards, it opened. I saw her soul, and my feelings changed. I couldn't help but love her. Now, back to her fear. What was it about?

As I held the cards, I gradually received more psychic impressions. I felt impatience, even urgency and anger. I took a breath and said so. "I feel that you're angry and impatient and really scared about something." *But what?* I wondered. I needed more.

Theresa stared at me, still faking her smile. She laughed. "Yes, that's me. Angry and impatient."

I felt stuck, then *bam!*—a flurry of information hit me, and I had to dash about quickly in my mind to gather it up or I'd lose it. I started speaking a mile a minute, not knowing what I was going to say. "I feel that you're afraid and angry because your husband is spending all your money, and he isn't telling you about it. I feel that he lies and keeps secrets from you, and he isn't letting you know the real situation with your finances." *Finances* was quite a word for me to use, but it's what I heard, so I said it.

"I feel that you take care of an old woman who is very frail, but not sick, and that you need the money to make sure that she'll be okay and not uncomfortable. I especially want to tell you that it's true that your husband spends too much, but he won't go broke, and you won't have to live on the street again."

This sudden avalanche of words came so fast that I didn't really know what I was saying. Afraid to look at Theresa, I fixated on the cards, hoping to God that some of it made sense. When I looked up, I waited for her to laugh and tell me I was no good as a psychic. Instead, her mouth fell open and she said, "Why did you say 'again'?"

"I don't know. I just said it." The words had simply bypassed my brain and flowed directly out of my heart. I was just glad some words *did* flow.

Theresa again asked, "Why did you say that?"

53

I responded with a question of my own, again coming from out of nowhere, certainly not from my brain. "Why do you ask?"

"Because absolutely no one knows I came from the slums of Rio de Janeiro and lived on the streets for the first 12 years of my life until my mother brought me here. Not even my husband. No one. It's my biggest secret. My greatest fear is that I'll end up back there. It's irrational, but it has been consuming me. And you saw it."

The second most surprising thing about this reading was that in a split second she went from treating me like a kid to becoming the kid herself. As for me, in that same instant I felt her pain and saw her as she really was, a lovable person who needed comfort. And I wanted to do my best to give it to her.

Again my guide spoke through me. "Don't be afraid. You deserve what you have now. Trust." And that was that. The reading was over. I looked at my watch. Ten minutes had passed. I was done.

"Can I go now?" I asked my mom.

Theresa said, "Can I ask you another question before you go? Will my husband make us move?"

I thought about it, waiting for an answer. I couldn't feel a thing or hear a word. I was as cold now as I had been red hot with vibes five minutes earlier. I'd never had that happen, where I didn't get a single feeling at all. I considered saying anything just so I could get out of there, but I knew better. That was definitely my adolescent self coming through. I took a chance on being honest and said, "I don't know." I got up and left.

If Theresa's greatest fear was being homeless, mine was getting nothing in a reading. I asked Rose, "Why didn't I get a vibe on her question? What did I do wrong?"

I prayed and waited for an answer. One didn't come so I started my homework. An hour later, while I was reading about the history of the American Revolution, Rose answered. "Because she didn't care about that question."

That made sense. So I let it go.

Chapter 10

MOVING TO GUAM

After my reading with Theresa, the word continued to spread that I was psychic and did card readings in our dining room. Before I knew it, the phone was ringing off the hook, and it wasn't just my mother's friends who were calling. It was now *their* friends who were trying to get readings with me. Soon both my family and I accepted my readings as a regular part of my life.

It became a routine. I'd come home after school, grab a glass of milk or a quick snack, and start my homework. Within an hour, someone would call, and in a panicked voice explain that they'd heard I was psychic. Then they'd pour out their troubles in a torrent of words and ask if they could get a reading with me right away because it was an emergency. And I'd say yes.

Even though it was normal for me to do readings at this point, I was terrified of the possibility of failure and letting my clients down. I felt deeply responsible and didn't want to disappoint anyone. What made it worse was that callers often said they'd heard I was great and desperately needed my help.

The trouble was, I didn't feel that great. I measured being great with being confident, and that was definitely not part of my self-image. What drove me to do readings was that I cared a lot about people even at my young age, and I wanted to help. I didn't *decide* to do readings. There was never a moment where I made a conscious choice to follow this path. It was as if it had already been decided before I was born, and it was simply a matter of getting on with it.

So I said yes to these people, trusting that it would all work out. Sometimes it did and sometimes it didn't, for reasons I didn't understand until much later. I took my responsibilities as a psychic very seriously. People needed help, and I had to help them. I prayed intensely to Mother Mary, who was a great source of comfort and assistance. I said rosaries to her before each reading so I wouldn't make any mistakes or do any damage as a result of anything I said. I asked my angels and guides, whom I now began to work with on a regular basis, to help me as well.

56

Rarely did I allow myself to think when seeing a client. Doing a reading involved *not* thinking. It involved intense inner listening and feeling, sometimes seeing images in my mind's eye, then sharing what I picked up no matter what I thought. Thinking interfered with the process. What I felt and heard from my guides was far more important than anything I might have thought anyway, because these higher forces were better informed than I.

I also never questioned what I got in a reading, either. My vibes, in whatever way they showed up, were the final word, just as my mother had insisted. This, too, was an understanding that I was born with, and my psychic experiences only confirmed it.

This situation often led to times when what I saw in a reading didn't make sense to the client and they dismissed it as wrong. They wanted me to say things that they knew were true in order to establish my credibility. This posed a huge and frustrating problem because I regularly saw things in the future, and there was no way of confirming them at the moment.

The only type of psychic information that could be confirmed immediately was anything I could obtain by telepathy—reading someone's mind. I did have telepathic abilities, and they did come through on a regular basis, but why would a client want me to tell them what they already knew? I sometimes did it just to appease them, but I thought it was silly and useless.

The kind of information I wanted to give clients wasn't obvious or immediately verifiable, so sometimes they had a hard time accepting it. And, quite honestly, some of it did sound outrageous, and even *I* had to stop, pause, and wonder what it all meant. I had no control over what I got, so I had to take what came through because the guides controlled that department, not I.

I was no good at explaining this to anyone because I didn't understand the difference between the various channels of guidance yet. Until I studied with my teachers later and learned about the differences, a reading was a reading; you got what you got, and you had to sort it out for yourself.

In retrospect, my early readings were a lot like channel surfing—a little telepathy, a little channeling, a little clairaudience, a little clairvoyance, even psychometry—all particular skills I'd learn to differentiate from when I began training. At the time, however, I received and conveyed a regular smorgasbord of information, and if a client didn't have a good imagination, it could be unappetizing and hard to digest. I wished fervently that I could make better sense to my clients, because when I couldn't, sometimes they were mean and hurt my feelings.

I remember reading for a woman named Maureen whose girlfriend recommended me. She was very businesslike on the phone, asking for my schedule, which made me very uncomfortable because I didn't operate on such a structured timetable. I just went with the flow. She sounded impatient, sighing a lot when I hesitated while answering some of her questions. She worked at a bank and could only come on Saturday afternoons after it closed. I was glad because I had a volleyball game that day—we were in the championship finals, and I couldn't get home until then.

I remember racing home after the game, feeling very unhappy because we'd lost by only four points. But I didn't have any time to wallow in my disappointment. I took a quick shower and put on my best dress (I always dressed up for my clients). I ran to the reading room, lit the candle, dimmed the lights on the brand-new chandelier my father had recently installed, and placed the deck of cards I kept in a red handkerchief in front of my chair. The new light reflected off the mirror, creating a shimmering, almost magical, atmosphere.

She should like this, I thought, remembering her crankiness and hoping it would cheer her up.

Maureen arrived exactly on time. She wore a beige two-piece twill suit, tan low-heeled shoes, and cream-colored hose. Her blonde hair was pulled back in a tight ponytail that stuck out of her head like a whisk broom. She had light brown eyes framed by large beige-pink glasses in need of tightening—in a round, ruddy face with a rash on her cheeks. She looked about 35, and was overweight and sweaty. I couldn't help but notice that everything about her was more or less the same color: beige.

She walked past me into the reading room, stopped, and wrinkled her nose. "P.U.! What on earth is that smell?"

I wondered if she meant me. I *had* taken a shower after the game, but maybe I hadn't washed as well as I should have.

"Um . . . uh, I don't know," I stammered.

"That sweet smell, like candy," she said.

"Oh, *that*," I said, relieved that it wasn't me. "It's my candle. I light it for good energy and blessings as we work."

"Well, I think it stinks, and I don't like it. Can you please blow it out? Otherwise I won't be able to concentrate," she harrumphed, waving her hand back and forth under her nose with her face all scrunched up.

"I'm sorry. Do you mind if I burn another candle that doesn't smell?" I said, not sure that I even had one.

"If you're absolutely certain that it's unscented."

I smiled, and prayed and prayed. "Rose, I need you." I said to my guide. "This lady is scaring me."

To my relief, I found a white, tapered candle in the credenza against the wall and grabbed it. "Here. Smell it. This will be good."

"It doesn't matter. It still stinks in here."

Struggling not to take her comments personally, I showed her to a chair and asked her to sit down. She did, keeping her purse on her shoulder and her arms folded defensively across her chest. Taking my chair, I carefully unwrapped my cards and handed them to her. "Okay, Maureen, please shuffle the cards for a few minutes and then cut them into three piles."

"You use *cards?*" she screeched. "I thought you were psychic, not a card reader. "

I was confused because it was all the same to me. "I *am* psychic," I said, "and I use my cards to help me focus on your vibration. I don't actually read the cards like they're telling me something. They just help me feel your vibration," I repeated.

"Well, can you just not use the cards in my case? I don't like cards. I just want your psychic feelings."

"Not really. But if you don't want to shuffle, you don't have to. I'll just do it for you."

"Fine," she conceded. "Whatever."

I carefully shuffled, looking straight ahead and not at her. I prayed to Mary, and asked Rose and all my guides for help. Then I asked Michael to protect me. This woman was hurting my feelings and making me angry. It was hard to focus.

I pulled a card, laid it down, and listened. "She's getting a new job," one guide whispered to another. I relayed the message to Maureen.

"Well, you're wrong. I just got a job. So why would I get a new one?" She folded her arms, daring me to answer.

I turned back to my cards and took a deep breath. *Keep breathing,* I told myself, still staring at the deck. *Please give me something good,* I prayed.

"You're going to move as well," I said, the words falling out of my mouth.

"That's wrong, too," she snorted. "I have a two-year lease on my apartment, so I won't be moving anywhere. Unless, of course, you mean at some point in my life, years from now." She laughed uproariously at her own joke.

"I don't know what it means. The guides gave it to me, and I don't ask for explanations," I said, surprisingly unfazed by her chiding.

Staring at the cards again, listening and hoping for something meaningful, I heard, "You are very lonely and wish that you could have a boyfriend." I shared this with her.

"No, I don't," she said defensively. "I don't need a boyfriend. Do you see one in there?"

I wasn't sure how to answer, but thankfully the words fell out of my mouth before I could think about them.

"Actually, yes." I said, waiting for my guides to fill me in on the details. They did, and the words flowed through me. "I see him, and he's big— 5'10" or so—and he looks like he's dark, like he's not the same race as you. He's kind of severe [*like you,* I thought, but didn't say], he's younger, and you'll marry him."

She eased up a little, now intrigued and maybe a bit hopeful, but not willing to let me know that.

"When?" she demanded.

"Soon."

"Soon. That's pretty general. Like when I move?" She burst out laughing, enjoying her own private joke.

"Probably," I said, feeling that was exactly right.

"What does that mean?"

"I don't know. I don't think it means when you're 50." I told her a few more things that she immediately dismissed with the rest, and then she decided she'd had enough. Frankly, so had I.

She stood up. "I don't know what you're talking about. I'm not getting a new job. I'm not moving. I'm probably not getting married. (I could see pain in her eyes when she said that one.) And I do not date younger men. Are you sure you know what you're doing?"

Ouch, I thought, feeling that verbal dagger right between the ribs.

"Do you have anything else to say?" she demanded.

"Only one. My guides tell me you're moving to Guam."

"Guam!" She nearly reeled. "Oh, for Pete's sake! Now I've heard every-thing. How ridiculous! I may not be psychic, but I want to give *you* a read-ing, honey. Get a different line of work. You obviously don't know what you're doing. Now show me the door."

She slammed down five bucks. I wasn't going to accept it, but Rose said, "Do." So I did. She walked out without another word.

I closed the door to my bedroom and cried. What a miserable day. We lost the championship game, Maureen was so mean, and my life's mission had been challenged. I wondered if she was right. Maybe I *should* get a new job.

"No!" my guides said in unison.

Three years later, after I'd been studying for a while with my psychic teachers and was getting ready to graduate high school, I got a postcard. On the front was the picture of a beautiful island. On the back, it said:

> Dear Sam,
>
>   You may not remember me, but I came to see you several years ago. You told me I would get married and move to Guam. I thought you were nuts! Since then, I met a younger man who was a sergeant at Lowry Air Force Base on a blind date, and we got married. He's Filipino, not white like me. We just got transferred to Guam. Isn't that weird?
>
>   Maureen

There was no return address.

I sure did remember her. It took me nearly six months to get over her barbs and attacks. In fact, there were still slivers from her anger lingering in my aura. But I appreciated the fact that she'd sent me the card. Read-ing it provided a type of healing for me, and it lifted my spirits. I knew that I had to have faith in my life's work and believe in the guidance I received even when it didn't make sense, but I didn't know how difficult my tests would be—or how painful. I was starting to learn.

I must admit that I was glad that Maureen had found love. It was all that was missing in her life.

"And don't forget color," my guides piped in (referring to Maureen's overwhelming beige-ness).

Chapter 11

SOLVING PSYCHIC RIDDLES

Doing readings continued to be both an adventure and an education. Staring at my tattered cards day after day, I not only learned about guides and how the spirit world worked, but I was learning about people and how *they* worked as well.

I was also beginning to discover, quite by accident, that while some guides were literal, others were metaphorical—they referred to our world and everything in it differently than we did. They gave information in forms, symbols, metaphors, hints, and clues, rather than direct, specific linear and logical explanations. Most of the time I knew what the guides meant, but sometimes I didn't. There were times when I was as confused as my clients, receiving information in riddles and puzzles that were hard to understand. While I conveyed all of it, sometimes I wished that the guides would just speak plain English.

That's how I felt when I read for a guy named Kurt.

When I first saw Kurt through the front-door glass, I was immediately impressed by his light, friendly vibration. He fidgeted from one foot to the other as he waited on the porch, partly out of impatience and partly because it was a cold afternoon and he wasn't dressed warmly enough. He wore blue jeans topped by a puffy, bright yellow down vest over a white (or at least it used to be white) waffle-patterned long-underwear top with a rounded collar. It looked as if his arms and torso were sticking out of a quilted balloon.

His jeans were tattered, with patches sewn all over them, including a peace sign, two marijuana leafs, and my favorite—a funny-looking man with a big nose and bald head leaning backward with one leg forward, the other behind, and shoulders back, with the words "Keep on truckin'" underneath.

Kurt's hair was brown and curly and fell in corkscrews over his face, shoulders, and down his back, cascading like a mop. His reddish, pimply cheeks poked out underneath his eyes, which were shaded by mirrored aviator sunglasses. He was like a permed version of Cousin Itt from *The Addams Family*. Spying me through the door, he smiled, showing off a set of dazzling white, perfectly straight teeth and two deep-set dimples on either side.

"Hi, are you Sam?" Kurt asked as I opened the door to let him in.

"That's me," I answered, a little bit intimidated because I'd never read for a client who was so cute and friendly. "Come on in."

"This is cool," he said, looking around the hallway, his hands still in his pockets. "Man, you're young!" he remarked, really looking at me for the first time. "How long have you been doing this, uh, what do you call it, anyway?"

"You mean readings?" I asked. "About a year, maybe a little more. I'm not that good at it, but I do my best."

This was the first time I'd ever publicly admitted to anyone what I thought of my own talent, but Kurt seemed so easygoing that it felt like the natural thing to do. More often than not, doing a reading for a client felt a lot like slow dancing with a boy—stiff, awkward, and uncomfortable, with both of us moving to different rhythms, trying to get the other to follow with no success. I didn't want him to think I could easily tango through his reading and then find that I had two left feet instead, like most of my other clients did.

I asked Kurt to follow me to the reading room, trying to act as professional as possible, but he took his time, peering into the living room where Noelle was watching TV. "Hi, how's it going?" he said, which startled her because my clients were usually whisked in and out without interacting with the family or venturing into our personal space.

"Fine," she said, giving me a who's-this-weirdo look.

Kurt casually strolled into the kitchen, studying every detail, and went to look out the window. I thought he was procrastinating. I stood at the open dining-room door, motioning with my head for him to get moving in that direction. Taking no notice of my now not-so-subtle hint, he smiled and enthusiastically said, "Cool house."

"Thanks. It belongs to my parents," I said, as I sort of shoved him in the dining room.

Still moving slowly, hands wedged into his pockets, Kurt maneuvered around me, turning his entire body sideways like an armless man, and stepping into the reading room where I had the chandelier set on dim, my unscented (taking no more chances) votive candle lit, and the cards set out in their red handkerchief, all waiting for us.

"Wow! This is so wild!" he gasped, as if he had just been ushered into an altered reality. *At last,* I thought, *someone finally got that I had set the stage for the reading.* "Man, you even lit a candle for this. Far out. So where do I sit?"

I pointed to his chair, which he slid into without the benefit of his arms, which were seemingly glued in his pockets. He was mashed uncomfortably against the edge of the table, but he sat that way until I gave him permission to move the chair.

"Thanks," he said, and withdrew his arms for the first time, pushed himself back, settled in more comfortably, and took off his glasses. Two beautiful brown eyes lit up his face. Surprisingly, he appeared nervous.

"Ready?" I asked, handing him the cards, not sure whether to be coolly professional or friendly like he was. "Please take the cards and shuffle for a few minutes, and when you're finished, put them down and cut into three piles. I'll take it from there."

Giggling like a four-year-old, he picked up the cards and shuffled. And shuffled. And shuffled. He must have shuffled for ten minutes without stopping, neither of us saying a word. Finally, I asked tentatively, "Uh, Kurt, are you finished shuffling yet?"

"Oh, I'm sorry," he said, embarrassed. "I was waiting for you to tell me when to stop. Should I have stopped before this?"

"Well, sort of, but don't worry. It's okay," I said, taking the cards away from him before he wore the faces off. We both laughed.

"I'm so sorry," he apologized again. "I don't know how to do this reading thing, so I was waiting for you. I hope I didn't mess up the vibrations or anything like that."

"No, no," I assured him, "it's fine. No problem."

"Maybe I should tell you why I'm here," he offered. "My mom sent me because she thought you could help me discover what my career is. You know, the usual 'what I should be when I grow up?' stuff. She's worried about me, so here I am." As he spoke, I listened to my guides, getting a feel for his vibration and the answer to his question.

"So, what do you see in those cards of yours? Do you think I'll ever find a job that I like and make some money?"

I could tell that underneath his cavalier attitude he was really troubled—desperate, in fact, to know the answer, but he wasn't sure I could give it to him. I could actually hear a voice in my head saying, *You're hopeless, Kurt. Absolutely hopeless.* I knew it was his mother speaking.

"I'll ask my spirits and see what they say."

I pulled out several cards and laid them out in front of me. Staring at their faces, I heard my guides whispering as if they were talking to each other *about* Kurt rather than *to* me. Then I saw the faces of some very old people all around me.

"I see old people," I said. "Very old people everywhere." He leaned forward and inquired, "Really?" as if I'd said, "Martians."

"Like doing what?" he asked. "Am I working in a nursing home or something like that?"

I didn't know. I looked at my cards and listened. I heard the guides say excitedly, "Carrying old people. He's carrying old people." I relayed that to Kurt.

He looked as if he were being sentenced to prison. "Jeez," he said, shaking his head, puzzled. "I don't even know anyone that old." With both trust and confusion on his face, he said, "And you think that will make me happy?"

"It's not what I *think.* It's what I *see,*" I said, trying to explain that anything that came through in the reading was not what I personally thought. If anything, I thought he should go to the mountains because he was certainly dressed for it.

"And you think I'll make some money doing that? I mean usually very old people don't have money."

"That's what I hear. My guides say you'll make money and take these old people around the world."

That confused Kurt even more. Me, too, for that matter. "What? You mean I'm going to take old people on a cruise or something? If they're that old, how are they going to walk? I'll have to carry them."

My guides piped in, "Yes. Yes. He will carry them. He's a carrier."

"You're right, " I said. "I guess you'll just have to carry them."

"No way," he said, laughing. "Let me get this straight. You say I'm going to be happy *and* make some money carrying really old people around the world? Can I at least use a wheelchair or something? They might be heavy."

I started laughing, too, because it did seem ridiculous, but the guides were adamant. "No wheelchair. Just carrying them."

"I guess you definitely can't use a wheelchair," I barely got out.

65

"Ask those cards if at least I'll carry *small* old people." By now we were both convulsed in laughter.

I listened. "The old people will be very large and very fragile," I said.

"Ask your guides if they're at least *rich* old people. If I gotta do that, I better get paid a lot of money."

Wondering why my guides were giving me such ridiculous information, I pulled three cards out of the deck—the three, nine, and ten of diamonds—and listened very closely. The guides were laughing, too. "They are very valuable. Very valuable," they said in chorus.

"Well, I'm told they're valuable," I said. "This probably means they'll be rich."

Kurt shook his head in disbelief. "It all sounds pretty weird to me. I'll just have to wait and see."

I thought he was being extremely generous by not dismissing what I'd said outright, as many others had done. I felt bad, though, that I couldn't come up with a more exciting career, like ski instructor, airline pilot, or rock star. Carrying old people around didn't even seem like a real job.

After Kurt left, for the first time I dared to question my guides. "I hope you guys are right, because it made no sense to either of us." But as always, good, bad, or indifferent, I had to let my reading go.

I went back to the reading room, blew out the candle, turned off the chandelier, put my cards back in my handkerchief, and closed the door. Still, I couldn't stop thinking how much I'd enjoyed Kurt, his energy and his vibration. He was fun, creative, and curious. *Like me a little,* I thought.

Twenty-seven years later, in 1997, I was on tour with my first book, *The Psychic Pathway*, at the Tattered Cover bookstore in Denver. As I was signing books after my talk, a man with bright eyes, a great smile between two deep-set dimples, and a bald head with curly fringe, approached the table.

When I asked him his name, he said, "It's Kurt. You probably don't remember, but I actually met you years ago. You read for me when you were very young. You told me I was going to carry old people around the world."

"Oh, I remember you," I said, blushing. "What a bust that was, huh? Thankfully I've improved over time."

"It didn't make sense for years, but guess what? I got married eight years later, and my wife and I opened the Southwest Art Gallery and Studio. One of the things we sold were paintings of Native American elders. People from all over the world bought them. One day as I was packing one to ship to Germany, I looked at the old man's eyes in the painting and thought, *Man, you're old.* Then I suddenly remembered what you'd told me.

"Here I was shipping this old face halfway around the world and loving it, when I thought of you and that reading. It was so right on that I laughed all over again, just like I did the first time."

"Thank God I've refined my skills since then," I said, and inwardly thanked the guides who had been with me so many years ago.

I signed Kurt's book and said a prayer for his continued success and mine.

Chapter 12

PSYCHIC ATTACK

When I started doing readings for others, I assumed that all of my clients wanted to know what *my* vibes picked up about their life. Much to my surprise, I soon realized that this was not necessarily the case. Sometimes they only wanted to hear what *they* wanted to hear—to confirm what *they* thought about their life.

I encountered this problem again and again. The worst example occurred when I was asked to read for a woman named Kerry, who found her way to me through my next-door neighbor, Grant.

Grant worked the night shift at a hospital, and Kerry was his boss. In their frequent conversations during the long hours, Kerry had confided to Grant that she had quite a few problems in her life, was miserable and confused, and didn't know what to do about it.

Wanting to help her, he told her about me, and that although I was only a kid (I was 13 at this point), word had spread that I was psychic and did readings. Grant told Kerry that he'd never had a reading from me, but he thought that I might see or feel something that would help her.

I had just finished watching *Rowan & Martin's Laugh-In* and was about to go to bed one night when I got Grant's call.

"Hi, Sam," he said. "This is Grant. Do you have a minute to talk? I want to ask you a favor. My boss is having a hard time right now, so I suggested that you could do a reading. Actually, I talked her into it because she's skeptical, especially after I told her how young you are. But I said your readings are great and that she should give it a try. Do you think you could do it?"

"Sure," I said, not knowing how to feel. If she had real problems, it made me nervous that she'd look to me to fix them. Also, I never did a reading for someone who had to be talked into it. It made me not want to do it. What if my vibes wouldn't come? What if I made things worse? But I found myself agreeing anyway.

I didn't realize what I was in for. Already the reading was set up for trouble—first, because Grant had to talk Kerry into it; and second, because I really didn't want to do it. Later on, my teachers taught me how to better protect myself against such negative energetic imbalances and set up readings on the right vibration based on the client's sincere receptivity and my feelings of being safe and grounded. But for now, I had to learn the hard way.

"How about tomorrow night at eight, before we go to work," he suggested. "Will that work for you?"

It was late, but I was too insecure to say so. I usually did my readings after school, between four and six, when the house was quiet. Instead I said, "Eight o'clock is fine. I'll see you tomorrow."

My usual reading jitters kicked in as I hung up the phone. These jitters went with the territory; they were the usual insecurities that came from my ego. Would I do a good job? Would my clients be nice? Would they listen to me despite my being a kid? Doing a reading put me in a very vulnerable position, asking me to open my heart, drop my defenses, and listen to my guidance—all in the face of someone who might or might not believe a word I'd say. It wasn't an easy position to be in, but I did it anyway because it was what I was supposed to do.

Fortunately, jitters stopped the minute I started a reading, so they didn't interfere with my ability to focus. At least they hadn't so far.

I also worried that I wouldn't be able to create a quiet atmosphere, because the late hour meant that the rest of my family would be home watching TV. The fact that I did readings didn't give me special rights, such as asking for quiet.

As I waited for Kerry to show up, I started getting seriously bad vibes. Being psychic is like being the main character in the Princess and the Pea fairy tale. Whenever I felt a bad vibe, like the pea, it was unbearable and impossible to ignore. Like having sand in your eye or a sliver in your finger, the only relief I could get, other than identifying the source and removing it, was to at least notice and admit it was there. That relieved it some. Ignoring a bad vibe was like ignoring a huge rhinoceros in the room.

I asked my guides what the problem was. Scanning for trouble, they said it was my client, even though I hadn't met her yet. All I could do was fret and wait. It was 8:05, and no one came. At 8:10, still no one. I had never had someone who wanted a reading arrive late before. If anything, they usually showed up early and eager.

At 8:15, I began to question myself. Did I make a mistake? Did I mix up the day?

When 8:20 came around, my bad vibes went from a simmer to a full boil. Just as I was about to plunge into the "they must have gotten into an accident" theory, which I knew, psychically, wasn't the case, the doorbell rang, and in both Grant and Kerry strolled, laughing and talking, acting quite casual and a little too loud for my comfort level—as if there were nothing in the world wrong with being so late.

They didn't even apologize, but I said nothing.

"Hi, Sam," said Grant. "This is Kerry, my boss." His arm was around her in what I thought was a pretty familiar embrace, given that she was his boss.

"Hi, hon," said Kerry, looking me up and down. Then, playfully squeezing Grant's arm, and nearly howling with laughter, she said, "Jesus, Grant, you said she was young, but you didn't say she was a baby."

"You're right, " Grant said. "She does look like a baby, but I hear she's good, so wait and see."

This infuriated me, and I was seized with a horrible vibe from both of them. I looked at them, stone-faced, until they noticed I wasn't sharing the joke.

Grant apologized. "We're sorry, Sam. Just ignore us."

A wave of cool detachment came over me as I observed them acting like fools, and I felt sorry for them. Then I heard the beautiful voice of a man whom I'd never heard before. "I am Joseph. I am with you." A warm feeling of light and protection wrapped me up and took all the stress out of my body. The two of them no longer bothered me.

A new guide. I loved having my guides come to my rescue. No matter how fragile and shredded my aura or my ego became, every time a guide showed up I felt so loved by their energy that I was instantly woven back together. A guide's presence and love made me feel immune to the insensitivity of the world, because, for me, the hardest component of being psychic was that I was so raw-edged sensitive.

Thank you for being here, Joseph, I silently said to him. He was to become one of my main spiritual teachers from the other side and a great source of protection from other people's negativity, disappointment, sorrow, anger, fear, and pain—the basic terrain of a psychic's work.

I continued my message to Joseph: *Just in time, I might add, because judging from these two, I'm going to need all the help I can get.*

Kerry and Grant both stopped laughing as if something had suddenly sobered them up (which Joseph just had), and asked quite seriously, "Are you ready for us?"

Feeling Joseph just behind me, I said, "Yes, please come in. I do my readings in the dining room."

I led them to the dining room and showed them where to sit. My deck of cards wrapped in my handkerchief and the lighted votive candle were in front of my chair. Kerry glanced toward the living room, hearing the TV and the laughter. "That's my family," I said. "I know it's a little noisy, but I hope you won't mind. I can't do anything about that."

Chewing gum, she said, "Nah, that's okay. I'm fine with it."

As she sat down, I studied her for the first time. She was tall, very skinny, with a stiffly lacquered black bouffant hairdo that looked like a Roman helmet. Her thin lips were slathered in ice-pink lipstick, and two deep purple stripes were drawn across each cheekbone, intended, I think, to be blush, but looking more like war paint. Her crystal-blue eyes were smothered in heavy eyeliner and mascara, and her front teeth were slightly crooked and discolored—from smoking, I assumed, as she took a long drag on a cigarette that she'd pulled out from her large white purse.

"Do you mind?" meaning the cigarette.

"No." I sure did, but it was too late.

Kerry wore a black ribbed turtleneck under a white rabbit-fur vest, missing a rabbit or two because it had a few thin spots.

As I tried to get a feel for her, the image of a worn, shaggy bathroom rug came to mind.

Grant wiggled in his seat. "Great. This is exciting." He looked boyish even though he was 45. His eyes crinkled and shut when he laughed non-stop, more of a nervous twitch than genuine laughter. He had high cheekbones and straight, very white teeth. He exuded a happy, bright aura. He was clad in a black T-shirt and jeans and had a set of keys in his hand.

Slamming his hands down on the table once again, he said, "Let's get to it."

I picked up the red handkerchief with my cards, untied it, and handed Kerry the deck.

"Please shuffle for a minute or two, then put the cards down into three piles." Every time I did a reading, I invented a new shuffle-and-cut routine. This was mostly for my entertainment and allowed me to get a feel for their vibration while they busied themselves. I actually never read the cards. They were just a point of focus.

Kerry shuffled, cigarette still in hand. I worried that she'd burn my cards, but she didn't. I heard Joseph say, "Don't worry. I am watching."

She finished shuffling, I picked them up and randomly pulled out a card and laid it on the table. It was the six of spades. As I studied it, I prayed for guidance and listened for directions. I started to get images.

I saw Kerry in a garage, looking at a rather homely blond man with thinning hair. He looked bored and red-faced, like he worked outdoors. He was smoking. Behind her was another man who was bald, dressed in a white shirt, but no suit coat, and he was sweaty-looking, large, but not fat. I knew that Kerry was the blond man's girlfriend—at least she wanted to be, but he wasn't interested. In fact, he didn't seem to like her at all.

Yet they were together. My inner vision told me she was very pushy, and he was pushing back. Meanwhile, the large man seemed to be looking for her and didn't know she was with this other guy. I felt sorry for him.

All this information flooded into my head at once, leaving me to put it in order. It wasn't clear what was going on quite yet. I asked Joseph to help me out. As if a lightbulb had been switched on, I realized that she was married to the large man.

How awful. I'd never been introduced to the idea of an affair before, and the discovery was very disturbing to me. After all, I was a very Catholic girl, and as I understood the rules of life, if you were married you didn't have boyfriends. I didn't know how I could suggest that she had a boyfriend, knowing she was married, without embarrassing or insulting her. But it was worse. The blond man wanted her to leave him alone.

Dragging on her second cigarette, she said, "Well, honey, see anything in that card?" Silently, I asked Joseph, *What do I say to her? I don't know how to say this.*

Tell her what you see and feel, I heard. *Tell her the truth.*

So I took a breath, mustered my courage, and said, "I see someone I think is your husband," I started, then paused. "A large bald man in a white shirt."

Her face fell the minute I mentioned her husband. It was clear that she wasn't interested in hearing anything about him. "And . . . ," she said, waiting for more.

"I see another man." I hesitated. "I'm not sure who he is. He might feel like your boyfriend, but he isn't." I had to tell the truth. "You want him to be your boyfriend, but he doesn't seem to want that as much." I softened it a bit. I just got scared to tell her the entire truth.

"These two men are looking at you," I continued. My heart was pounding hard as I said this. I looked at her fearfully, waiting for her reaction before I dared go on.

She excitedly took a drag of her cigarette, happy to hear that I'd picked up on the blond guy. "You're right. What do you see about my boyfriend? I want to know everything."

This threw me even more. She didn't hear a word I said about him not being her boyfriend. She wanted me to use my vibes to tell her all about him, and I didn't want to, mostly because all I could see was that he didn't like her too much.

She wanted to know where he lived. She wanted me to describe his wife. She wanted me to see if he had any other girlfriends she didn't know about. He did, but I didn't want to say. I tried to do what Joseph wanted—that is, tell her exactly what I felt instead of what she wanted to hear.

To get her to stop talking, I pulled another card. It was the ten of spades, and with it I had a feeling of complete "yuck" about her. *Oh, great! I can't say that to her. Help me, guides.* I prayed intensely.

"I get a bad feeling from him," I said. "I can't explain it, but I do. Maybe you shouldn't have him as your boyfriend."

This annoyed her to no end. "I didn't come here for your opinion," she said. "I just want you to do the reading. Tell me what you see about him. Go on."

That was a new one. I'd never had someone tell me to ignore what I saw and try to take control of the reading.

I pulled another card, the nine of diamonds. I could see the husband clearly. I saw that he worked in an office that looked pretty boring, and he wasn't too happy. Admittedly, he didn't look too exciting to be with either. (Again, my personal opinion—but then I didn't marry him, she did.)

"Does he love me?" she asked.

"Your husband? Yes," knowing full well she meant the other guy. Her husband did love her, and Joseph said to tell her so.

"I don't want you to talk about my husband," she snapped. "I don't want to know anything about him. I mean my boyfriend."

"Uh, I don't really get that feeling," I said, hedging.

"Sure, he loves me," she insisted. "I know he does, so I don't need you to tell me. Do you think my husband will find out about him?"

More embarrassed now than ever, I looked in my inner eye. "No," I said thinking what does it matter, "he won't."

Then I got a terrible feeling that something might happen if she kept sneaking out to see her boyfriend, but I couldn't tell what it was.

All the while, Grant sat on the sidelines and laughed at both of us. Some neighbor he was. He could at least help me out and not laugh at me.

This went on for a while. Kerry kept pushing me to look for information to support her fantasy that her boyfriend loved her. "Joseph, what am I supposed to do with her?" I silently pleaded. In a clear, loud voice, he simply said, "Tell her to go home."

"You should not see the blond man anymore," I said to Kerry. "I have bad vibes, and you have to go home." I said this at least ten times, and each time she ignored me.

She only wanted me to use my psychic abilities to spy on this guy and tell her the details.

Completely exasperated by this tug-of-war, I threw my arms in the air, and nearly in tears from the feeling of being forced to use my psychic abilities in a way that didn't feel right, I shouted, "I didn't say go back to your husband. I just said go home!"

"Don't worry, I know what you mean," she said, defensive and angry. "Anyhow, thanks for the reading, honey. I know this must be confusing, but when you love someone, you can't help it. I don't want to go home. I want to be with this man."

She grabbed her purse and cigarettes and gave me five dollars. I didn't want it.

"No, thanks," I said. "You can keep it." They left, and I went to bed.

This whole episode really frustrated me. Never before had someone asked me for a reading when they really wanted me to spy for them and tell them only what they wanted to hear. Or argued with me about what I saw.

Praying for my guides to help me calm down, I heard Joseph's voice say, "You said the truth. That's all you can do. Be peaceful." That helped a lot. But still I wondered what I could do to prevent this from happening again. The experience left me feeling so bad, manipulated, ineffective, and misunderstood.

Three weeks later, Grant called me, all worked up. "Sam, do you remember how you kept telling Kerry to go home? Well, last night she was meeting her boyfriend and left her ten-year-old son home alone figuring he'd be fine for a short while. While she was gone, the house caught on fire and her son died."

That news was bad enough, but several days later Kerry herself called, angry and hysterical. "Why didn't you tell me this would happen?" she screamed. "You might have helped me prevent this."

"I tried," I said. "I told you to go home." She hung up, and I never heard another word from her. But I didn't have to. The weight of my guilt nearly suffocated me. *She's right.* I told myself. *Why didn't I see it? Why couldn't I see more than I did?*

What happened left a searing impact on me. If only I could have done a better job. If only I could have seen more. I knew there was more to every puzzle. I knew the pieces I found weren't enough. Like an archaeologist on a dig, I was no longer happy with just picking up on the shards lying around. I wanted to pick up on the most valuable information, the kind that could have spared her son's life, and then learn how to communicate it so that my client would listen. Nothing less would satisfy me.

I kept this event a secret and didn't tell anyone, not even my mom, partly out of guilt, partly not wanting to worry her. And partly out of the need to forget it.

In the long run, however, it was a major and necessary learning experience that my soul needed. It would drive me to learn all I could about getting the right information, what my responsibility was, and what my client's responsibility was. It made me want to learn to be the best psychic I could be and not get pushed around by people or caught in their deceit or confusion.

For now, however, I just felt bad.

~❧ PART 11 ❧~

My Psychic Training

(1970–1974)

Chapter 13

MEETING CHARLIE

One fall afternoon when I was in the ninth grade, I came home from school to find my mother on the phone, excitedly making plans with someone to come over for dinner the next evening. When she hung up, she said in a thrilled voice, "Tomorrow we're going to have an honored guest for dinner, Sam," but she wouldn't say who. "You'll see," she said, always one to enjoy a little mystery.

The next day my siblings and I were told to clean the house from top to bottom, including our bedrooms and closets, which I thought was excessive. "My God," I said, complaining to Noelle, as I waded through the junk at the bottom of my closet, "is this person coming for dinner or to do a house inspection?"

Mom bought a turkey, so I knew that the mystery guest must be important, since we had turkey only once a year on Thanksgiving, and it was only August.

I was told to get the dining room ready for company. I snatched up my cards and my candle and replaced them with a white linen tablecloth. Then I set the table with our good china and silver and my grandmother's best crystal. The dimmed chandelier, reflected in the mirror, gave off a warm glow. The room took on an aura of festivity and gave me good vibes.

"It is rare we prepare to receive royalty," said Rose, my guide.

At 5:15, Dad was sent to pick up our guest, who Mom finally told me was a professional psychic. I got really excited, as I didn't know that there was such a thing. His name was Charlie Goodman, and according to my mom, he was very famous. He was old and retired, living on a limited budget, and didn't have a car. *Why doesn't someone that famous have a car?* I wondered.

My father returned with Charlie a half hour later. I stood at the front door watching as they got out of the car, excited to meet him, but a little afraid. Even though I was psychic and felt things about people all the time, except for my mother I'd never met another psychic person, someone who could read *me*. I wondered how much of me he could see, and if he'd think it was good. Or worse yet, I wondered if he wouldn't bother to look at all because I was unimportant and not worth his while.

As he approached the house, my heart started beating faster than normal, probably because I was scared. My mother came up beside me as we both watched this aging, handsome man slowly climb the front stairs. He looked 70 or so and very fit. He was six feet tall, ramrod straight, with a full head of long and unruly gray hair, a wrinkled face, and bright blue laughing eyes peering through thick black horn-rimmed glasses.

He wore a white button-down shirt, a tired brown tie with white flowers, and a burgundy cardigan sweater, a bit threadbare at the elbows. He had on charcoal gray trousers and black wing-tip shoes, scuffed but shiny. He wore a thick silver bracelet, which seemed out of place for someone his age, and a pack of cigarettes bulged in his shirt front pocket.

As Charlie climbed, he saw Mom and me waiting for him like two kids waiting for Santa Claus, and he let out with what I came to know as his signature booming laugh. A mouth full of gleaming teeth flashed in the porch light.

"I'm so glad you made it," said my mother, reaching out to hug him, but pulling back, offering her hand instead.

"So am I." he said. "So am I."

"Welcome to our humble abode," she said.

Oh, please, I thought. *No one talks like that.*

My mom ushered Charlie into the living room, offered him a seat on the sofa, and sat down opposite him. I followed. "This is my daughter Sonia, but we call her Sam. She's the one I told you about."

He leaned forward, smiled, and extended his hand. "It's a pleasure to meet you in person. I've heard such wonderful things about you." Smiling stupidly, I shook his hand, at a loss for words because I didn't know what to say to a famous psychic.

Charlie laughed as I stood there with my mouth open. I turned uncertainly toward my mom, looking to her for direction, but she had that "Okay, now get lost" look in her eye, which disappointed me. I wanted to stay, but I took the hint. "Nice to meet you, Charlie," I said and left the room. I went as far as the hallway, where I stood and listened in on their conversation.

I heard Mom explain to Dad that her friend Mary had introduced her to Charlie several months earlier, that Charlie was a very famous medium in Denver who did psychic readings. "After dinner he's going to give me a personal reading," she said.

A reading from a real professional psychic? Wow! Although my mother and I did readings all the time, we were rank amateurs and certainly not famous. I wondered if he used cards like we did and saw the same things we did. I knew as sure as anything that I was going to be there and watch a real pro. And maybe even learn something.

Soon after, my mother summoned everyone to the dining room and asked us to take our seats. Charlie was given my father's usual seat at the head of the table, and my father sat at the other end where my mother usually sat. My mother sat at Charlie's left because she was essentially deaf. She had slightly more hearing in her right ear, and every little bit helped her to lip-read better.

My brothers and sisters were not nearly as fascinated with Charlie as my mother and I were. Although they were on their best behavior, he was just another of Mom's new friends and nothing more, so they paid him little attention.

My mother went into the kitchen to bring the food to the table, expecting us kids to help her as usual. Noelle and Neil took the cue and followed her, but I stayed right where I was, standing right next to his seat, watching and listening, not wanting to miss a thing Charlie said, knowing I could get away with it because my mom was trying to impress him and would never reprimand me in front of him. I took full advantage of the situation.

When dinner was on the table, we all sat down. Charlie said grace, and we started to eat. During dinner, Charlie told us all about himself. He was single, 68, and had never been married. He'd been a civil engineer before he retired and was originally from South Dakota. He'd spent many years in England where he trained with master psychics who taught him the psychic arts (I loved that expression) of clairvoyance, clairaudience, and trance channeling.

Charlie had moved to Denver some time ago, and after retiring began doing professional readings full time, leading, I figured, to what was his now-famous reputation. One of his regular clients was a single, elderly, wealthy woman who had a passionate interest in all things spiritual and whom he'd helped through many difficult periods. She had a son in another state whom she hadn't seen in years, and no other living relatives. She lived in a large, redbrick mansion on Colfax and Jackson, about 20 minutes from our house, on the east side of Denver. It was one of many built during the gold rush in the late 1800s. In the past few years, she'd become senile and now lived in a nursing home. Charlie had moved into her house and was taking care of it in exchange for rent until her son decided what he wanted to do with it.

As he spoke, Charlie lit cigarette after cigarette, and I noticed that his fingernails were very long, though clean. He seemed a bit shabby, but neat and clean-shaven. His most distinctive characteristics were his deep voice and booming, contagious laugh that erupted with such unexpected suddenness that we couldn't help but laugh with him.

Bruce listened to Charlie between bites of turkey, especially when he talked about his readings, then said, rather bluntly, I thought, "So you do readings, too? Like my mom?" (I noticed he didn't say "like my sister.")

"Yes, that's right," said Charlie, nodding and lighting another cigarette.

"What do you see about me? Can you tell me anything?"

I cringed at Bruce's directness, fearful that he might have offended Charlie, but at the same time I was glad he'd asked because that's exactly what I wanted to ask him myself but was too scared to do so.

But Charlie just laughed, not seeming to mind Bruce's question at all. He said, "I see quite a bit about you, and I'd be happy to share some of it." He paused. "You, young man, are like your mother—feisty, creative, artistic—and you'll do what you want, not what anyone else will tell you. [*Boy, did he get that right,* I thought.] You've been given the gift of music, and you have a guide, an African chief named Henry."

We all laughed at this. His guide must be Henry, our house guide who acted as our burglar alarm.

Bruce <u>*does*</u> *have the gift of music,* I thought. *He's a drummer.*

To Noelle, he said, "You, young lady, are very blessed. Your life will be very comfortable." He chuckled to himself as he observed her life, his head nodding. "Yes, very comfortable. And you will create beautiful things in this life. You are a designer like your mother, and your guide is Catherine."

That's good, too. Noelle did sew, just like Mom, all the time. She made me angry because she made such great clothes, and she wouldn't let me wear them. *Wow, and my mom's mother, Ecaterina, is her guide.* I was even jealous for a moment.

To Neil, he said, half observing him, half looking inward, as if seeing through him, "Like your father, like your father . . . a salesman at heart, the guides say. But there's gold in your hands. Use your hands. Your guides are Ezekiel and Michael, angels who watch over you. And should."

We knew of Michael, but Ezekiel was new.

Neil, my rock'n'roll-guitar-playing, want-to-be-in-a-band brother, raised his eyebrows as he listened, then shook his shaggy head as he took this information in. "Thanks, man. Cool."

All I could think of (besides, of course, what he was going to say to me) was how smoothly and easily Charlie did these short readings—without hesitation, without cards, without anything at all. He seemed to be listening to his guides as I did, but with no apparent difficulty. How I admired him and wanted to be like him!

Charlie turned to my dad, who laughed nervously. It surprised me to see him looking so vulnerable.

"Paul, you are an old soul. Your gift is rare, the gift of patience. You have one purpose, to serve and love your family."

That made a lot of sense, too. All my dad ever did was work hard so we could have a nice home. He never complained. He was never late for work. He never missed a day. He did everything for us without saying much about it. He would pick us kids up anywhere at any time without a word of irritation, no matter how late or how far, just wanting to be sure we were home safe and sound. I was so caught up in my own world that I didn't think much about my dad. But the way Charlie described him made me suddenly appreciate him a lot. "That is right," said my guide, Rose.

Next was Soraya, only eight. "You are young, but already powerful, an artist like your mother, a builder like your father. You are a free spirit. You like to fly. Your guide is Raphael, the archangel. But don't be too wild." He laughed so hard that his eyes got teary, apparently seeing something funny that we couldn't.

This laughter business was getting a bit on my nerves. I never knew anyone who laughed so much at everything. And yet, Charlie was so good at readings that I couldn't be critical. *I don't know about the artist and builder stuff for Soraya because she's so young,* I thought. *But then again, her favorite games were "paint the house" or "electrician," so maybe Charlie was right.*

To my mother, he said, "I'll get to you later," chuckling more than laughing. Then he turned to me.

Will he notice Rose? I wonder if he can see her. "Rose, can he see you? Will you let him?" All of a sudden, I felt naked, as if Charlie were an x-ray technician who could see straight through to my bones. He studied me for a full minute and lit another cigarette.

"Sonia, you have the gift of psychic awareness. Your path is to follow a long tradition of healers and teachers and help people find their way, using your vision and your inner channel to find their path and peace in their heart. You have many, many guides and will come to know them all. Your guide right now and your companion for life is Rose."

"Rose!" I couldn't believe he said this. I knew Rose was my guide, but there were days when I wondered if I was making it all up, especially when people I read for said so. When Charlie confirmed Rose, he confirmed everything. He confirmed that I was psychic and not crazy like some people said.

I was flattered, happy, relieved, and intrigued all at once. Charlie said he had teachers who helped him. He said he'd studied with masters. I, too, wanted teachers. I wanted to be able to read like him—straightforward and without cards—without trying as hard as I did, without being afraid. I nearly burst out crying from the torrent of emotions rushing through my body. Instead, I took a bite of now very cold turkey.

All I could say in such a weak, pip-squeak voice I couldn't believe it came out of me, "Really, Charlie? You think so?"

I wasn't questioning him. I just wanted him to repeat it. All he did was laugh and laugh and laugh.

We'd hardly finished dinner when Mom got up, eager to get to her reading, and said, "You kids clear the table and clean up. Charlie and I are going downstairs because we need some privacy. You're all excused."

Everyone started clearing the dishes. Everyone, that is, except me. "Can I go with you? I want to watch."

My mother didn't look too happy at my request. "I don't think so. I'd rather you didn't. I don't want to disturb Charlie."

Then, for the first time in my life, I challenged her. "I'd rather I did," I said, turning to Charlie. "May I watch? I'll be quiet."

Once again, he laughed. "It's fine with me. In fact, the guides say, 'Yes, yes, of course.'"

My mother, now resigned, whispered, "Okay, but I want you to be absolutely silent and not interrupt." I assured her it would be no problem. *After all, I've been doing your readings for years,* I thought.

As I followed them downstairs, my siblings, stuck with cleaning up, jeered at me. Too happy to care, I ignored them. As we entered her photo studio, my mother placed two chairs in the center of the room. I sat in the corner where my mom and Charlie couldn't see me but where I could hear them. I felt that Rose was with me.

My mother dimmed the studio lights and asked Charlie if he needed anything before they started. "An ashtray," he said. I jumped up and quickly fetched it and retreated back to my corner.

Charlie sat back, took off his glasses, and closed his eyes. My mother leaned forward, notebook and pen in her lap. I knew that she couldn't hear and would struggle to follow him, and I considered offering to take notes for her in case he said something she'd miss. But Rose said no, she'll hear what she needs to.

Charlie took a deep breath and became very still—so still that I thought he might have fallen asleep. Suddenly he bolted upright, shuddered (which scared me), tilted his head to the right as if listening, then said, with his eyes still closed, nodding, "They are here. They are ready." The hair stood up on the back of my neck. I swear I could feel his guides almost next to my skin.

"They say hello and welcome," Charlie said. I silently said hello to them as well.

I watched and listened, absorbing everything. Charlie appeared to be having a conversation with his guides, waving his left hand in gentle, soft circles as he listened and spoke. I listened to my guides, but I never waved my hand. I wondered if it would help. He nodded his head a lot as if he were agreeing with his guides, or maybe to keep a connection with their presence. The more he did this, the more I felt the guides in the room. I strained to see them, but I couldn't.

Then he began to speak. "The guide is John. He's an accountant. He's here to help. He says it's okay to move. The house will sell in three months. There will be no intermediary. Just you."

Our house? I didn't know we were selling our house. I looked at my mom, but she was just furiously writing down everything he said.

Charlie continued. "No middleman. You'll find a larger house from an older couple. Not far. Much nicer. Very lucky price. Very lucky. A gift. It will all be fast. Easy. Time to go. Time to go now."

He continued, but I didn't hear much more. I was too busy watching him, trying to absorb what I'd just heard. His eyes were still closed, his head cocked to the left as if listening, his hand gently waving in tiny circles as he spoke. My mother was writing so fast that her fingers were flying off the paper. Then Charlie stopped and lowered his hand to his lap. He shook his head like a swimmer shaking water out of his ears, stopped, opened his eyes, and guess what? He laughed.

"They left," he said. "There's no more." I felt it, too, like a whoosh out the door. He reached for a cigarette and lit it.

My mother sat back, looked at her notes, and thanked him. Profusely. She seemed satisfied with the reading, so apparently it must have made sense to her. She told Charlie that my dad would be happy to take him home.

As he got up to leave, I stopped him. "Charlie, will you teach me to read like you do?" I somehow found the courage to ask. "Like your teachers taught you? Is that possible?"

He looked at me, then at my mother. She nodded to say it was okay with her, although she seemed surprised that I'd asked.

He looked deeply at me, thinking about it. I waited.

"Perhaps," he said. "But there's a *but*." His gaze bore down on me with great intensity. "Although you may have psychic ability, that isn't enough. You must also have the intention and the discipline to be a student of mine. I won't waste my time otherwise."

"Yes, of course." I said, eagerly. I wasn't sure what he meant, but I wanted to learn from him more than anything in the world. And I would do whatever it took to do so.

He must have believed me. He told me to be at his home at noon on Saturday and plan to spend three hours. "Then we'll see."

I was ecstatic. This felt so right. I knew in my heart that without Charlie's help I'd be standing still and my readings wouldn't get any better. I knew there was more, much more, to learn.

Upstairs all was quiet. My dad was waiting in the living room watching the news. He got out an umbrella to escort Charlie to the car because it was drizzling outside. Then they left.

That night in bed I eagerly talked to Rose. I thanked her for bringing Charlie to me and for getting him to agree to teach me—or to at least think about it. I fell asleep wondering where and why we were moving.

Chapter 14

LESSON ONE

The following Saturday I got ready to go to my first class with Charlie. I had no idea what was appropriate to wear to a psychic apprenticeship. I changed outfits three times before my vibes felt right. I settled on a long scarf skirt; 15 silver bracelets on each arm; a black, short-sleeved sweater; and black platform shoes. It was my best outfit, and because this was so important to me, it felt appropriate.

I left the house at 11:00 and walked the 13 blocks to Colfax Avenue. There I caught a bus to Jackson Street where Charlie lived. I brought my large canvas purse in which I put a notebook and several pens in case I needed to take notes. I had no idea what we were going to do, so I wanted to be prepared for anything.

The bus ride only took a half an hour. I found Charlie's house without even looking at the address. It was just as he'd described—a gothic, red, three-story mansion with a huge stone porch. There was a small patch of yard in front with dried grass and weeds, looking as if no one had taken care of it for some time. Through a large picture window, with heavy curtains on either side pulled back, I could see a small, lighted crystal chandelier.

Just to be sure I wasn't making a mistake, I verified the address, 1610 Colfax. Yes, this was definitely Charlie's house. I didn't want to be too early; he might be reading for a client and I didn't want to disturb anyone, so I walked around the block. Eight times. I was right about the reading. As I approached the house, sweating from the laps I'd just done, I saw him shaking hands with another elderly man who said, "Thanks again."

Seeing me, Charlie started to laugh. "Hello, Sam," he said. "Come in. Did you enjoy your workout?"

Embarrassed that he knew what I'd done, but excited to be there, I replied, "Yes, thank you," and left it at that.

The foyer was heavy with wood paneling and an impressive oak stairway with carvings all over it. On one wall was a floor-to-ceiling smoky mirror above a built-in seat. Next to it was a massive velvet and oak armchair that looked like a throne. On the other wall was a bronze coatrack near a small round marble and oak table.

Looking ahead, there was a long hallway leading to the back of the house, but it was too dark to see much. To my right were doors leading to the room where I'd seen the lighted chandelier.

In this room was a massive marble and oak ornately carved fireplace on top of which I saw partly burned candles in small glass holders. A threadbare, red brocade loveseat with fancy legs sat under the window. It looked too fragile to sit on.

To the left of the doors was another large, overstuffed upholstered chair badly in need of refilling crowding a short coffee table with two cups of half-drunk coffee, an overflowing ashtray of Marlboro cigarette butts, a pair of glasses that I assumed were Charlie's, and a glass of water. Across from what must be Charlie's chair was a smaller upholstered chair that had seen better days, but was not nearly as tattered as the other one.

"I'm delighted that you're here on time!" boomed Charlie. "Are you ready to begin?"

"Oh, yes," I said, happy as a lark and ready to get on with it.

"That's fine," he said, smiling. "We're ready for you, too." I assumed that "we" meant Charlie and the guides.

And so we began. First Charlie sat me in a blue-and-white chair and asked me to tell him about all my psychic experiences up until now. Just asking that question burst open a dam I wasn't aware was so ready to flow. Having had so many psychic adventures and no one to confide in or advise me for so long, I didn't realize how much I'd wanted to share.

I told Charlie about my vibes, and about Rose and Joseph and my other guides. I told him about hearing people think and about hearing the voices of my guides, sometimes out loud, always in my heart. I told him how I'd done readings with cards, but not feeling that I'd done a good job.

I told him how at times I saw vibes, but mostly just heard them, and some-times they flew through me and just showed up.

Then I told him about the woman whose house had burned down, and I burst into tears. I couldn't stop crying, not realizing till now how scared I'd been, how much I carried for others, and how terrible I felt that I'd made a mistake in not preventing the tragedy from happening.

Charlie listened without interruption, although at times he closed his eyes and nodded his head like he did when he read for my mother, as though listening to both me and his guides at the same time.

When I finished, I felt as though I'd just been to confession. It was cathartic, as if a heavy weight had been lifted off my shoulders. After sit-ting peacefully in my own inner silence, I said, "Gee, Charlie, it felt great to tell someone all that. So do you think I can ever develop my abilities like you have and get any good at this?" I held my breath, fearful about hearing his answer.

He answered by laughing, and his laughter relieved me. Like a squeegee on my mental windshield, it cleared my emotions.

"Sam," he said, "it depends. Of course we both know that you have the natural ability to be a great psychic. But do you have the discipline that it requires? I can teach you, and have been guided to do so. But I cannot instruct a student who isn't present."

"But I'm here, Charlie," I said, not fully understanding what he meant.

"Today you are, but we'll see. It's clear that you're lit up like a Christ-mas tree most of the time, with every psychic channel in you turned on at once."

"Every channel?"

"Yes. You'll learn that there are many psychic channels, which are all valuable and important, but that can be overwhelming if you're not dis-cerning and keep them under control. Right now they're all partially active, spontaneously opening and closing at random, which is why you're expe-riencing such a psychic free-for-all.

"In working with me, I'll teach you what each channel is and how to open it and close it discreetly," he continued. "Just because you pick up on something with your psychic sense doesn't mean it's of any value. What you've mostly been doing, unbeknownst to you, is wading through a lot of psychic garbage and debris. It's psychic, but most of it hasn't been the best information you can get.

"Don't get me wrong. You have beautiful guides, and they've worked hard for you, and quite frankly, for an untrained channel, you've done an impressive job. But now we're going to refine your skills, and I'll teach you how to control what you get and how to shut it off when you're done. This is just as important as opening it up."

Charlie explained that we are physical beings, but we have a soul body as well, and in that soul body we have seven *chakras,* corresponding to different points in the physical body. *Chakra* is a Hindu word meaning "wheel," and each has a function to keep your spirit healthy, balanced, and functioning. When activated, these chakras open up our psychic ability, our ability to tune in to vibes. He also said that the main psychic channels center on the top four chakras (the order of chakras correspond to the floors in a house, top meaning the top floors and the attic), while the first three (basement and bottom floors) relate more on the physical, emotional, and intellectual parts of ourselves.

"The heart is your main psychic channel," he said, "where everything happens. And when the heart chakra is open, you get vibes. You feel energy from others and from your guides. When this chakra is wide open, the energy opens corresponding chakras in the hands, and your hands become psychic, too."

"Really?" I asked, fascinated with that idea.

"Yes," he said. "As a matter of fact, your hands are already psychic. You use the cards as a point of focus, but it's not the cards that give you the information. It's your hands and the chakras in them.

"The word for this psychic skill is *psychometry,* and it's what I'll teach you first. That way you can give up the cards and just hold things for your guidance. Cards are fine, and I've used them myself, but psychometry is more refined and will help you become more accurate and detailed."

"How do you do that?" I asked, thinking that without cards, I wouldn't have to stay in the dining room. Don't ask me why, but they seemed to go together.

"Just take an object that belongs to someone, and hold it," Charlie said, "and then the information will come into your hands directly."

"And you think I can do that?" I asked.

"Absolutely," he assured me. He reached for an envelope on the coffee table and handed it to me. "Try it," he said, putting the envelope in to my hand. "Tell me what you get."

I tried. "I-I don't get anything," I stammered

"Nonsense. What you must do is get organized. Now follow my direction. Who sent it, a man or a woman?"

I hesitated, afraid to be wrong.

"Come on," he pushed. "It's just day one. You don't have to get it right—just get it."

"A woman," I said.

"Okay. Is it mailed from Denver or farther away?"

I hesitated again.

"Let's go," he insisted.

"Far away," I said.

"North? South? East? West? What do you feel?"

"East," I answered, getting excited because I did feel east.

"Happy news? Sad? Business? Pleasure? Personal? Impersonal? What do you feel?"

I concentrated on the envelope, searching for the answers. I repeated his questions, measuring my response when holding the envelope.

I got a click feeling in my hand for *happy,* a click for *personal,* and a click for *business,* which confused me, but unlike any other time I had searched for a vibe, Charlie's questions provided structure, and I was snapping out answers

My God, I thought, *this is easier than staring at the cards. The only question is—is any of it right?*

"Very good," said Charlie. "Is there anything else you want to add?"

The minute he said that, I got an overwhelming urge to say the word *cake.* "It's stupid, but I want to say cake."

Charlie laughed. "Never, ever say that something's stupid. You have spirit guides that you're unaware of giving you this information, and you just insulted one."

"Oops," I said. "I'm so sorry."

"You're forgiven, but don't do it again," Charlie said on my guide's behalf. "Now let's see how you did." He took the envelope out of my hand and held it in his. "But first, how did you like the feeling of doing this?"

"I liked it!" I said exuberantly. "I even loved it. Once I got over being scared and wasn't afraid to tell you what I got even if it was wrong, it felt easy."

"You said the magic words. You might have a chance at this after all." He chuckled.

"What were they?" I asked.

"You said you got over the fear of being wrong and said it anyway. That means you were willing to trust your feelings no matter how I felt about it. That is the hardest test, and you just passed. Very good."

Then he handed the envelope back to me, and said, "Open it and see how you did."

Feeling like a contestant on a game show going for the grand prize, I wanted so much to have done a good job that my hands trembled as I opened the envelope.

It was a letter to Charlie. It was personal. It was from a person who was talking about a reading Charlie did several years ago and meeting the right man. That meant it was from a woman. It said they were getting married in Texas. Not east. *Rats.* Would Charlie come to the wedding? it asked.

90

Well, I got some things right. It was a woman. It was personal, a wedding. "Hey, maybe that's why I got cake. Does the cake count for the wedding?"

"Of course," he answered. "Everyone knows it's the best part." There was the laugh again.

"But I was wrong about east. It's in Texas."

"Don't worry. I haven't even shown you how to do this. This is what you can do without help from me. You'll improve." He took the envelope.

"I want to tell you what my guides say to you now. You have the capability of being a fine psychic, and this is your purpose. But for now, you're *too* psychic. You're *too* open. You have great guides, and some lower guides talking to you. We want the great guides. We want to let go of the lower energies.

"So until you clear your energy and you learn more about what you're doing, I want you to stop all readings. Just for a week or two. I want you to start over, like resetting your system. You'll enjoy the break." Charlie paused. "Now stand up."

I did.

"Stand in the center of the room under the light, and hold your arms out to your side."

I complied.

He stood up, rubbed his hands slowly together, and then shook them out as if he'd just washed them and was letting them air dry. He ran his hands all over my body about a foot away, occasionally grabbing on to some invisible knot, shaking it loose and yanking it out. It was as if he was pulling leeches off of me. I felt a warm rush of energy.

"What are you doing? Pulling psychic bugs off of me?"

"Exactly."

I felt better by the minute. The whole afternoon was like an exorcism. I felt for the first time in my life that I was standing alone under the chandelier without a bunch of people crawling all over me.

"There," Charlie said. "All clear." He lit a cigarette and looked at his watch. It was nearly three. I couldn't believe it. It seemed like I'd just arrived.

He closed his eyes, tilted his head, and listened. "Okay. We'll work every Friday evening and Saturday afternoon 7 to 9 and 12 to 2:30. That's when your teachers are available."

"My teachers? Aren't *you* my teacher?"

"Your teacher spirit guides. That's when they'll come."

"I'll be here next Friday. Do guides have schedules like we do?"

"Apparently yours do," he said.

I thanked him profusely. This was only my first lesson, and everything had already changed so much for the better.

I had so much on my mind I couldn't even wait for the bus. I walked all the way home.

Relief was the only way to describe how I felt. I was also excited. Charlie got me organized, and he lifted all those people I'd read for out of my aura where I still carried them, even though I didn't know it.

And psychometry! That was so exciting. I couldn't wait to try it again. Only Charlie said wait two weeks before I tried anything. *I'll just have to wait, but it's going to be hard,* I thought.

Feeling so light, so free, I had to skip a few steps even though as a 5'8" teenager with platform shoes, 30 bracelets, and a shoulder bag, I knew I looked ridiculous. "Oh, what the heck!" I shouted out loud. I skipped for an entire block, laughing like Charlie.

That night as I lay in bed, I asked Rose why I felt so incredibly, amazingly, totally, and absolutely high.

She said, in my heart, "What you are feeling is joy, the joy that comes from entering your true path and your life's purpose. Now go to sleep."

She was right. It was pure joy. And up until now, I had never felt anything quite like it.

❈

Chapter 15

HELP FROM THE
OTHER SIDE

Taking a breather from readings was absolutely liberating. I'd always had my radar on—and on high—so the quiet and calm I felt toning it down was like a soothing balm to my nerve endings. It gave me some space. Having Charlie remove the connections I held on to with clients was also a relief. I had no idea I was still attached to their energy, but once released, I felt like I'd just gotten out of a crowded madhouse.

I had a sense, for the first time, of inner space. I had no idea that there was even such a thing, but now experiencing this, I didn't want to lose it. I also became aware of how much I stuck my nose into other people's business. Being told not to do readings made me realize how I was reading everyone all the time. By not patrolling the borders and spying on others, my awareness actually sharpened, especially of my guides. Now I felt much calmer in my heart and head. I began to feel the presence of many other helpers besides Rose and Joseph.

My first new guide was Dot, whom I named because I saw her in my mind's eye as a bright violet-white light, almost too intense to look at. She (I knew it was a she) hovered over me like a glowing orb. She usually showed up at night in my room, but also appeared once when I was relaxing in the bathtub.

Dot wasn't like other guides that I'd come to know. She was attached to me in a manner that I can't describe. Later Charlie told me that Dot was my *oversoul,* my spirit self, as opposed to my body and personality. As I grappled with the concept, he said, "Don't make it so difficult. Just consider that Dot is you, your soul, at its best." That worked. It made cellular sense, if not intellectual sense—as if what he said I somehow knew in my bones.

Dot followed me everywhere, and I must say, she helped me develop a larger, more objective viewpoint. With the help of her energy, I began to look out, look back, and look forward all at once. My awareness changed from being two-dimensional to spatial, global, orblike—moving in all directions at once.

Joseph became more defined. I was more aware of him both at night and during the day. He followed me and gave me instructions. He guided me on what was important, such as what to study for a history test, for example. I had to prepare for an essay test on World War I, and because the war didn't interest me, I hadn't paid attention most of the time in class. There was so much material I didn't know where to begin, but Joseph helped me sort out what to study and what to ignore. He did a good job. I got a B-plus, which was great, considering that three days before the exam I couldn't have answered a single question.

Joseph told me he was an Essene and that I was, too. I didn't know what that was, so I read about them. They were an esoteric tribe of philosophers and healers during Jesus' time. Jesus was an Essene.

Joseph also taught me a code of ethics. If I gossiped, he admonished me. If I lied, he'd make me get caught. Three minutes after the only time I ever played hooky from school, went out to lunch with my friend Vickie, and called in a phony excuse, the principal called my parents to tell them I'd won an award for exemplary behavior. He wanted to present it to me over the phone even if I was home sick that day. My mom told him I was at school. Needless to say, I didn't get the award. I knew that Joseph had orchestrated the bust. He told me that to become a clear channel, I had to live in truth and integrity. When I didn't, I was stopped.

The most astonishing guides descended upon me one night just before I fell asleep. In my head I was saying my usual prayers, but in Latin, and I didn't know Latin. What's more, I found myself surrounded by a trio of Catholic bishops, and we were praying in unison. Then I was no longer in my bedroom. I wasn't even me anymore. I was one of these Catholic bishops in the middle of a massive and secret ritual, and the scent of frankincense was everywhere. We prayed and chanted, and I was filled with an intense desire to understand my soul.

Then, three bishops dressed in white robes, with gold scarves draped around their necks, wearing huge white miter hats with elaborate gold stitching, began to speak to me. I can't remember what they were saying. It wasn't English, and it was more like they were telepathically filling my mind with knowledge and understanding.

I just kept chanting and praying in Latin. Somehow without saying it, they conveyed to me that they were my teachers and were there to help me understand the soul and how it grows. They had names—De Leon, Lucerne, and Maurice—and they told me to refer to them as just The Three Bishops.

Not all of these guides came through the first week after I met with Charlie, but they did show up during the first month. Because there were so many, I affectionately called them "The Gang." *My* gang. And I loved them.

The big thing I got while connecting with these guides was that being psychic was no longer about seeing superficial information. It was about understanding the soul. At least it was for me. So I ran to the library and checked out everything I could find on the soul. My life and psychic perspective were changing at lightning speed. It was so exciting that I could hardly sleep. But I did. More peacefully than ever before.

❋

Chapter 16

DISCOVERING MY
PSYCHIC BODY

I saw Charlie for my second lesson the following week. He told me that our meeting the week before was only an opportunity to get to know one another officially, it wasn't a class. (But for not being a class, I sure learned a lot.)

"Today," he said, "I'll lay out the ground rules and expectations I have in working with you. Then we'll proceed from there."

The first thing he said was that he was willing to teach me to be a channel and medium, but he'd never work harder for my success than I did. And he meant it.

"Therefore," he continued, "my first requirement is to always be on time." He glared at me because I'd barely been punctual that very day, skidding in at 12:05 after having walked too slowly to Colfax, thereby missing the bus.

"We have to be respectful of the spirits' time. So if you're late, I will be *most* unhappy." He said he never wanted to know *why* I was late. "Spirit guides don't care. If they bother to gather enough energy to come through our plane of consciousness and we're not there, or not prepared, they'll decide that we're not serious and leave. And then lower entities will come in their place."

I learned that riffraff, as he called them, were useless guides who offered poor, worthless, or misleading information. They were wandering souls who weren't from a higher channel.

I told Charlie that I didn't know there was a difference in the quality of guides.

"Just like there's a lot of junk on the radio, there's also a lot of junk on the psychic airwaves. So you have to know what you're doing and maintain very high standards when channeling, or lower entities will grab your ear, fill it with all sorts of nonsense, and not let it go."

That idea scared me. "How do I know if my guides are riffraff?"

"Several ways," he said. "One, they *offer* riffraff—flattering you, telling you that you're important, criticizing others, all nonsense.

"Two, they *feel* like riffraff—not warm and uplifting. A higher guide is there to help you, but will never flatter your ego, compare you to others, claim you're special, or criticize anyone in any way. Remember, the guides are supposed to be *higher* forces. If they don't feel higher, they aren't."

Then he went back to our schedule. "As I said, we'll meet twice a week, Friday and Saturday. And you must be serious. Are you?"

"Yes, I am," I assured him, knowing I'd have to rethink how I managed my time and commitments.

"The key to being a good medium," Charlie said, "is to be organized about your priorities and never waste time."

I got it. Or at least I thought I got it. Once, several months later, I showed up on Saturday at 12:10. It was in the middle of the winter, it was snowing, and the bus was slower than usual. *Charlie would surely allow for weather,* I thought. When I rang the bell, there was no response.

He's old, I thought as I waited. Maybe he just didn't hear it or was slow in answering. I rang again, waiting, getting a little cold standing there. Still no answer. I rang the bell again, holding it down for several seconds in case he hadn't heard. No one came. I got worried because this was so unlike him. Maybe he was hurt or sick. *He seemed fine when I was here last night,* I thought, *but you never know.* Freezing, I went to the corner coffee shop and called him. There was no answer.

Great, I thought, unsure if I should be angry or worried.

"You lecture me all the time about being on time, and now you aren't even here," I grumbled into the phone. "How dare you hold me to such a double standard." I hung up and walked past his house one last time, just in case he showed up before I gave up. He didn't, so I left and caught the bus home, angry and fearful.

I called him later that night and again throughout the week, but he never answered. This was before the days of answering machines, so I had no way of knowing whether he was even alive except by using my vibes, which were like scrambled eggs as a result of all my emotional distress.

Friday arrived, and once again it was time for my class. That afternoon I called Charlie, by now fully expecting to find him either decomposed, senile, or kidnaped. He answered in a cheerful voice on the second ring. "Charlie," I gasped. "Are you all right? I've been worried sick about you."

"Why? I'm fine."

"You are?" I could hardly believe it.

"Of course. Why do you ask?"

"Because you weren't at our lesson on Saturday. I waited and then I called and then I had no idea what happened to you and I was worried," I gushed out in one big breath.

"Nothing happened to me," he replied.

"Then where were you last week?"

"I left," he said without any sign of guilt.

"You left? You *left?* Why? You knew I was coming. And you left?"

"Actually, no, I didn't know if you were coming. We had an appointment at noon, and you weren't here, so I left."

"But I came just after 12," I said. "What time did you leave?"

"12:03," he answered, cheerfully. "We said noon, so at 12:03 I left."

I was silent. Now I got it. He *was* serious.

"Can I expect you on time tonight?" he said. It was 5:48.

"Yes," I said. "Yes, you can." I hung up the phone and ran the entire 13 blocks to Colfax—in my platform shoes at that. I arrived at 6:50, flustered, but on time. I waited until two minutes to seven and rang the bell.

He opened the door.

"You're early," he said, laughing.

I didn't see the humor.

❈

Chapter 17

OM! SWEET OM!

During the summer of 1972, Neil and Bruce started a rock'n'roll band and disappeared into their room for hours after school to practice. Noelle began sewing and took her first job as a cashier at La Posada, the Mexican restaurant three blocks away. Soraya spent summers in Kansas City with Cuky, who was now married to Buddy and worked at the training academy for TWA. And Stefan moved to California to study engineering in graduate school at Stanford. He also eloped with Susie, his college girlfriend from Denver.

Mom became very involved in photography and spent most of her time shooting weddings or retouching prints. Dad still worked at Ward's seven days a week.

As for me, at 15, my life was consumed with classes with Charlie and becoming the best psychic I could be, although no one even noticed or seemed to care.

The first thing Charlie taught me was to focus and meditate. He explained that meditation was essential to creating a proper atmosphere for giving a safe and grounded psychic reading, and until I could do it, he wasn't going to teach me anything more. Meditating would clear my aura of negativity that I may have picked up during the day and would protect me from any bad energy that a client would bring to a reading. It would strengthen my ability to tune in to spiritual guidance of the highest, most healing nature and keep me from attracting low-level entities posing as guides.

As far as Charlie was concerned, unless I was able to tune in to quality guidance, I was wasting my and my clients' time. He said that although I had significant natural psychic talent, if I didn't learn to control it, direct it, and shut it down when I wanted to, it would control me and make my life miserable.

"Being bombarded by psychic information about other people all the time is taxing to your nervous system and isn't healthy," Charlie explained. "You can learn to choose when to open your psychic sensors and when to close them down, as well as how to discern the quality of what you're channeling, giving you command of your gift.

"Otherwise it's confusing and tiring, like listening to 15 radio stations at once and sorting through a jumble of messages. This is way too much work."

Charlie assured me that with meditation and training, readings would become easier, less taxing, and far more direct and clear than they already were.

That would be nice, I thought, knowing how much effort readings took. "I'd love for it to be easier," I told him.

Our meditation class began with Charlie sitting in his overstuffed chair, back straight, palms faceup in his lap, his glasses off and eyes closed. I sat opposite him on the floor because he said that this was the best position for meditating. He was too old to sit on the floor he said, but "*you* must because it grounds your base chakra and strengthens your connection to your source of Divine support."

It wasn't easy to sit on the floor in my velvet scarf skirt and chunky shoes, but I managed. Just as I did, my new contact lenses started to bother me, making it nearly impossible to close my eyes for more than 30 seconds without feeling stabbed. I told Charlie, but he was deaf to my complaints. Seeing that I wasn't going to get any sympathy from him, I shifted around the floor until I settled down and took my lenses out. "I'm ready," I said.

We sat with our eyes closed, not moving, just breathing. Once or twice I peeked, seeing if Charlie was still sitting there like Buddha. He was.

After an eternity of silent breathing, Charlie suddenly boomed in his deep voice: "Om, Mane, Padme, Om!" In surprise, my legs jerked out in front of me, nearly kicking him in the shin. I opened my eyes and apologized, but he remained motionless with his eyes still closed.

The chant caught me off guard and made me laugh, which I tried to muffle. He still didn't move. When I managed to regain my composure, Charlie said, "Now you do it."

I stiffened and was speechless. I couldn't do that! I didn't even know the words. I burst out laughing instead. I tried to suppress it, get over it, and breathe through it, but it only got worse. I was laughing so hard I couldn't speak.

Charlie didn't flinch. He kept his eyes closed and ignored my teenage meltdown. He just sat there, waiting until I stopped. Then he started again. "Om, Mane, Padme, Om!" He paused and said, "Now it's your turn."

Jeez-us, not again. I took a deep breath, keeping my eyes shut, and determined to get myself under control, I opened my mouth to say the words, but collapsed into another fit of laughter, this time to the point that tears were now rolling down the corners of my eyes onto my cheeks.

Charlie sat perfectly still. Unfazed, eyes closed, he waited until I was finished. Then again, "Om, Mane, Padme, Om!" This time I managed to open my mouth and squeak out the tiniest "Om," but it sounded so weak and pathetic that it only sent me into another round of hysterics.

Charlie waited for me to calm down, then he did it again. "Om, Mane, Padme, Om! Your turn."

We went through this ridiculous dance for two and a half hours. And that was all we did. He never lost patience or reprimanded me. He never opened his eyes, laughed, or got angry. He just waited and repeated, "Om, Mane, Padme, Om!" and asked me to repeat it.

Finally, all laughed out and tired of my own silliness, I fell into a deep sense of calm. Charlie chanted again and waited. This time I said it loud and clear in a grounded voice of my own: "Om, Mane, Padme, Om!" and it felt so peaceful. Energy swept right through me. We did this ten more times, and I began to drift into a sea of blue light in which I was floating. It was better than the best night's sleep I've ever had.

Then both Charlie and I spontaneously opened our eyes at the same time and smiled at each other. "Very good," he said. "Now we can continue."

We meditated together this way for 20 minutes at the beginning of every class. Each time Charlie added another element of instruction.

"Tilt your head to the left. It activates your right brain."

"Breathe slowly. It opens your heart."

"Sit on the floor, cross-legged, it grounds you."

"Chant the 'Om' chant. It clears you of all negativity and cuts any psychic cords that attach other people to you."

"Meditate because it strengthens your clairvoyant channel. There's a reason we're doing this."

Charlie was extremely disciplined and expected me to be the same as we worked. It was rigorous, but I saw results. I was becoming better and gaining a little confidence.

Charlie explained, "The difference between a trained psychic and an untrained psychic is the difference between a transistor radio and a stereo receiver. Your work will be richer, more developed, and ultimately more beneficial than reading random psychic emissions coming your way from who knows what kind of guide." I wanted that very much.

104

I was quickly learning that just because a person hears a guide, it isn't necessarily a guide worth listening to. Charlie said that there are many levels of guides: angels, healers, helpers, teachers, joy guides, runners, and masters, all serving in various capacities to elevate our consciousness, help our daily experience unfold peacefully, and advance our soul's evolution.

Each of us has 33 guides working with us at any one time. But, he said, there are also displaced dead people who haven't found the light, and negative entities that drag us down. They would be more than happy to bend my ear and give bad psychic advice if I allowed them to. I needed to know the difference so that when I worked, I didn't let these rascals slip in. Charlie said that meditation and focusing blocked the gateway for this type of negative energy to come through.

Charlie asked me about my guides. Luckily, he said that they were all beautiful spirit helpers. He thought that saying rosaries as often as I did is why I attracted such high-caliber help.

"Prayers are natural filters, eliminating negative entities and attracting positive helpers," he explained. He added that a lot of what he was teaching me I already knew on a soul level because I came into this incarnation to use my channel for soul healing and had been trained in past lives in these very matters. That's why I was such a good student and got the hang of psychic readings so easily.

Charlie also advised me to say the Lord's Prayer, the "Our Father," every morning just as I woke up and right before I went to sleep.

"This prayer is really a secret formula for balancing the chakras and clearing the aura." He broke down the formula to show me.

"Our Father who art in Heaven"—opened the chakras.

"Hallowed Be Thy Name"—balanced the seventh chakra.

"Thy Kingdom come, Thy will be done"—balanced the third chakra.

"On Earth as it is in Heaven"—balanced the second chakra.

"Give us this day our daily bread"—balanced the first chakra.

"And forgive us our trespasses as we forgive those who trespass against us"—balanced the fourth chakra.

"For Thine is the Kingdom, the Power, and the Glory"—balanced the sixth chakra.

"Forever and ever. Amen"—balanced the fifth chakra.

He said that the "Our Father" was an instant tune-up for the energy body and the perfect way to prepare for a reading. I was in such a habit of saying rosaries before readings that we agreed I should continue. But I would add the "Our Father" immediately upon waking.

Charlie said that the Catholic faith understood spirit guides and helpers from the other side, and it was one of the best things about that religion. He said that it was a good choice for my soul to have made when I came into this incarnation.

I asked Charlie if he was Catholic.

"No. But neither were Jesus and Mary."

Then he laughed.

Chapter 18

IN EARNEST

Once I learned to meditate and concentrate to Charlie's satisfaction and could demonstrate my ability to raise my vibration and connect to my true spiritual guides while effectively blocking out riffraff, he said I was ready to move on to more sophisticated lessons. It took a long time to get this far. I was thrilled.

I was just shy of 16, and I spent every Friday night and Saturday afternoon with few exceptions in three-hour classes training in the "psychic arts," as Charlie called them. I was taught in the tradition and method of the English theosophists in which Charlie had been trained 50 years earlier when he was a young man in his 20s studying in England.

I loved it. I hated it. And I loved it.

Charlie was strict, structured, and demanding, and I felt at times that I was in psychic boot camp because he required so much of me, wanting me to be as disciplined and as demanding of myself and my psychic skills as he was.

Just as I began to get into my routine with Charlie, we sold our house on Bannock Street, as he'd predicted, and moved to Dexter Street on the east side of town. It was a fast and furious move, and clearly a step up in the world. The new neighborhood was much more modern and sophisticated. Our house, a sprawling ranch with a parklike backyard and a huge family room in the basement, was far better for my teen years because we were now located on the "good side" of Denver.

My trek to Charlie's was just about the same as before, only this time I was coming from the opposite direction, and I had some very close and harrowing calls with being late, because as Charlie warned me, "Three strikes [late] and you're out." That requirement alone made me get organized pretty fast.

The classes were broken into three parts. Part one was meditation and a brief check-in, during which Charlie would give me a two- to three-minute reading or progress report from one of my guides, such as if my aura was getting stronger, my etheric body was gathering more light, or once, in a rare, and I mean *rare,* moment, that I was doing a good job.

After meditation and check-in, Charlie would lecture me for 30 minutes, teaching me the nuts and bolts of my spiritual body, including the fact that everyone had three auras—causal, etheric, and oversoul—and how each one dealt with different aspects of a person.

The causal dealt with the physical body; the etheric dealt with the emotions; and the oversoul, the one that would eventually be of the most concern to me, with the path and purpose of our soul in evolution. Charlie said before I started with him that I'd only been tuning in to the causal and etheric auras of my clients. This was fine, he said, but not my highest goal. My highest goal was to help people understand their soul's purpose, but he warned me that this isn't what people were interested in when they asked for readings. My challenge was to give them enough of what they wanted to hear so they would then be able to discern what my true message was regarding their path and purpose. In that way, I'd stay on track with my own mission as well.

Charlie was absolutely adamant that I understand why I was psychic and that I use my channel for the correct reasons.

"You are *not* an entertainer," he scolded, "and to entertain others with your gifts solely as a means of being the center of attention is a gross violation of your talent, and you will suffer for it."

Charlie constantly warned me, "Your gifts are to serve spirit and God, and not *ever, ever* [and he meant it] your personal ego." I understood.

After the lecture, which, thankfully, was always just long enough to keep me fascinated and was never tedious, we then moved on to the practicum part of our class, as he called it. This was the best part because it was when I got to practice what he'd just taught me. Charlie always said, "If you can't *do* it, you don't *know* it."

First came my lessons in sensing auras and energy with my hands. Charlie said that the hands are psychic receptors and can very accurately read if the energy in them is open. To that end, he had me place my hands out, rub them together, open and close the fingers rapidly to activate my psychic feelers, and then with my palms held outward, approach his body, and without touching him, feel the edges of his aura.

At first I couldn't feel anything, but within 20 minutes of my first try, I could feel his energy body. It felt like a marshmallow—spongy, but thick, soft, and mushy. In time, I began to distinguish between the causal, the etheric, and occasionally the oversoul as I felt for them. They felt like water in three forms: liquid, steam, and mist.

Charlie also taught me how to remove psychic cords—energetic attachments from other people that dragged a person's energy down, drained them, or kept them connected to someone on a psychic level in a way that wasn't good for them. He said that it's perfectly natural to "cord" to people; we do it all the time. When these connections are loving, they're positive; but when they're controlling, they're unhealthy and keep a person from being who they really are. A positive cord would be between a mother and her child, a negative one between a woman and her ex-boyfriend. I loved de-cording, because I really could feel them, like snakelike ropes wrapped around a person, and I could also feel a great difference when they were gone, like getting out of a ball of string.

Distinguishing between auras and de-cording was useful, Charlie said, for preparing for psychometry, which was the skill of doing readings by holding an object instead of using cards. This was the psychic art I'd rely on most for many years to come. It sensitized my hand chakras and taught me to discern various types of energies to a very fine degree.

We worked for an hour and a half, then took an exact 15-minute break during which Charlie turned on the chandelier, making the room very bright. He sat in his chair, smoked two Marlboro cigarettes, and drank a very large glass of water. He insisted that I drink the same.

"Psychic work is very rigorous on the body," he told me, "and it taxes your nerve endings quite a bit. This is because most psychic information comes through your emotional system and uses up all your water. Water keeps your body hydrated and keeps your vibration charged, like putting water in your car battery to keep it running." It delighted him to use this analogy.

During breaks, Charlie would sometimes share stories about his past psychic life. He told me he was psychic as a child, just like me, but he had to hide it. "In South Dakota, they thought I was a spook." He told me he spent ten years studying with the Theosophical Society, a group of meta-physicians who trained in India and then returned to England to advance their studies and teach others what they learned.

Charlie spent most of the breaks, however, counseling me on how to be psychic in a world that doesn't understand it. He constantly empha-sized that I needed to dedicate myself to the service of others and only use my skills for clear and ethical assistance to empower others. He said that when people use their psychic gifts to manipulate or entertain, they attract negative karma because the psychic part of us is intended to help us grow spiritually and not to flatter our ego. I would face tests of character regard-ing my gifts all through my life, he warned. (Boy, was he right!)

"There will be people who flatter you, and just as many, if not more, who condemn you," he said, reflecting on his own experience. "In either case, just ignore them and do your work. Don't waste your time focusing on anything anyone thinks.

"When it comes to our work [I loved that he was now calling it *our* work], very few people understand it to be the spiritual channel that it is, and less are interested in your using it to evolve their soul. There will be a day, however, when what I'm teaching you will be taught in schools every-where," he said. "But in the meantime, you can expect to face all sorts of discrimination. Just keep your integrity intact and your heart pure, and you'll be protected from ignorance and judgments.

"God gave you this talent. Work for God, and all will be well."

No matter what story he shared, or what counsel he offered, when break was over, Charlie stopped and we resumed the practicum. The chan-delier went off, softer lamps went back on, the spirits filed in, and we went back to work.

Charlie was a great teacher. He was devoted, consistent, demanding, and eccentric. He always had a snack for me during break, yet sometimes these snacks left something to be desired. His favorite treat for me was mini cocktail hot dogs on toothpicks, but he also had single pieces of chewing gum, sliced (but turned brown) apples, and peanuts, but only seven or eight. Needless to say, these snacks didn't appeal to me, but I felt his love and affection in preparing them for me, and it warmed my heart. So I ate every single one.

Once I learned to clear and sense auras, Charlie taught me to open my chakras. We said the "Our Father" in every class to balance the chakras, and then he explained the function and psychic purpose of each one. We skimmed the first three, which he said were designed to fuel and balance my physical body. The ones he was concerned with were the top four chakras, because those were the ones I utilized in psychic work.

The first and most important of these was the heart chakra, where Charlie said my soul lived. He told me that the heart chakra was the main psychic epicenter, where everything happened first. If the heart was clear, the readings would flow. If it wasn't, the system would shut down. Keeping the heart clear was easy, according to Charlie.

"Forgive. Forget. Laugh. This opens the heart and lets the highest energy possible—love—flow like water."

No wonder he laughs so much, I thought. It all made sense. I began to join him.

Our class in the heart chakra started with Charlie teaching me that forgiveness is the gateway to the soul. He had me visualize everyone who had ever upset me and forgive them. Then the opposite—psychically ask anyone I may have upset to forgive me.

Then for a full five minutes we laughed. And laughed. It was fun, and I was getting the hang of it. Charlie called this a "shower for the soul, and the best de-corder of them all."

He said that when I used the heart chakra correctly, it automatically opened my other higher psychic centers in my throat and in my forehead, which is why I began to hear guides and see images automatically. These centers worked together.

For now, we worked on psychometry. In each lesson, Charlie put a tray full of objects in front of me and then asked me questions about the owner of each object.

The first was a pen. I put it in my hand, first the right, then the left, as Charlie had advised, choosing the hand I was most comfortable using. It was my left.

Then he asked me questions. "Who owns this pen? A man or a woman? Feel the vibration, don't guess."

"It was a man," I said. "A heavy man."

"Where is this man? Where does he live? Feel it from the vibration. Don't guess."

I started to ask my guides to help me, but Charlie interrupted.

"Don't use your guides. Not now. Use your chakras. Open your channel more before you invite them in. It's easier for both of you."

Rose said, "East, in the mountains," while Charlie said, "Don't ask her."

"East in the mountains," I said. Charlie laughed.

"What does this man look like? Describe his features. Any thought that comes to mind. Describe what you feel. Is he short, tall, round, stocky, young, old?" He fired the questions at me so fast it made me dizzy.

"Charlie, stop it," I pleaded. "You're going too fast. I can't think."

"Good," he said, delighted, "that's just what I want to happen. I don't want you to think. I want you to feel."

The infuriating part is that Charlie rarely confirmed anything I picked up, even if I begged him to. "Not now," he said. "Later. I want to train you to trust what you feel and say so regardless of what I tell you. You may be picking up something very accurate, and I may not know it. If you need me to verify it, you become dependent on my approval instead of your feeling. My job is to teach you to trust *your* psychic impressions. That's when you become a true professional. Do you understand?"

I did, but I didn't want to. I wanted him to tell me how great I was.

"That's stupid, Charlie," I said once, tired of his refusal to give me any feedback. I'd just done a reading on a pair of glasses. They were just glass, no rims, and then gold ear wires. I knew they belonged to the lady that owned the house where Charlie lived. I knew that her name began with an *E*, and that she was rich because of her dead husband. I also knew that her son thought she was crazy (and she *was* a little), and that she loved Charlie, even though she never really said so. I also knew that she was happy he was in the house. I wanted Charlie to tell me I was right.

He wouldn't. He laughed, even teased me a little, and laughed even more when I pushed him to give me feedback. He lit a cigarette, indicating to me that class was nearing the end.

"Why do you need me to confirm this?" he said. "If this is what you feel, it's what you feel. Are you right or not?"

"I'm right," I said, with more certainty and authority than I'd ever owned before. "I know this is right, but I want you to admit it."

"And if I say you're absolutely wrong?" he said. "If I say, 'I don't believe you,' then what? It doesn't matter."

"I know in my heart that what I felt was correct," I said, before I even thought about what I was saying. It turned out I'd just agreed with him. Rats!

Charlie burst out laughing. "Excellent," he said. "Now we're getting somewhere. This is exactly the confidence I'm seeking. You'll need it in this field of work. Believe me."

"But why not tell me how I did?" I asked, still wanting feedback like a kid wants candy as a reward for good behavior.

"Because if you need someone to verify your psychic feelings, you become a slave to their perspective. You may say something I'm unaware of or not willing to hear, so I may not agree with you, or I may tell you that you're wrong, when in fact you aren't.

"I don't want you to require feedback to avoid this very likely probability. Consider feedback an unnecessary bonus, Sam. It's always pleasant if positive, not so pleasant if it isn't. And you'll soon discover that more times than not, it isn't positive. Let feedback be unimportant, and keep your interest in it to a minimum. Never require it. I assure you that it will block you and hold you back."

With resignation, I let it go.

"See you next week," I said in a flat tone, pouting a little over my failure to get a compliment on my psychic progress.

"Yes," he said, ignoring my tone, "see you next week."

"Hey, Charlie," I said as he walked me to the door, "do you think I'm ready to try psychometry on a client?"

"What do you think?" He winked at me.

"Never mind. I think I am," I responded snottily. And so did my guide, Rose, who said, "Yes, you are. Yes, you are."

Charlie opened the door and watched me start down the stairs. My large purse with my notebook was slung over my back; my bell-bottom jeans were dragging on the ground over my new black platform shoes; my 30 bracelets, 15 on each arm, were jangling; my ornate chandelier-looking earrings were nearly brushing my shoulders; and my now very long, perfectly straight hair was falling down my back under my red bandanna scarf tied gypsy-style.

Just to make sure he knew I wasn't happy with him, I said good-bye without fully turning to wave as I usually did.

When I reached the sidewalk, I could feel him watching me and laughing.

As I was about to start across the street to the bus stop, he yelled, "Oh, Sam." I stopped.

"Her name was Emmeline. Her husband is dead. He was a wealthy, retired cattleman. She was just a little crazy, but aren't we all? See you next week."

"Yes!" I screamed, brandishing a fist in the air. I knew it. My reading was clear. My reading was accurate. My reading had the right details. And best of all, it was easy!

I could hardly wait to try psychometry on my next client. I turned to thank Charlie. But the door was already shut.

Chapter 19

BE DETACHED

As I rode the bus home, I thought about Charlie's insistence that I trust my psychic impressions no matter what. I was so sure about the vibes I got from that pair of glasses I held that I would have defended those feelings to anyone. That's what Charlie was talking about— the importance of being focused enough to get high-quality, clear psychic impressions and then believing in myself and not being dependent on anyone for validation.

"Remember, Sam," he said, "when people come for a reading, they're more often than not feeling confused and upset. In that mental and emotional frame of mind, they may or may not recognize something you say as meaningful. They may need time to think about it when they're less emotionally worked up.

"Also, you may be given information in ways that don't match up to the way they see things. Or you may both be talking about the same thing and yet have completely different perspectives, so you can't rely on your clients to verify a reading immediately.

"And you may be given information they don't want to hear, so they won't. You can't control that part. You can only be responsible for *your* part. It may take time. It may take a lot of time, in fact, for your readings to make sense.

"Just remember that you're only the messenger," he said, over and over again. "It's not your job to make a person understand the message. It's only your job to deliver it—and to deliver it with love and detachment."

I knew that Charlie was right. I'd done too many readings that didn't make sense to my client at the time, but did make sense later. That was the nature of the psychic world—to see what isn't obvious, or what hadn't materialized yet on the physical plane. How could most of it be verified in the moment? *That's why most people don't trust their vibes,* I thought, *because they have no guarantee they're right.* Charlie was training me to not need a guarantee. Not from anyone. Not even from him.

When I told Charlie how hard it was for me to read for some people, he said, "It *is* difficult to be psychic and help people through their challenges, because when they come to see a psychic, they're usually at their last straw. They're often very emotional and not thinking clearly, and if they hear something other than what they want to hear, they can be quite unpleasant.

"So never take their behavior personally, and never be tempted to tell them what they want to hear just to relieve them for the moment. They'll only resent you later for it.

"Face it," he said. "A person comes for a reading when they're really stuck. Even when they say it's for fun, remember, a reading isn't fun. It's an invitation to explore the deeper part of their lives, something they aren't used to. If what you see is something they don't like, it isn't fun for anyone. This can make people testy because they're vulnerable. It's your responsibility to love and support them, to encourage and offer hope while never misleading them in any way."

Meanwhile, guides were also coaching me on the fine line I had to walk between encouraging a person and keeping them looking forward to life and to their dreams, while not being influenced by their fears and their preconceived notions and ideas, which I was coming to discover were very strong.

Like holding the center in a storm, and sometimes a tornado, I had to give what I felt in a reading regardless of the emotional weather that followed. And at the same time, I had to learn not to react or be influenced by a client's energy, which was really tricky because as a psychic I was so sensitive. Charlie simplified all of this by repeating over and over: "Observe and don't absorb."

What a dance! I loved the challenge, and I was devoted to learning.

All these lessons were gelling inside me at the same time. I was beginning to get why Charlie came into my life. My guides sent him to teach me more than how to improve and refine my skills, although that certainly was our primary goal for now. He was also teaching me how to be ethical, responsible, and grounded while entering the murky waters of the psychic world; and also how to take care of myself.

The idea that being psychic was *fun* and made me *different and special* was rapidly giving way to a deeper, more accurate understanding of the challenges and serious nature that my life purpose presented. I felt grateful for all of my guides and how much they were transmitting this awareness to me. I felt it and thanked them.

I was euphoric at the thought of doing psychometry readings without cards. I was ready to be the messenger and not worry about whether a client got the message.

Apparently the Universe was ready to test me to see if this was true, because when I got home I received three calls in a row to do readings for the next day. That had never happened before. "Okay, gang," I said to Rose, Joseph, The Bishops, and Dot. "I'm ready."

The next day was Sunday. I got the reading room ready. I lit the candles and burned a stick of my favorite incense, patchouli, which my dad said stunk like marijuana. The new dining room didn't have a chandelier, but it did have wall sconces that reflected a warm, soothing light, and I think I liked it even better. I studied the space on the table where I had once placed my cards. Feeling insecure, I opened the top drawer of the credenza. There they were, in their red handkerchief as always, staring up at me. *Just in case,* I thought.

I'd never done three readings in a row for clients, although I had for Charlie. What I discovered is that the more readings I did, especially with psychometry, the easier it became. Like warming up a cold engine, the first was always tough, but once I got going, it became easier and easier.

I was ready now to try psychometry on real clients. I wondered if the years of training with Charlie classified me as junior professional. "No," said my guides in unison. "Not yet."

"Okay, okay," I argued back. "But I'm getting there, aren't I?"

Silence. Then Charlie's voice, saying as he always did every time I asked for verification of something I knew. "What do you feel?" Then laughter.

The doorbell rang. It was my first client. Her name was Alicia, and she was with a friend who came along for moral support. She was 5'2", dressed in lime-green hot pants with a matching Nehru jacket, and bright green-and-yellow platform shoes with a bunch of plastic flowers stuck to the top. I thought she looked really cute, or at least her outfit was.

She, on the other hand, was chewing gum and looked a little annoyed. She had short black hair in a Beatle cut, thick false eyelashes that looked like furry caterpillars stuck to her eyelids, and bright green eye shadow that matched her outfit over dark brown eyes.

Her girlfriend was exactly the opposite. She was as tall as I, skinny, waist-length straight hair, bell-bottom jeans, sandals, and a tie-dyed, tight-fitting T-shirt. They both looked like they were in their mid-20s.

I showed them into the dining room and asked them to take a seat. Feeling nervous without my cards, I told Alicia, "First I need to hold your watch."

"My watch?" she asked, irritated. "Why?"

"Because I read it."

"I thought you read cards."

"I used to, but not anymore [I hoped to God this was true]. Now I use psychometry. It's another psychic art." (I loved how that sounded. It made me sound so sophisticated.)

"Weird!" she commented flatly, undoing her wristband and flipping the watch to me. "Whatever you say."

"Don't get distracted," Joseph whispered in my ear. I was grateful for his presence. Her friend smiled at me as if to compensate for Alicia's rude behavior.

I closed my eyes, and summoning my guides I began the "Our Father" to balance my chakras. Then I took a few deep breaths and focused on the watch. It became very hot, and images and feelings began flowing very fast. I had the urge to wave my hand in circles like Charlie did, but didn't for fear the two young women would laugh at me.

I breathed and asked Rose to help me sort it all out. The pictures began to slow down. I saw Alicia standing in a room surrounded by a pile of broken glass. The guides said, "Crystal," so I assumed I was right. I said, "I see you in a room full of broken glass. A lot of it." I looked at her to see if this made any sense. She looked at me, completely blank, save for the hint of irritation around her mouth.

After ten seconds, looking me dead cold in the eye, slowly and deliberately she said, "I have absolutely no idea what you're talking about. Why don't you try again?"

Ouch, I said to myself, feeling the full sting of her remark.

I heard Charlie saying, "No need for approval. Just deliver the message" and thought, *I will, Charlie.* I hoped his spirit was with me.

I closed my eyes. Shards of glass were still there—on the floor, the ceiling, the shelves—waiting for her. I heard Rose say, "This is a gift. It's a gift for her."

Telling her the broken glass was a gift certainly didn't sound like something to get excited about. If anything, it made it worse.

"I'm sorry," I said. "This broken-glass image is very strong, and my guides say it's a gift for you."

All the more unimpressed, she blinked in boredom. She said sarcastically, "Then tell your *guides,*" raising her hands in quotation marks, "that I don't know what they *mean.*" Again, quotes.

I wonder why she's so upset, I thought, mentally putting quotation marks around *her* as well. "Steady," said Joseph. "It is your job to send love."

I breathed and went back to my assignment, asking Joseph to step in. The same images and feelings flooded my mind. The glass was everywhere. She had received it as a gift, and she was here to ask me what to do with it. I knew it. I was right, and this is what I had to tell her. But seeing her glaring contemptuously at me, I didn't want to. I smiled as a way to soften her resistance. No luck. She was cold and defensive and looked scary. "Just the message," whispered Joseph.

"I see what I see. It must mean something."

"Oh, for Gawd's sake!" she said, losing all patience and slamming her hand on the table so hard the candles flickered. "Let's go," she said to her friend. "This is a waste of time."

"Go ahead if you must. I can only say what I get, and I get that's why you're here."

She got up to leave, but her friend stopped her. "Wait, Alicia, you aren't giving her a chance. Ask her about the business. What you came here for."

Alicia rolled her eyes and shot me a pitying glance. "Oh, all right. Do you get anything about the business I just inherited? I have no idea what to do with it?"

"Do you think that's the gift I just mentioned?" I asked hesitantly, knowing full well it was.

"I have no idea," she said. "It certainly doesn't feel like a gift to me. It feels like a drag."

With nothing to lose, I cautiously asked, "So what kind of business is it?"

To which she impatiently replied, "It's a junk shop really, old china and crystal."

"Crystal? I heard 'crystal' from the guides."

"I told my boyfriend last night it's just a bunch of broken glass if you ask me. Worthless."

There it was, broken glass. My jaw dropped open, and so did hers.

"Oh my God," she said, as if suddenly connecting the dots. "I just said 'broken glass,' didn't I? In fact, I always call it broken glass. That's really good. That's actually very funny."

"Well, I guess the guides call it what you do," I said, trying very hard to see the humor.

"Breathe. *Breathe*," said Rose. "You're doing a very good reading."

I told Alicia that the guides had said this broken glass was a gift, and that those items in the shop were not junk, they were valuable.

That's when her friend piped in, "That's what I told her. They're collectibles and antiques."

Alicia got the message. The shop was a gift. It was worth keeping. And she should work there. She left satisfied. One down. Two to go.

I didn't even have time to properly thank my guides or celebrate my victory when the doorbell rang again. This time standing in front of me was a short, stocky, eccentric-looking man, around 35, dressed very conservatively in a black pinstriped three-piece suit, with a gold pocket watch pinned to the lapel, and black spit-polished, wing-tip shoes. He had a large briefcase in his left hand, a pocket watch in his right, and was peering out at me from behind horn-rimmed glasses, a lock of his bushy hair falling in his face. Alicia flew a million miles out of my mind as I saw him stop his watch the minute I opened the door.

"Exactly on time," he said, pocketing the watch and extending his hand. Nodding, smiling, and eyeballing me in my bell-bottoms and denim vest with pirate-ruffled blouse, he said, "Milton J. Weiner, as in 'hot dogs,' here. Glad to meet you." Then hesitating a moment, he said, "I assume you are the resident psychic, Ms. Choquette?"

He was so quirky, so formal, and yet so friendly, it made me laugh. I immediately felt at ease. Not like I felt with most of my clients.

"That's me. But you can call me Sam. Come on in."

He stepped in and looked around, assessing everything in the room very carefully. "Cool digs," he said, nodding in approval, trying to sound hip. He didn't.

"Thanks, it belongs to my parents."

"I assumed so, considering that you're too young to sign a mortgage."

Who is this guy? I wondered as I pointed him toward the dining room. He stepped aside and gestured for me to go first. "Lead the way, madam. I'll be right behind you." Everything about this odd man was understated and humorous. He had a pleasantly refreshing and original vibration.

I felt his energy. It reminded me of "Snap! Crackle! Pop!" from the Rice Krispies cereal commercial.

"I sit here," I said pointing to my chair, "and you sit there."

"Very well, but are you sure you don't want me to sit at the other end of the table? Sometimes people say I'm a little much to take, and I don't want to overwhelm you."

He was serious. He was too much in every way, but I liked him. No other client had ever before cared what might make me comfortable, and I appreciated it.

"Not at all," I said, relaxed all over. I sure didn't feel like I had ten minutes ago with Alicia.

"So what do I do when you do what you do?" he asked. "I hope I'm not creating too much 'do-do.' I've been known to do that in the past." This guy was a regular comedian.

"You just give me something to hold," I said, "and I 'read' it. It's called psychometry."

"I'm familiar with psychometry. I'm an amateur student of it myself. Fascinating stuff. I can hardly wait to observe a pro."

That was also a first—an educated consumer. And an eager one at that. And he called me a pro. I wondered if I should correct him, but my guides said, "No."

He opened his briefcase and took out a yellow legal notepad and a fountain pen. Then he turned to me, paused, and said, "Uh . . . may I? I don't want to miss anything important."

"Of course," I said, thinking it was a very good idea, and one I might even suggest to other clients. He removed his watch from his vest pocket and gingerly handed it over to me, cupping it. "My most prized possession," he said. "Belonged to my dearly departed grandfather," he said.

Milton held the watch suspended in air for a moment, then said, "Unless, of course, you think Gramps might try to hog all of your attention. He was known to do that, you know. He's dead now, so nothing you say to him will be of any value to me, you understand. Don't want to confuse your psychic antennae in any way. What do you think?"

All I could think was, *You're a goof, a completely eccentric goof, but I like you.*

"Gramps's watch should be fine," I assured him. "If not, we'll try something else." He laid the watch lovingly in my open hands. It was gorgeous and heavy, and clearly one of the finest pieces of craftsmanship I'd ever seen. I loved the feelings it gave off. It was talking to me already.

Milton sat back and whispered, "I'll just sit here and be quiet. I don't want to interfere with the spirit." He smiled and nodded, apparently in some way trying to help me tune in. He put his finger to his lips and said, "Ssh! I'll be very quiet."

By now I nearly became hysterical because Milton was so funny. I closed my eyes and concentrated hard on focusing because he was so distracting.

I held the watch in both hands and then shifted it from hand to hand. The left hand felt the strongest, so I left it there. Impressions flooded in. Images flew across my mental screen a mile a minute.

Then Dot started talking to me, helping me capture the images—sheets of paper swirling around my head—and bring them to the table. I kept my eyes closed so as not to lose the connection.

"I see you in a courtroom," I said, surprised at what I heard from my guides. "You're fighting with someone, but I don't see the other person. You're alone. There are only a few people there. I think it's a lawsuit of some sort, but I can't find the other person."

Milton was furiously writing down every word. I could tell because I heard scratching on the paper. "This is good. This is good," he said, nodding as he wrote.

Encouraged, I continued, "Whatever you're going to court over, you'll win."

He stopped. "Are you absolutely sure I'll win?"

This was scary. I was sure, but *absolutely?* "Yes," said Joseph through me. "Yes, absolutely," before I could even decide if it felt absolutely to me.

"This is powerful," he said. "Go on."

I saw many people congratulating him. Some were asking questions. It looked to me like they were interviewing him. "I think whatever you'll win in court, people will congratulate you and then it will be in the newspapers," I said, my eyes still closed.

Milton squirmed with excitement. "Are you *absolutely* certain about this?" he pressed. Joseph said sternly through me, "Yes. Don't ask again."

"Anything else?" asked Milton. All I saw was him standing alone and a bit sad. But was that *me* feeling sad for him? I wasn't sure.

"You win, but you're still alone." Then the reading abruptly ended.

I opened my eyes. I blinked, and reoriented myself to the room, to my body. I felt as though I'd been flying and had just landed. Milton's eyes were like saucers.

"Do you realize that if what you're saying is correct, I might single-handedly change the laws of America concerning alimony," he gushed, drooling with anticipation at the thought.

Not knowing what alimony was, this made no sense to me.

"You see, I'm an attorney," he explained. "My wife and I are divorcing. She wants alimony. I, on the other hand, do not want to give it to her, so I'm challenging the law that says she's entitled to it. If I succeed, I have a chance at avoiding alimony. But you say I'll succeed. Are you sure?"

I hesitated, "Well, let's put it this way," I said. "My guide, Joseph, is sure."

"I'm writing it as we speak," Milton said. "I hope to make history," again mouthing the word *history* silently for emphasis, "and I will if this goes the way I want it to."

"Well, it feels like it will," I said confidently.

"If it does," he said, then paused, thinking about that possibility . . . "If it does, then I'll be back with a present for you."

Jeez, no one ever offered me a present before. I didn't even want one. "That's not necessary," I said. That he made it so easy for me to read for him was present enough.

"If things go as you say, you'll hear from me," he emphasized. "With pleasure."

He took his watch back and returned it to his vest. "By the way, how's Gramps?"

"Uh . . . fine, I believe. I didn't hear any complaints."

Milton put away his legal pad and snapped his briefcase shut. He stood up, shook my hand, and clicking his heels together and bowing ever so slightly, said, "Thank you, Mademoiselle, and much appreciation to your spirit helpers. Now I'll be on my way."

I showed him to the door. He stepped out, looked at his watch, and said, "Adieu," then strolled to his old, boxy Mercedes parked in front of the house.

I shut the door and laughed out loud. Shaking my head, I blurted out, "That was fun," thanking my guides.

I got a glass of water in the kitchen, remembering what Charlie had said about drinking enough. I was in the process of downing the second glass when the doorbell rang for the third time.

123

I opened the door and found myself looking at another man, Tony. He was 40, short, bald, with a few strands plastered on top in a comb-over. He wore a blue velvet suit, white shoes, and a white belt. He was loaded with jewelry. I was taken aback by his appearance. He looked like Elvis without the hair.

He seemed to have the same reaction to me. "Who are *you?*"

I knew I was once again up for a challenge. "I'm Sam," I said. "And you?"

"You're Sam? The psychic? Je-sus! You're just a kid."

"And you must be my client," I said, silently calling on Joseph.

He stepped into the living room and looked around quizzically, almost embarrassed to be there with me, and said, "Okay, kid. Do your thing."

I led him to the dining room and started the process all over again.

I asked him for something to hold, and he debated for several minutes before settling on a pinky ring.

I took it in my hands, looking for his energy, when he interrupted, "Mind if I smoke?"

I opened my eyes and said, "No," then handed him an ashtray from the credenza. I started all over again.

Luckily, the interruption didn't matter. Images flew across my mental screen. *Slow down,* I breathed to myself, *slow down.* The images decelerated.

"I see you getting married this year," I said, seeing a wedding.

"Ha!" he said. "Did my girlfriend tell you to say that?"

"No, I just see it," I said quietly, trying to hold on to the image. "I see you selling your house and moving this year as well. To a house in the eastern half of Colorado away from Denver."

"Ha!" again. "Are you sure my girlfriend didn't put you up to this, kid? That's her idea. Not mine." He dragged on his cigarette, one arm slung over the back of the dining-room chair, slouching back as if to say, "Go on, try me."

I shut my eyes again. I held on to his ring. Suddenly, a flood of information shot through. "I see a beautiful blue car. It's very old."

"Hey!" he said, straightening up. "That's very good. I collect cars, and I just bought a pristine old Edsel today. One of the originals. It's parked outside. What else do you see?"

I heard Rose say, "This car is very expensive because it will be damaged while you're driving it." I told him.

"Damaged? No way. I just picked it up today. I parked it just around the corner out of the sun to keep the finish nice. I'm driving it straight home after this and putting it in the garage." He insisted, "This isn't a car, it's a work of art, a masterpiece. You don't drive a car like this. You admire it."

"Is it insured?" I asked.

"Not yet," he said. "I told you I just bought it an hour ago. And it's Sunday. Don't worry. It's not a problem. I'll insure it tomorrow. No big deal." He thought for a second. "Hey, do you want to see it? Go for a ride in it?" he asked, interrupting the reading, apparently having had enough of it. "It's a classic. A once-in-a-lifetime chance for a kid like you."

"Um, no," I declined, "but thanks anyway. Besides, you shouldn't be driving it. My guides say so."

"Come on. At least see it," he insisted. "You'll love it. It's one in a million. I'll take you around the block just so you can brag to your friends that you saw it in your reading. Let me show you the real thing."

He was up and heading for the door. He wouldn't take no for an answer. "Come on. You'll love it."

"Okay," giving in, "but I'm telling you to take it home."

We walked to the corner, and there it was. It was the most beautiful car I'd ever seen. "Nothing is going to happen to this beauty," he said, patting the car like a horse. "She's in mint condition. Absolutely perfect. Not a scratch on her."

He pushed me toward the door. "Go on. Get in. I'll give you a little thrill and take you around the block."

"I don't think we should," I repeated. "You need to take this car straight home."

He wouldn't take no for an answer. I found myself cruising down the street with him one minute later.

"Isn't this the thrill of a lifetime?" he asked, going far more than around the block.

No, not really, I thought, but smiled politely. "It's beautiful. Maybe we should go back now."

"Just a few more blocks," he said, turning onto Colorado Boulevard, a four-lane major thoroughfare. "I don't want to cut this too short."

He drove several more blocks, and I was getting more and more uncomfortable by the minute.

"I have to get home now," I insisted, as we pulled up to a red light next to a huge Safeway semi truck.

Just as I said that, the light turned green. We started to go, when out of nowhere, almost as if falling out of the sky, a huge chunk of metal slammed into the hood of the car and skidded across it, leaving a huge gash.

Then it bounced against the windshield and shattered it. It was so sudden I almost had a heart attack from surprise.

Tony screamed. We were both in shock, not knowing what had just happened. He became hysterical, and I started to cry. Just then the trucker walked up and said, "Gee whiz, what a shame," looking stunned himself.

What happened was his transmission somehow snapped apart as the light changed, and part of it hit the ground and ricocheted into Tony's car. It was just bad luck.

"I think this may have been what I saw in your reading," I said. That pushed him over the top.

"Go away!" he shouted. "Get away from me, you little demon. You're evil!"

That I didn't expect. I was crushed. It wasn't my fault he wouldn't listen. It wasn't my fault he was such a show-off. He created the problem, not me.

"Turn and leave," I heard Joseph say, so I did. I walked the six blocks home. I wished I hadn't gone with him. I wondered if this is what Charlie meant when he said, "Never be attached to your client's opinion."

Wow, what a day! I thought, thinking of Tony's meltdown. *Too bad. It was a nice car.*

As I walked up to my house, I looked at my watch. It was five o'clock. *It's not that late,* I thought. *I still have homework to do.*

Chapter 20

IN THE TRENCHES

One of the best things Charlie taught me was how to shut down my psychic sense and give my body a rest from the vibrations. He told me, when I was complaining about how much and how easily I cried, that psychic people have a terrible time managing their bodies and their emotions because of what he called their tendency to channel the pain of the world, thus overtaxing their nerve endings.

He said that psychic people must learn to give their emotions a rest. This is why many untrained, and even unaware, psychics are unhealthy and become depressed. Being psychic is energetically the equivalent of running a fire hose through your nervous system, and it can rip you apart. He was right—at times it had for me.

By working with Charlie, that was happening less and less. It took a lot of concentration, meditation, breathing, and focus, but more and more I began to feel in charge of my channel and not allow it to run my life.

"Remember, Sam," Charlie said, "psychic energy is above all energy, and too much of it running through your body is stressful. When you pick up a psychic vibration, you're tuning in to a real energy in the process of creating a real event. Your psychic antennae borrow your eyes, ears, emotions, fingertips, toes, stomach, even the hairs on the back of your neck to convey this real experience to you. And unless you control the valve on your psychic sensors, it overwhelms you."

One useful trick Charlie taught me for shutting down when I was getting psychically overloaded was to cross my arms over my solar plexus, as he called it, when doing readings, and never position myself directly face-to-face with a client.

"Turn your body and your eyes away from your client slightly when reading for them," he suggested, "so that you can pick up a clear vibration and not slip into a telepathic rapport and read their mind instead."

He also taught me to de-cord from my client to clear my aura, and to wash my hands after each reading to release myself from their vibration and energy field.

Charlie's basic rule was to observe and not absorb psychic energy from those I read for. One way was to strengthen my clairvoyant channel so that I could observe better. He said the ideal use of my psychic channels for a reading was 30/30/30/10—30 percent psychometry, 30 percent listening to my guides, 30 percent seeing in my mind's eye, and 10 percent just knowing.

"That way no one psychic channel is overtaxed," he said.

My clairvoyant practicum was fun. He told me that my inner eye was above my brow and the depth of two fingers into my forehead, and that I should regard it as my personal movie screen.

To activate this channel, first we meditated, and then he instructed me to envision a white light at the level of my sixth chakra. Next, Charlie stood behind me holding various objects close to my head and asked me to describe what I saw. We began with swatches of colored fabric that represented the seven chakras—red, orange, yellow, green, blue, indigo, and violet-white. With eyes closed, at first I just guessed. Then I tried to figure it out. Eventually, I started to see.

The first time I succeeded was on a particularly calm evening. I'd had a great day at school, passing my physiology and English literature final exams with flying colors. I got out of school early, and I felt light-headed and right with the world. We had a beautiful meditation where I led the Om chant, and I saw Rose brushing my hair and applying healing oils to my temples. I came out of the meditation almost smelling the scent of the oil, and I felt deeply peaceful and nurtured.

Charlie then held up the swatches behind my head one at a time. The first flashed on my screen. "Yellow." I definitely saw yellow. The next was purple, not too dark, a lighter purple. With the third, I said, "It feels like gray. No, green."

The next one I called gray. No, red. Next one, yellow. Then it felt like gray again. No, it was yellow. I settled on yellow.

We did this a few more times. Almost every image was clear. I wasn't guessing. I actually saw the colors in my mind's eye. Charlie laughed and laughed as we worked. He didn't have to verify that what I was seeing was correct. I knew it was. Except for the color gray. That confused me.

We took our break, and he lit his cigarette while I chewed my gum. As we relaxed, he said, very generously, "You're definitely getting the hang of this. I think it will make reading easier."

"I really am," I said, no longer searching for compliments. "Except for the gray. I kept seeing the color gray, and yet it wasn't there."

"As I've told you before," said Charlie, "you never know quite what you're picking up with your inner eye. You just have to trust it. It could be something from next door for all you know. That's just the inexact nature of clairvoyant seeing. It doesn't matter. You did a good job."

He finished his cigarette, I spat out my gum, and we were just about to return to our practicum when I noticed that peeking through Charlie's open collar was a snippet of gray.

"Charlie," I asked, peering more closely at him, "are you wearing a gray T-shirt?"

He looked down and said, "Why I believe I am."

"That's the gray I saw," pointing and laughing.

"Good thing it wasn't my underwear." And we both laughed so hard at the idea that it was hard to compose ourselves and get serious. I don't think we quite did that night.

Our classes changed. We skipped Friday nights and just spent Saturdays together. The classes were also less formal as we worked less on practicum and more on coaching me how to conduct myself as a professional. Charlie shared his list of psychic "do's and don'ts for being a true professional psychic."

Ever cautious, he started with the don'ts: "First of all, don't ever offer your psychic input to anyone without being asked. Even if you have a strong feeling about something, don't. Remember, unsolicited advice, even psychic, is unwanted."

He said it was okay for me to let people know I did readings, but he warned me not to brag—instead, I should be low key and humble. "It is isn't you who does the work, anyway. It's the guides. You're a channel and not the source for guidance and direction. It's best that clients come to you instead of your going after them.

"Always work by appointment, and preferably wait at least three days before you see a client. This isn't to be controlling, it's to be respectful. The time between the call and the actual appointment helps the client get better prepared to listen and get organized about what it is they're seeking direction and guidance on.

"It's to their benefit to wait. Never do emergency readings. Emergencies require doctors, lawyers, and firemen—not psychics," he said. "An emergency reading means someone wants you to fix something, change something, or see something that isn't there, none of which you can do. Or it means someone wants you to make a decision for them, also something you don't ever want to do. Know your limitations."

Charlie also advised me not to read for the same people too frequently because that invites dependency. "Our job is to offer direction, support, and encouragement. We don't interfere with a person's path, which too many readings can do." His suggestion was to keep readings for a client to twice a year at the most.

More than anything, Charlie discouraged me from being too available. "Above all, never be tempted or flattered into letting people depend on you. It's a gross misuse of your skill and weakens your client. It's very seductive to be told you're needed, so be careful. You'll get into a lot of trouble if you fall prey to flattery, or think anyone ever *needs* you for a reading. They don't.

"Our job is to be quiet helpers and assist people on their spiritual journey. We are to offer encouragement and support, and hope they find their way back to their soul. We're helpful and can be healers, but we're not rescuers."

Around that time, I got a call from a man named Alex who wanted a reading right away. He'd heard about me from my brother Neil, whom he'd met at a concert the night before. I was surprised that Neil would give him my name because I didn't think my brother paid much attention to my readings or thought much of them—but apparently he did, because Alex said Neil told him I was really good. He said it was an emergency and since he was a friend of Neil's, he wanted me to see him that afternoon. After all, he said, they were buddies.

I was ready for him. "No," I said, "I don't do emergencies."

"Well, what do you do? I'm in a hurry for some answers now."

"I can see you in three days. Not before." He reluctantly agreed. "I'll agree for now," he said, "but three days from now might be too late." It wasn't.

He rang my doorbell as scheduled three days later. He was looking at his watch, still racing against time.

Alex was about 30, 5'7", just a shade shorter than I, with a receding hairline surrounded by a head of thick, bright red, tightly curled hair. He looked like Bozo the Clown with an afro. He wore a multicolored, flowered shirt with a large open collar and bloused sleeves, and a brown leather vest with long fringes on the bottom. His tight jeans looked uncomfortable because he was chunky. He had on scuffed cowboy boots. Everything about him said "stressed." I wanted to tell him to breathe and relax.

I invited him in. Seeing me in my new white-and-orange linen pantsuit and Nehru jacket, my long hair tied back in a ponytail, and my new platform sandals, he said, "You're pretty cute. Want to go out sometime?"

"Uh . . . no . . . you're too old!" I said, taken aback.

"You're probably right. Too bad. Let me know if you change your mind, though. I've got some really good pot."

Yikes! That's even worse. I didn't do drugs, and that scared me a little. Some of my friends had started smoking pot, but I wasn't interested. I was high enough in my psychic world.

Staying composed, my arms wrapped over my third chakra for protection, I said, "That's very nice of you, but I don't smoke pot."

"You don't?" he asked incredulously. "Too bad," he said. "It's really good stuff."

"I'm sure it is," I said, "but no thank you, I'll pass."

I'd never had a client hit on me or offer me drugs before. But Charlie's training came in handy: "Don't react." I calmly showed Alex to the reading room. He sat down, started drumming his fingers on the table, and asked, "How long does this take? I've got to be somewhere in a while."

"It depends," I said. "Forty minutes to an hour at the most."

He looked at his watch again and said, "I guess I've got time."

I asked him to give me his watch to hold and then turned my body away from him, avoiding eye contact for self-protection, asking all my guides to stand between him and me. I didn't trust him. I'd never before been in a situation where I was feeling unsafe. I wasn't sure what to do. Just then, Rose said, "It's okay. He's not harmful. You can relax."

I switched my focus to the reading, and as I did, my guides filled the room. I was grateful to see them. They lent me support as I worked, and I felt I could use every bit with Alex. Psychic feelings started rushing in. I saw Alex with a very tall man who looked like a cowboy, with long hair and a long handlebar moustache. He had a receding hairline as well, but he was young. It seemed like they were business partners of some sort, or were going to be. Alex appeared afraid of the other guy. I told him this.

Alex sat up. "That's right. That's the guy I'm meeting in a while. We might go into business together. Do you think I can trust him?"

I closed my eyes. The energy was very dark between them. I didn't like how it felt. Both of them were scary. Joseph stepped up to help me, and it popped in my mind that they were both drug dealers. *Oh my God! That's illegal!* And my vibes said they weren't like some of the kids at school who sold baggies of pot for ten dollars. These guys were big-time.

132

And both were scared. I knew my reading was accurate. "Be detached," said Joseph. "Don't judge." I opened my eyes and looked at Alex. His drumming fingers sounded like a racehorse's hooves.

Taking a deep breath and summoning my courage, I said, "No offense, but is your business illegal or something? Like drugs?"

He stopped drumming. "Why, what do you see? Trouble?"

"Not really. Well, I don't know yet. But it feels illegal, and you're scared."

"Should I be?" he asked, leaning way forward and breathing in my face.

"I don't know," I said. "Let me see." I closed my eyes and took a breath. The Three Bishops stepped in and in a flurry said, "His business is selling marijuana. His partner is not trustworthy. Alex is not trustworthy either. He wants to travel to acquire more marijuana, but he should not go. If he stays here, he will not get caught. The partner will get caught. He will not go because this is not his path. He is protected. He takes another path."

I told all this to Alex. "What do you mean, 'he'll get caught'? Will I get caught, too?"

"Apparently not," I said, "but only because it's not your path. You're lucky. You shouldn't go."

"He wants me to go to Colombia with him. I have to let him know by tonight. He's leaving on Friday, and he's pushing me to go with him. He says it's totally safe. Should I go?"

"No," I said, "unless you want to get caught, because he *will* get caught doing whatever he's doing."

"Are you sure?" he said. "It's a chance to make a lot of money."

"I'm sure," I said, for some reason wanting to protect him. "Don't go. It's not your path."

He smacked his hand on the table and bit his lip. "Man, I have a bad feeling about this, too," shaking his head. "I was going to do this just this once, then quit. Don't you think I can do it just once?"

I shook my head. "No, I don't. He's going to get caught."

"Should I tell him?" Alex asked.

I shrugged. My guide told me to stay detached. "I guess. Maybe. I don't know. You decide."

"But you're sure about me?" he said.

"I see you being protected by not going because it's not your path."

He slammed his hand on the table again. "You're a good kid. Stay out of trouble. Thanks." He popped a stick of gum in his mouth and left.

I hoped he wouldn't get involved with that guy, but Rose said, "Let it go."

Shortly afterward, I got a call from Milton, the eccentric attorney I'd read for several months earlier.

"Milton R. J. Weiner here, as in hot dogs. I called to inform you that I owe you a present."

"What do you mean?" I asked, laughing at this very strange man.

"I've just received approval to have my case heard at the Supreme Court level. It's unbelievable, but it's just as you had predicted. And if you remember, I told you that I would be back with a present if things worked out as you said. So I'd like to arrange to make good on my promise."

"You don't owe me anything," I said, feeling very uncomfortable. "So never mind, okay?"

But he insisted. He showed up that evening, thrilled with his success, and in want of a celebration. His victory was significant, although I didn't fully appreciate its ramifications because it didn't make any sense to me. I didn't know about alimony or care about it, but apparently he did. "I just saved myself a lot of money," he said. "I want to thank you for that."

"I don't think I had anything to do with that," I said.

"But you did," he insisted. "I'm not so sure I would have made my argument so confidently had you not assured me I would win. And I'm determined to fulfill my promise to buy you a present, as this is such a historic moment for me. So, what would you like as a reward for a job well done?"

"Nothing." But he wouldn't take no for an answer. I checked with my guides, and surprisingly, they said it was okay to accept his present because he had a need to give something back to someone, and that someone was to be me. I asked him to agree that if I accepted his gift, I didn't owe him anything in return. This was part of my training.

He assured me that he agreed. "What would make you really happy?"

"A car," I answered flippantly, joking (but not really).

"Then a car it is."

My jaw hit the floor. "You aren't serious. You shouldn't joke about such a thing."

"I am serious," he said, "assuming said vehicle is of the used persuasion, of course."

"You are absolutely kidding, aren't you?" Pulling my leg like this really wasn't funny.

"I *am* known to be a practical joker at times," he said, "but I'm not someone who misleads anyone or reneges on a promise. However, I'd like to put parameters around said vehicle's price. Let's say a thousand dollars, if that's okay with you."

"A thousand dollars!" I screamed, nearly falling off my chair. It was hard to even comprehend the figure, let alone realize that someone would spend that on me for a reading. "Of course it's okay with me, but I still can't believe it's okay with you. Are you absolutely sure?" He was.

So we agreed that I'd look for the car, and then call him when I found a suitable one.

Getting that car was the first miracle of many in my life, and the first affirmation from the Universe that my work as a psychic had genuine value to someone.

"Obviously my reading helped him in some way, or why would he be doing this for me?" I said to my guides.

"It's a well-deserved gift from your Creator," they said, "and he's just the delivery boy. You are doing important work helping others, so just accept this as a gift from God."

I looked for the car for a week. I knew exactly what I wanted. And I found it—a 1963 beige VW bug without a scratch on it. The price was $620. It had 107,000 miles on it and a rebuilt engine, but the dealer assured me it was in perfect condition and was ready to roll. I thought it was magnificent. Milton sent the car dealer a check and appreciated that I didn't spend the full budget. Two short weeks later, I was a psychic on wheels.

Newly emancipated from the bus, I felt as if I'd just sprouted wings. It was a rite of passage and helped me graduate from "queer" to "cool" at school. I was now in charge of where I was going and how I got there. That car gave me power.

A month later, I drove home from school, now a junior, and fixed myself a snack. I started to watch the six o'clock news on TV when there was a short item about a man being arrested at Stapleton International Airport for trying to smuggle a suitcase with a false bottom full of Colombian marijuana. I felt sorry for him but didn't know why.

I got dressed and went to work at the little pizzeria where I had been recently hired to work one or two nights a week. With my new car, getting to work was easy, and I didn't have to leave until the last minute.

When I got home that night, I found a note on the refrigerator, left for me by Noelle. "Some guy named Alex called and he said to tell you thanks a lot."

I stared at the note for a full minute, not knowing who Alex was. Then I remembered it was the drug dealer that I'd read for. His thanks meant that he hadn't been arrested. He must have listened to me.

"Thank you," I said out loud to the guides, glad he hadn't been arrested, too.

Chapter 21

GRADUATION

One Saturday I showed up for class at Charlie's house, having just washed my car, with the Rolling Stones' new tape, "Goats Head Soup," blasting on my stereo at full volume, feeling like a million bucks. Instead of finding Charlie in his white shirt, ratty brown tie, and burgundy sweater waiting for me, I found a note taped to the door.

"Dear Sam, there will be no class this afternoon. I had an unexpected change of plans. I apologize for this cancellation. See you next week. Charlie."

A wave of dread swept over me as I read that note, killing my good mood. I didn't know why, but the minute I read it, I knew something was terribly wrong, and I felt sick in my heart. Charlie was always waiting for me, always on time. Always predictable. Getting this note was definitely not a good sign.

I struggled with my feelings, thinking I was just being too Romanian in my reaction—overly dramatic and reactive.

"Oh, for heaven's sakes, Sam," I admonished myself, trying to get a grip. "You're being ridiculous. It's probably no big deal. He's probably gone to the horse races or something."

But try as I might, I knew it was something more. I got back in my car, and "Dancing with Mr. D" was blaring as I turned on the ignition.

I shut off the radio. My own psychic sensors were going haywire. Mick Jagger was too much to bear. I drove home in silence.

This change of routine threw me for a loop. I didn't know what to do with myself. I spent the next few hours cleaning my room. Noelle, with whom I shared my room, was on the bed, sewing.

"What's up with the cleaning?" she asked. "And why are you home?"

"I don't know," I said, and that was the truth. Eventually, I settled down and thought about the note. Charlie had written: "I'll see you next week," I reminded myself, so everything is fine. He just ran into a little glitch.

I considered telling Noelle, but she didn't know Charlie very well, and she didn't seem to be all that interested in my readings. I sighed and said nothing.

"You okay?" she asked, hearing my sigh.

"Sure. I just have bad vibes."

"I hate that. Don't worry, they'll pass," she said, trying to cheer me up, then going back to her sewing.

"I hope so," I said, talking more to myself than to her.

That week I went to school and to work as usual. I even did a reading for a guy who wanted to open a restaurant. In it, I saw that he had the right idea but the wrong partner. This made him very upset because they were signing papers that week.

"Your partner isn't who he says he is. He doesn't have any money."

My client called me stupid and said his partner was one of the richest guys in the state of Colorado.

I said, "Maybe. But I see what I see, and I don't see enough money."

He taped the entire session, and when we were finished, he rewound the tape and tried to play it back. For some reason, the tape recorder never recorded. The whole session infuriated him. I didn't care. *I must be getting good at detachment,* I thought, feeling absolutely neutral as he stormed out the door. "Good-bye," I said to his back as he walked to the stairs.

For the past two months, Charlie and I had stopped meeting on Fridays mostly because of my job and school schedule. Saturday came around, and I got ready for class. This time I was playing Led Zeppelin's "Stairway to Heaven" as I drove to Charlie's house. I parked and bounded up the front stairs, forcing an almost too-happy smile as I rang the bell, I could see Charlie through the glass in the door. He was in his usual white shirt, brown tie, and now very tattered burgundy sweater, and was smoking a cigarette as always. He, too, was looking just a little too cheerful, and my heart quickened. Suddenly, I was afraid.

"Hi, Charlie," I said, overly eager as I walked in. "Boy, I'm glad to see you today. I really missed you last week."

He laughed, but it didn't have its usual sparkle.

"Is everything all right?" I asked. "The reason you were gone last week wasn't serious, was it? Is there a problem?"

"No, there's not a problem," he answered, avoiding my eyes. "But something significant has changed, Sam. Come in and sit down for a minute. I have something to tell you."

My heart sank. As I sat across from him, my eyes teared up, and I didn't quite know why. The salt water was burning my contacts, and everything became a big blur.

Charlie lit another cigarette. "The reason I wasn't here last Saturday is that Emmeline, the lady who owns this house, died that day. The nursing home called, and I rushed down, which is why I only had time to leave you a quick note. I went to the funeral on Thursday. The son is selling the house. I have to move out by next Saturday."

"Move?" I asked, shocked, "Where to? Do you want me to help you find a new apartment? I have my car. I can drive you around, and we can use our vibes to find you a great new place."

Charlie sighed and smiled. "That's a nice idea, but it won't be necessary. I already have a place to go. I own a small trailer in South Dakota where I'm from, on some land that belongs to my nephew. That's where I'll be moving. I've been planning to go there for a while now."

"South Dakota!" I screamed. "No!" I felt as though someone had just punched me in the stomach. "You must be kidding, right? What about . . . our classes?" I wanted to say "me," but all I could get out of my mouth was "our classes."

I could see the pain in his eyes. "Sonia [which he never called me], I've taught you everything I know. The next step for you is to just continue on your own and do what I said."

"But what if I make mistakes? What if I really mess up?"

"Plan on it, Sam, "he said, laughing. You *will* mess up. Believe me, you will. There's no way around that. That's just the next classroom. You'll learn along the way."

He lit another cigarette, but only held it, smiling at me. It wasn't a genuine smile. It was sad and heavy. My heart broke. As much as I tried not to, I started to cry.

Charlie awkwardly patted my shoulder. His hand felt heavy. He said, "Sam, you know that we will stay connected. You only have to find your angels, and my spirit will be with you. And besides, there's always the mail. You can write. Or even phone. I promise just as soon as I have one, I'll let you know." But I knew that wouldn't happen. I knew I wouldn't see him again.

"Now, don't worry," he insisted. "This is a good thing for you, too. You have lots of fun ahead of you in that little car of yours, and you'll be glad you're free to do things now." I couldn't speak because I was numb.

"You have beautiful guides, and there will be more to come. Experience is the best teacher, you know, and it's time to move on and gain some."

"Well, Charlie," I said, still devastated that this was it, "if today is our last class together, what are we going to work on?"

Charlie perked up. "I have that all planned out," he said. "Today, as a special treat, we're going to the horse races. Let's go use our psychic ability and show 'em what we're made of."

I choked back the tears as he climbed into my Volkswagen and adjusted his seat to get more comfortable. Led Zeppelin kicked back on at full blast, and I reached over to turn it down. Charlie stopped me. "It's nice," he said. "Let's listen to it."

I tried to smile as I looked at Charlie, nodding his head to the beat of "Stairway to Heaven" between puffs on his cigarette. His skin was wrinkled, and he had deep creases running up and down his face. His glasses were a little smudged and slightly loose and crooked on his nose. His hair was freshly cut and looked a little too short on the sides. I could see his scalp through the stubby hairs. He took another drag and stared straight ahead. Then he closed his eyes. He looked old and tired.

We drove. The song ended, and the tape automatically shut off. The car was silent. Charlie patted his shirt pocket, looking for his cigarettes, I assumed. Instead, he pulled out a race program. "We're here. Come on, Sam," he said as we parked. "Let's put some of that training to work and make some money." His heavy mood had passed. He was ready to have some fun.

We settled into our seats in the grandstand up front, Charlie's favorite spot. He ordered a beer, and I ordered a coke. There was so much I wanted to ask him and tell him, but he was already absorbed in the races.

We bet two dollars on every race, ten in all. In spite of everything we knew between us, we lost every one. Somehow that didn't surprise me at all.

Charlie moved the next week. He said he was moving on Saturday, so I got up early and went to see him off, maybe help him out, and say good-bye. When I got there at 8:30, the door was locked. I knew Charlie was gone. He never really said good-bye to me; he just disappeared.

I slumped on the stairs, trying to sort out my feelings. A man in a brown overcoat and a black fedora walked up. "Can I help you?" I knew he must be the son Charlie talked about.

"No," I said, getting up, "I'm sorry."

I walked back to my car. Led Zeppelin kicked on again, still in my tape deck from the racetrack excursion. This time it was playing "When the Levee Breaks." I shut it off and drove home.

Charlie didn't write as he had said he would, but it didn't surprise me. He wasn't the writing kind. I did feel his spirit from time to time, and I knew he was thinking of me. There were many times I heard his voice so loud in my head that I thought he was in the room with me.

Two years later, my mom heard from her friend Mary, the one who'd introduced him to us, that Charlie had died.

�֍

Chapter 22

THE MURDER

Charlie was right. My life was taking off in a lot of new directions. I worked two after-school jobs, one at Angelo's Pizzeria on 6th Avenue and Washington Street, and the other at Michelle's Ice Cream and Coffee Shop on the bridge between what used to be the Denver Hilton and the May D & F department store. I continued to do readings, and they continued to get better. I even met several other psychic people, some of whom were professionals and seemed fairly interesting.

I began to spend time with two in particular even though they were a bit odd. One was a woman named Phyllis who called herself a "trance channeler," and then there was Howard, a professional astrologer.

Phyllis was single, 55 or so, 5'5", carrying about 180 pounds. She looked a lot like the Pillsbury Doughboy—white skin and a soft, puffy body, only she wasn't quite as sweet or cute. She had a very red face caused by rosacea; and a straight, pointed nose on top of tiny lips and teeth. Her thin hair fell just below her ears and sat on her head like a stocking cap. She wore red-and-white-striped T-shirts that dropped over her hips, and straight-legged blue jeans and white canvas shoes over her very tiny feet. She looked a lot like an elf.

Phyllis lived alone in a one-bedroom apartment in a new apartment complex on the southwest side of Denver near the foothills. She worked during the day at a wholesale-distributor warehouse, but nights and week-ends, she did readings. Phyllis talked to spirit guides just as I did, but jerked her head and jumped off her chair every time they spoke to her. Having a conversation with Phyllis was like talking to a Mexican jumping bean—I just wanted to grab her and tell her to sit still. I asked her why she jumped like that, and she said she didn't really know. I think it was for show, because I once watched her talking to her friend Howard when they didn't know I was there, and she didn't jump once.

Despite her eccentricities, Phyllis was very nice to me. She repeatedly told me what a good psychic I was and how important I was, which I admit I liked. Once she read for me and told me I was a high priestess from the planet Saturn, where I was held in near pop-star status because of my beau-tiful singing voice. She said that when I incarnated into this lifetime on Earth, I brought my voice with me because it pleased so many people on Saturn. She said that I hadn't understood that Earth operated on a differ-ent musical system from Saturn, so my gorgeous voice sounded terrible to the human ear. That was by far and away the best explanation I'd ever heard for why I couldn't sing a note. I began telling my family and friends to quit complaining about my singing.

"On Saturn I was famous," I informed them. "If we were on Saturn, you'd have to pay a lot of money to hear me."

As I said before, Howard was Phyllis's friend. Tall, husky, and 50 years old, he wore horn-rimmed glasses beneath wavy, black hair, which he plas-tered across his head with Dippity-do. His pasty skin complemented a mouthful of teeth with a big gap between his two front ones. He bent slightly forward when he walked, as if the briefcase he carried were too heavy. In it, he had several large astrology books and a pack of gum, which he chewed constantly because he was trying to quit smoking. He wore dark brown corduroys with a plaid wool shirt tucked inside, and thick-soled, black suede Hush Puppies with plaid socks.

Howard was consumed with astrology and wanted to quit his job sell-ing insurance and make his living doing charts exclusively, so he spent almost all his free time poring over them. He was particularly fascinated with my chart and told me I was a born psychic with many planets in the 12th house, which signaled psychic ability.

I met Phyllis and Howard through one of my clients who had given them my name. They called me for a reading, coming to see me together, then kept calling me just to talk. Soon after came frequent invitations. I accepted them all, partly because they were so enamored of me, partly because they were so invitingly peculiar, and partly because Howard was teaching me quite a bit about astrology, which I wanted to learn.

After a while, the novelty wore off. I found them just too eccentric. Phyllis was preoccupied with aliens and talked incessantly of evil spirits, neither of which my psychic radar ever picked up. Howard was just plain annoying and talked nonstop about money and finding ways to quit his job and make money in the "psychic biz," as he called it.

Their most recent business endeavor was selling small black boxes filled with crystal chips that they claimed protected a person from bad vibes. They sold them for $75, which to me was a small fortune. They insisted that I buy one because I was at "risk for a negative attack," and I consistently said no. It wasn't that I didn't believe the box did what they said, I just didn't feel the bad energy Phyllis warned me about. I didn't feel anything from the box either.

Eventually, Howard and Phyllis got on my nerves. What began as flattering attention became overbearing and controlling, yet I was immature and naïve and didn't quite know how to politely ditch them. I became increasingly uncomfortable whenever they were around, and I thought that most of Phyllis's readings were too far out to make sense.

One August afternoon, Phyllis called me at home, excited and breathless. The police had just contacted her and asked if she'd be willing to help them solve a murder in Salida, a town about 60 miles southwest of Denver in the mountains. Two people had been found gunned down in front of their fireplace in their gorgeous mountain home, and the authorities had no leads or clues and needed some assistance.

"Sam," she said, "you must come with me to work on this murder. It's your big chance, and you mustn't miss it. You'll get lots of recognition for helping solve this case."

Flattered that Phyllis recommended me to help (after all, I was only 16), I said, "Great. Count me in." I wasn't clear what "big chance" meant. I told my mother the story, and she strongly advised me not to go. But being a typical headstrong psychic teenager, I insisted that she not interfere with my life. "This is not a game, Sonia," she said, using my real name to emphasize how serious she was. "It is *not* a game!"

Howard picked Phyllis and me up early the next morning, and we drove the hour and a half to the Salida sheriff's department. Phyllis carried a huge black bag, Howard brought his briefcase, and the two talked nonstop the entire way. I sat in the backseat empty-handed, feeling more and more trapped, and worried that I was getting into something way over my head.

We followed the sheriff to the murder scene, another 20 minutes down a winding road toward a beautiful, newly built, isolated two-story mountain home with a large porch and gorgeous wildflowers all around it. We entered through a low wooden fence and continued to drive toward the house, which was still about a fourth of a mile away. I could see two more sheriffs waiting for us. I also saw three other people, two guys and a woman, all in their late 20s or early 30s, standing beside them. From their expressions, I knew at once that these people were family members of the victims. All three looked completely shattered and desperate. Their auras were gray and brown, and their hearts were broken. The minute I saw them, I realized the enormity of the situation, and I was suddenly overwhelmed. Until then, this was only an opportunity for me to be a star. Seeing their faces, I felt ashamed of myself. My mother was right. This was no game.

Howard and Phyllis, oblivious to the family and their grief, chattered inanely about evil spirits and the mountains. All I could do was say rosaries and beg my guides to protect me and forgive me for being so self-absorbed.

We pulled up to the house and got out of the car. Phyllis and Howard marched ahead with the sheriff. I hung back, desperately looking around, trying to figure out how to escape. I was scared. I knew I'd be of no use, and I wanted to cry. The next thing I knew, I was being introduced to the family. The daughter said, "I'm so grateful you're here. We hope you can help us find who murdered our parents. Please, please try to help us."

I shook her hand, but I didn't say a word. I couldn't find my voice because I was so heartbroken for her, for all of them, and so embarrassed and frightened for myself.

How could I tell them that I'd made a mistake in coming? How could I tell them that I didn't think I could help because I was too emotional and scared to tune in to anything? How could I tell them that I thought Phyllis and Howard were nuts and they shouldn't listen to them because the things they said only happened on Saturn?

The next thing I knew, the sheriff led us three psychic sleuths into the house, the family members following behind. In the living room, I saw many dark stains splattered all over the fireplace and the wall, which I realized was dried blood. The hair stood up on the back of my neck as I fully absorbed the hideous nature of the situation. On the floor near the fireplace, I saw the outline of a body in thick white chalk just like I'd seen on TV police shows. I heard the sheriff say that the victims must have been sitting or sleeping in front of the fireplace when the intruder or intruders entered the house.

Pointing out the first body, the sheriff said that the father was shot at the fireplace before he could escape, and the mother, apparently trying to run from the killer, was shot in the chest and the back many times and then fell into the basement stairwell head first.

I slowly walked to the stairs and looked at the place where the woman had fallen. Again, I saw the outline of a body, this one sprawled on the stairs, and blood everywhere, including a huge stain where her head had been. I could see her crash downstairs in my mind's eye. I could actually feel her trying to escape her killer, and I gasped in horror, clapping my hands over my mouth to muffle the sound. Everyone turned to look at me. I dropped my hands to my side and just stood there, frozen. Turning to the family, feeling as though I were in quicksand, I managed of all things, a smile. Never before had my psychic ability absorbed something so completely awful. Despite all the admonitions by Charlie to remain detached, to observe, and not absorb anyone else's energy, I absorbed everything, and it made me feel faint with terror.

Before I even had a minute to register the situation or try to get grounded and detached, Phyllis and Howard were mobilizing into action. They asked the family to wait outside along with the sheriffs so we could "get to work." I was speechless.

Once everyone was outside, I meekly asked Phyllis, "What do we do?" Completely freaked out and looking to her for protection, my heart pounded through my chest. What followed unfolded like a bad horror movie.

Phyllis threw open her bag and pulled out a huge crucifix and started swaying it in the air, screaming, "Get out, evil demons, get out. Out!" Then she started saying the "Our Father" very loudly and screaming at me that the house was filled with evil energy. Howard, at the same time, was wailing at full volume. They seemed to be performing some sort of exorcism.

Paralyzed by their antics, I watched as they marched around the room chasing the demons out. All I could pick up over the thunderous boom of my own heart was feeling as though I were drowning in the absolute terror the two people must have felt before they died. I couldn't separate myself from the murder victims, especially the woman. I felt her fear course through my veins. I felt her horror take the breath out of my lungs, and absolutely felt, looking through her eyes, her disbelief and shock when she realized that she actually knew the person who was about to kill her.

Phyllis continued screaming, and she was scaring me to death. Suddenly she stopped, looked at me, and shouted, her eyes wildly darting back and forth, "Oh my God, the evil spirits are taking over your body. You're too young. You're not protected." Howard handed me a crystal box and said, "Hold this. Pay me later."

Phyllis shrieked at me, "Run! Run before they possess you!" and waved the crucifix violently in all directions to chase the demons away.

Needless to say, I flipped. Never before had I been so terrified and so unbelievably traumatized. I felt like I was drowning in the bizarre energy that filled the house. Dropping the box, almost as if in slow motion, I looked at the blood, I looked at Phyllis and Howard, I looked at the outlines of the bodies, the sheriff, and the family waiting outside, and I panicked. I ran out the door—by the family, past the gate, onto the road, down the mountain. I ran and ran. I couldn't stop.

I ran for almost 20 minutes when the sheriff drove up beside me and stopped. "Get in," he said. "Are you all right? What the heck happened in there?" Then, looking hard at me as for the first time, he said, "Jesus, you're just a kid, aren't you?"

I couldn't talk. I just got in. We sat for a minute, and then he said, "Would you like me to take you to the station?" I nodded my head and burst into tears. When we got to the station, I called my mom, and she came and got me.

Before I left, I apologized to the sheriff for running away and for not being of any help. I asked him to apologize to the family. I felt so bad for them. The last thing I told him before I walked away was, "Those people knew the person who killed them. They knew who he was, and they knew him very well, like he was a good friend or someone they trusted, especially the woman. I'm sure of it. That's all I got."

My mother had mercy on me. She didn't say a word in the car. I cried all the way home, trying to get the horrifying images of the blood—especially where the woman's outlined body was—the crucifix, and the stupid black box out of my head. And worst of all, I couldn't stop seeing the faces of the stricken family.

Then I heard Charlie's stern voice in my head and his endless lectures on not being flattered or manipulated in my work. I heard him warning me about keeping my ego out of things, and not starting to think that I was needed for any emergency. I felt like I had completely ignored everything he'd taught me, and I felt totally ashamed. I'd utterly failed every test he said I would face. This only made me feel ten times worse. *Serves me right,* I thought, personally devastated and psychically shattered. Charlie had warned me never to get involved with people or situations like this, and yet the minute he was gone, I did exactly the opposite. What a failure I was.

When we got home, my mother said, "Being psychic is not enough, Sam. You must also become spiritually educated to understand why horrible things happen. I had to learn that after all the things I witnessed in the war. It's time you learned it, too. Just don't lose faith in life."

Whatever happened to the family, or Phyllis and Howard, I'll never know. Nor do I know whether the case was ever solved. I was so traumatized by the entire experience that I nearly had a nervous breakdown. In fact, it was so deeply disturbing that I never wanted to do anything psychic again. I was angry with myself for having gotten in that mess. I wished I'd just listened to my mother.

The worst part was watching my back, watching the shadows, wondering if Phyllis was right and there *were* evil things around me. Certainly, what I saw was evil enough. And because the killer was on the loose, all sense of safety I'd had was shattered. My once-sheltered world of spirits, angels, and guides had collapsed, and it was now overtaken with demons.

My beliefs about life, people, and psychic interests turned black, and I felt that I was being punished for getting involved. Why couldn't I just be normal like other kids and ignore psychic matters? Why couldn't I tune out my vibes and ignore my feelings? And why had I been spending time with those nutty people? I beat myself up about the whole mess over and over.

After that, I walked away from all things psychic. I felt that my circuits were blown, and I couldn't take it anymore. I couldn't relax. I couldn't sleep. I couldn't watch TV, especially the news. I didn't feel safe with anyone. Someone did that horrible thing and was on the loose. He could be anywhere, and if he knew that I was at that house and was sure those people knew him, maybe he'd come after for me. That alone nearly paralyzed me with fear.

I tried to put the experience out of my mind by meditating. That didn't work. Then I went to church every day and wore a huge cross around my neck for protection. That didn't help either. Then I burned salt in a frying pan because I'd read somewhere that it dispelled bad vibes and would protect me. That didn't help. No matter what I did, I was completely afraid of evil spirits, evil people, and bad things happening to me and being unable to do anything about it.

I didn't feel my guides at all, and I didn't care. I blamed them for allowing me to get into this mess. If they were any kind of guides at all, they would have warned me. I became very withdrawn and depressed. I wanted to shut off my sensitivity and think about other things, like going to concerts, listening to music, and having fun. I didn't want to be bothered with the psychic world; I just wanted to live in the ordinary world and pretend there was nothing more.

Six or seven months later, a client who called me for a reading miraculously helped me recuperate. I told him I was no longer doing readings and explained why. He said that it saddened him to hear I had been through that ordeal. He referred me to a sweet, elderly gentleman named Tom Dougherty, who practiced biofeedback and emotional therapy and who said he thought he could help me.

I met Tom and told him what had happened in Salida. I couldn't even get through the whole story without crying and becoming extremely upset all over again. Tom explained that I was suffering from post-traumatic stress disorder, and that he could help me with biofeedback, a method he used to help Vietnam veterans recover from traumatic experiences.

I saw Tom twice a week. Through the use of biofeedback sensors, I began to recover my sense of balance. He had me place my fingertips on small sensors that made a high-pitched sound to indicate anxiety or stress. I had to talk the events through, with my fingertips on these sensors, over and over again, until I could tell the story without the sensors sounding once. It took several months to be able to do this—to have the entire event unfold in my mind's eye without any emotional reaction—but finally I succeeded. With the use of the biofeedback and a huge dose of good old-fashioned grandfatherly counseling, I finally began to heal.

One day as I recounted the Salida episode again with Tom, I felt as though the entire experience was more absurd and ridiculous than it was terrifying. And I realized that Tom had succeeded in teaching me what Charlie had tried to, but I'd failed to learn—to *observe* but not *absorb* psychic energy from the people and events around me.

Through my work with Tom, I could now do that with ease. I no longer felt pulled into anyone's energy and could observe entire past events with no reaction at all. This gave me my world back; it gave me space and breathing room. It allowed me to be aware of others' energy without being affected by it. Basically, it gave me freedom. Before, my psychic senses had taken me underwater with people as I swam in their vibrations; now I simply stood at the edge of the pool and looked in without even getting wet. What freedom! And with that, my psychic antennae began to rise again.

I woke up very early one morning near the end of the summer, and standing at the foot of my bed was my guide Rose, smiling, radiant, and full of love. I was thrilled to see her once again and realized how much I'd missed her. In fact, I'd missed being in touch with *all* of my spirit guides. "Welcome back," she said. "You made it."

I felt Rose's loving presence fill my body—that sweet, uplifting vibration that always left me feeling happy no matter what. "Sonia," she said, "you've just been through the dark night of the soul. Had you not made the choice to heal your spirit, your path would have changed, and your mission would not have been possible. We're grateful to have been able to love and guide you to Tom, even when you couldn't feel us with you."

"So you brought me to Tom?" I asked, thinking it had been a miracle.

"Yes, of course," she said, "we have always been with you, even when you turned away and shut down your heart."

Feeling Rose's energy once more, I decided that enough was enough. I was tired of being held hostage by my own fears and by the past. Yes, it had been unpleasant and scary, but it wasn't enough to keep me stuck. I knew that the only way to get over this completely was to learn everything I possibly could about why this had happened so it wouldn't happen again to me or anyone else. I was determined to reenter my mission, and this time be far more intelligent and discerning. If I knew more, I could help people avoid psychic traumas and unscrupulous people. I made a deep commitment to myself to leave no stone unturned in my quest for spiritual understanding.

I was no longer willing to merely use my psychic gifts to spy on people and peer into their future, or figure out answers to their questions. I was no longer interested in just being the messenger. I wanted to be the teacher.

Gradually, my other guides returned as well. In reality, they hadn't gone anywhere. Like turning off the television, the trauma had simply shut off my psychic channel, and I couldn't hear my guides for a while. As I began to heal, my channel was slowly reopening.

The Three Bishops began transmitting guidance to me once more. They said, "Your real mission is to learn and then teach others that we are not mortal beings. We are spiritual beings, operating through physical bodies, lifetime after lifetime. There is no real death. Your job is to use your higher channel to help people remember this, to recover their awareness that all people are Divine by nature, here on Earth to learn to love.

"In each lifetime, each person creates various dramas that teach them how to love. But the soul lives on. It does not die. You keep returning until you learn to love, and to create and to express your God Self.

"All psychic experiences are really our soul reminding us not to become so hypnotized by the material plane or our egos or our personalities, that we forget that really we are spirit, co-creating with God.

"All psychic awareness is ultimately meant to guide you back to that truth. It's your soul, the voice of your true self. And the more you listen to it, the more you heal."

That was a lot to think about, and I thought about it all the time. I didn't start doing readings again for some time, but I slowly began to realize that I was here to do that, that it was my mission. Hearing this, I could begin to see how the events of my life had been weaving together, leading up to the murder—and how, as horrible and traumatic as it was, and as difficult it was for me to recover, it was the best thing that could have ever happened to me.

That night, Bruce asked if I wanted to see the Rolling Stones in concert because he had an extra ticket. The fact that my brother was asking me to go a concert with him was such a miracle that I took it as an affirmation that the Universe wanted me to step back into the world and start enjoying myself once again.

I jumped at the chance, and we had a fantastic time.

I was back.

Chapter 23

MOVING ON

My searing experience in Salida left me with a lot more questions than answers. Although I was a highly trained psychic, I knew that I had more to discover about how the world really worked. In retrospect, I can see that the murder was a turning point for me, and one that was necessary to fulfill my destiny as a psychic guide and healer. Until then, I had approached psychic readings with no thought about why life happened as it did, or even why I did readings at all. I just did them because I could. Now I needed a reason to use my psychic abilities—and a good one at that—to motivate me to get back in the trenches.

I no longer had a desire to merely "see" the future as I'd been doing, especially when what I saw was often so frustrating and disappointing to my clients. I wanted to help my clients create a better future, rather than struggle with the one they had. I no longer wanted to say, "I see a train wreck coming." I wanted to say, "I see a train wreck coming, so you'd better change tracks."

I especially wanted clients to know that they *could* change their course, and that life didn't really work the way it appeared, unfolding randomly and chaotically, with no other choice but to accept it all as it came.

In pursuit of answers, I developed an insatiable appetite for reading everything metaphysical and spiritual that I could lay my hands on. I began to understand that we have everything to do with what happens to us, and as spiritual beings we actually co-create with the Universe all the events we experience. Every one. Even the two people who were murdered.

That's not to say that I felt the murdered people deserved their fate or intended it. Not at all. But it did mean that I knew that in some way they had a vote in their experience, even if it wasn't clear to the rest of us how that vote was cast to lead to such a horrifying outcome.

That became my new mission: to find the answers to those questions, because otherwise the world was just too random and scary to live in. If we couldn't direct our lives and prevent such heinous events, then we were doomed. And I wasn't willing to accept that because I knew in my heart and soul that we weren't.

I wanted to know how things operated behind the scenes of our lives so I could tell people how to better direct their own.

I also had another insight into my psychic readings and why clients sought them. I came to recognize that often when clients came to me for readings, they weren't *really* interested in my true psychic insights; rather, they came in the hopes that I would see a particular outcome in their future. What they wanted was a happy ending, whatever that meant for them at that moment. And that was what I wanted to give them as well. I wanted to tell them that their wishes would come true—easily and soon. Nothing else would have made life simpler or more rewarding. The trouble is, I couldn't do that because it wasn't true most of the time.

Before I even started a reading, I often knew in my heart that whatever my client wanted wouldn't happen no matter what. I could predict this unhappy outcome because their vibration, their energy, was "off." It was dissonant and discombobulated, moving in all directions and lacking any steam or power to create. It made their life wince and move away, rather than draw to them whatever they were seeking.

Once in a great while, however, I would read for a client whose vibration was just the opposite: peaceful and harmonious. I knew they would get their heart's desire—and soon. Unlike their off-key counterparts, these clients had such a positive and compelling, energetically on-key vibration, that it felt as though they were in the flow of life, easily attracting what they were seeking and more. This was the difference between happy endings and sad stories.

Discovering what created this kind of attractive vibration or energy became my main interest. If only I could uncover the secret and show my off-key clients how to create on-key energy and tune their vibration, they would begin to flow, and attract the positive things they were seeking.

In my drive to share how energy and vibration worked to either attract or repel life, my readings changed significantly. I began to use my psychic skills to more closely see each client's vibration and where and how it went flat or dissonant, thereby leading them off course. I then sought to shift it back to center with various suggestions, as if tuning a piano.

I spent hours at the library, poring over books on theosophy, religion, astrology, numerology, yoga, sound and color therapy, esoteric spirituality— anything I could find to help me discover more ways to bring a client's vibration back into harmony.

My search led me all over town and then some. I discovered a book-store in Boulder called the Pentagram, owned by Wiccans (followers of a pre-Christian western European nature religion), who made their own incense and had a fantastic collection of books and other esoteric mate-rial on the psychic arts. They blended incenses to help me restore balance in a client and taught me the best times each month to give a reading for heightened awareness, clarity, and harmony.

I discovered a group of astrologers who owned a store called the Nic Nac Nook in west Denver that sold texts that I couldn't find in the library, and also gave astrological classes. I frequented that store regularly, learn-ing how to cast astrological charts in my search to understand what made a person's vibration tick.

Just as I began to delve more deeply into my spiritual and metaphys-ical studies, my guides once again delivered a helper and friend as they had in the past. Even better, this one was delivered right to my front door. Well, almost—actually, he was delivered next door as my new neighbor.

His name was Pat Adamson, an offbeat professional actor, mostly play-ing bad guys in live theater and films. He was 23 to my 16-plus, and he was just as serious about metaphysics and spiritual and psychic things as I was.

Pat was an intense-looking man, over six feet, with wavy shoulder-length hair and a ruddy face pitted with acne scars. He had deep-set, dark blue eyes, an angular jaw, high cheekbones, and a strong forehead, all of which giving him a remarkable resemblance to the TV character Herman Munster. Pat chain-smoked Marlboros like Charlie did and was biding his time before moving to Hollywood to begin a career in horror films. He did land a few roles in local theater productions and two movies filmed in Denver, and he was so convincing that he even scared me a little when we first met.

The truth was that Pat was one of the most benign, peaceful people I'd ever met. He was easygoing and understated and spoke slowly, taking long pauses between thoughts, contemplating what he was saying before he said it to make sure it was what he wanted to say.

Pat was a student in a metaphysical mystery school and had been for a long time, and he knew how to read tarot cards. Everything he studied was fascinating to me, and I picked his brain for hours. He'd drop by afternoons before he went to work, and we'd drink coffee, he'd smoke cigarettes, and we'd do readings for each other. It was great to have someone to talk shop with. Having a friend to bounce my ideas and experiences off of made life a whole lot easier and fun for me.

I did psychometry readings for Pat, mostly to help him find acting jobs and girlfriends, and he read the tarot cards for me, mostly looking for new guides and boyfriends, a sad testimonial to the fact that neither of us was very successful at love. In my early teenage years, I was rather gangly and awkward, with thick glasses and spaces between my two front teeth, all legs and a skinny body a foot taller than everyone else in school, including my two brothers. All this coalesced into a more attractive arrangement when I got contact lenses and my teeth grew together—and the rest of the world grew a bit, too, evening up the height problem. I had long, always ironed, straight hair, and had developed an exotic French and Romanian look. I was even invited to model, which I did a little, so I could no longer blame my wallflower status on an ugly-duckling appearance.

As much as I hated to admit it, it was becoming painfully clear that my psychic abilities were to blame for my nonexistent love life. My esoteric interests scared guys, and when someone I liked found out that I was psychic, he usually ran. It was either because he thought I was a nut and he didn't believe in psychic matters, or because he believed that I *was* psychic and worried that I might see something about him he didn't want me to see. In either case, it left me sitting on the sidelines.

Even my sister Noelle, who was as geeky as you could get with her thick glasses and homemade clothes, had more dates than I did.

My problems extended beyond the romantic realm. The more public I became as a psychic, the more I noticed that people had some very superstitious and prejudiced ideas about the sixth sense and me as well. Many were extremely uncomfortable or intimidated by my psychic ability and the psychic realm, some dismissing it as ridiculous or nonexistent, others projecting that I was antispiritual or anti-Christian and avoiding or judging me in the process. While I knew that my gift was important,

God-given, and natural to all people when awakened, I was regarded as weird or unholy. Others' narrow-mindedness showed me that I had a long way to go in my mission to help people understand their own creative and spiritual potential.

Talking with Pat helped me realize that my psychic practice and spiritual and metaphysical pursuits were an indelible part of my nature. It wasn't something I did. It was who I *was*. And if people were uncomfortable around me, so be it. I'd just have to make do with the sad fact that I was scary to many, especially if they didn't understand that we were all souls with a sixth sense.

At any rate, in addition to my family, I still had a psychic and spiritual friend in Pat. And we had a good time. He wanted me to teach him psychometry, while I wanted to learn tarot, so we taught each other all we knew.

Pat began my lessons by explaining that tarot wasn't really intended for readings, but rather for self-reflection and personal guidance as a person worked to evolve their consciousness. He said that tarot was an ancient pictorial text with mysterious origins that embodied all the esoteric arts, including astrology, numerology, the ancient laws of western Kabbalah, as well as color and sound therapy. If I wanted to fully master tarot, he said, it would take years, possibly my whole life. He also told me that if I were to apply what I learned from tarot, I would raise my vibration into higher consciousness and manifest anything I desired easily. That was exactly what I wanted to do, so I began to study both with him and on my own in earnest.

I felt that studying with Pat was giving me a refresher course in things already familiar to me. In a few short months, despite Pat's declaration, I felt that I knew as much about tarot as he did. I can't explain why, but I knew tarot so well that I was sure I had studied it in another lifetime.

After several more months of readings and discussions, Pat announced that he was leaving for California to pursue his acting because Denver was a dead end. He said that I'd learned all he could teach me and suggested I meet *his* teacher, whose name was Dr. Trenton Tully. He was the director and primary teacher of a small private mystery school in Denver called the Metaphysical Research Society (M.R.S.). This was an offshoot of The Brotherhood of the White Light, a worldwide mystery school dedicated to the study and practice of raising spiritual consciousness and the goal of ushering in a higher degree of love and balance to the planet.

The Society had a centuries-old tradition, dedicated to the study of ancient metaphysical texts and lost wisdom—the Dead Sea Scrolls, the

Gnostic Bible, the Kabbalah, numerology, astrology, tarot, and the mystic arts, or the higher octave of the psychic arts—all aimed at helping people evolve into light-filled beings who bring balance to the planet. The more Pat spoke of the M.R.S. and The Brotherhood, the more I knew I belonged there.

This was the perfect next step in my psychic evolution. It would pick up where Charlie left off and help me fill in the blanks in my psychic and spiritual education. Dr. Tully must have thought so, too, because he agreed to let me come. The group met twice a week—on Tuesday evenings at seven and on Sunday afternoons.

Pat arranged to take me to my first class that Sunday. I knew it was right, and that it was what my guides wanted me to do next. It was all too synchronistic not to be. I was grateful to be moving on in my training. In fact, I could hardly wait.

Chapter 24

DR. TULLY AND
THE TEMPLE

The following Sunday morning, Pat picked me up in his run-down Opel Kadett and drove me to 1001 East Seventh Avenue, a beautiful three-story mansion sitting high up on a hill, with a commanding set of stairs leading to the entrance.

I'd never seen such a beautiful home, let alone entered one. It's interesting that again I had a teacher who lived in a mansion. I remembered one of Jesus' teachings: "There are many mansions in my father's house." I now knew of two.

This house was red brick, like the one Charlie lived in, with a classic portico of two white Roman columns. The solid oak front door had a brass lion's head knocker. As we walked up the stairs to the front door, I noticed that the lawn was impeccably groomed, with beautiful flowers gracing the front. I wondered who took care of the landscape because it was so obviously loved. The house was regal and grand, and I felt self-conscious. Following Pat's inelegant sartorial cue in his black T-shirt, jeans, and sandals, I wore my tattered bell-bottoms, a tie-dyed purple-and-white midriff top, and my espadrille platform sandals. It felt disrespectful given the elegance of where I was.

"Pat," I whispered, as we neared the front door, "aren't we a little under-dressed to be here?"

"No, Dr. Tully doesn't care—," Just then the door opened, cutting him off. I hoped this was true because I really wanted to make a good impression and feared that I wouldn't.

Out peered a sweet, gray-haired, little old lady with slightly wrinkled creamy white skin and hair swooped up into a casual bun. She looked like Aunt Bea on *The Andy Griffith Show.*

"Hello, Virginia," said Pat in a whisper. "This is the friend I told you about, Sam."

She mouthed hello, no sound coming through, and I understood that whispering was the order of the day. She smiled warmly, not seeming to notice my attire.

As I entered the house, a fragrant waft of incense beckoned me into another world. There were beautiful murals painted on the ceiling and the walls of the large foyer, giving me the feeling that I was in a European palace. A magnificent chandelier hung overhead, surrounded by a gold, blue, and white mural of a thousand-petaled lotus, which filled the ceiling. On one wall was a mural of a Tibetan Buddha sitting in a meditation pose next to a peaceful meditation garden. Ahead was a huge oak staircase leading to the second floor, with two floor-to-ceiling stained-glass windows at the landing, whose light cast a warm glow over the expanse.

To my right was a grand salon with beautiful antique table and chairs and a dark Queen Anne desk with a small Victorian brass lamp sitting on top. Murals of angels danced across the walls and ceiling. At the far end of the room was a massive oak-and-marble mantel with large, heavy brass candlesticks holding beeswax candles; and above, a large mirror with a gilded frame.

To the left was a small anteroom into which Pat motioned me to follow him. I walked past a dozen or so elegantly dressed older men and women, who eyed me in a lovely, gentle way. The atmosphere was exotic and mysterious, but I felt surprisingly comfortable and at ease.

In the anteroom I noticed two black-and-white photographs of two extremely handsome men on the wall. Pat whispered that the younger one was Dr. Tully, and the older man was his teacher, Dr. Doreal. On all sides were floor-to-ceiling bookshelves, filled with old metaphysical texts and what appeared to be bound lectures of Dr. Tully's and of his predecessor, Dr. Doreal. Small boxes with nine foil-wrapped pieces of what appeared to be chocolate, but were actually temple incense, sat on the shelves.

Pat motioned me to follow him back to the main salon, where he introduced me to the group. I was so overwhelmed by the beauty and mystery of everything that I didn't catch a single name. I just smiled and shook their hands, trying to soak everything in and loving every minute of it.

Classical music was playing in the background as Virginia signaled to us to move to the classroom on the opposite side of the staircase. Dr. Tully was ready to speak.

Students were already sitting there with notebooks. I asked Pat if I should have brought one as well. He said probably yes, because the lectures were part of an ongoing spiritual curriculum, and notes helped him to remember everything that Dr. Tully said. "But don't worry," he said. "Just listen today and bring one next time if you want to come back."

The classroom was incredible. At the far end was a small stage with velvet drapes pulled back in a tie, flanked by two white Roman columns. On the stage's back wall was a huge 12-pointed gold star *mandala* (a ritualistic geometric sign symbolic of the Universe) hanging against a golden backdrop. On either side of the stage was a large bouquet of fresh white roses and greenery in antique vases. In between sat a commanding oak podium with an Egyptian ankh painted on the front, a small blue light, and a glass of water. Overhead, Egyptian symbols were painted, and antique Persian rugs covered the floor.

On either side of the room near the ceiling were paintings of Egyptian wings, and on the wall next to me was an antique Tibetan painting of Buddha. Eighty folding chairs were arranged in rows with a central aisle. More antique rugs adorned the floor, giving me the feeling I was in a museum.

The mostly older students sat quietly, some with their eyes closed, meditating. The room was three-quarters full, and no one looked up or turned their head as Pat and I took seats in the third row.

I sat quietly for a few more minutes, soaking in the sensuality of the room, when the music stopped. I held my breath in nervous anticipation.

A deep, resonant gong sounded from behind the curtain and reverberated around the room, sending chills through my body. The sound lingered and lifted very slowly, as though it were soaking into my bones.

When the room was again silent, everyone now sitting up at full attention, wide-eyed with notebooks opened, out walked a solemn, cultivated, extremely handsome tall man whom I assumed was Dr. Tully. He had a head of thick, straight black, perfectly groomed hair; flawless wrinkle-free skin; dark brown eyes with thick eyebrows; and full lips on a symmetrical, oval face. He resembled one of the men in the photo I'd seen in the other room, but he looked older. It was hard to tell his age, but I guessed him to be a very young 45. Pat told me later that he was closer to 65.

Dr. Tully wore a white floor-length robe, and white leather moccasin-like slippers. He had a thick gold, ropelike brocaded belt wrapped twice around his waist. He walked past the podium to the center of the stage in silence, and then with outstretched arms said, "Let us close our eyes for a moment, please, and begin with a healing vibration."

I closed my eyes, and Dr. Tully began to sound a mantra that started out as a soft pleasant *oooo* . . . then became the deepest, loudest, clearest, most piercing *Ooooommmm* I ever heard. It felt as though my brain had been dredged by sound, and Dr. Tully had unclogged and purged every inaccurate thought, sensation, or feeling in it. His voice penetrated my bone marrow. I felt as though I'd been instantly tuned and was left buzzing with energy. It put any Om that Charlie and I did to shame.

Personally stunned and psychically mesmerized by the power and intensity of Dr. Tully's voice, I didn't dare move a muscle. With my eyes still closed, I heard, "Great One. Mighty Masters of Light, Truth, and Wisdom, open thou the way and the gate that lies between this temple and the Hidden Shambalas, that the Light, Truth, and Wisdom of the Great Ones may be opened into us as we are gathered together on this avatar day. This we command by the Unutterable Word! So Mote It Be!"

Again, silence filled the room for a full 15 seconds. Then Dr. Tully said, "Thank you. Let us relax and continue our lesson." His presence was formidable, his aura radiant. He actually glowed. I knew I was in the presence of a truly holy and learned man.

Dr. Tully went to the lectern and took a small sip of water. Then, for the next two and a half hours, he spoke without a break, without even a pause. He talked about consciousness, power, and how to attune to Divine Consciousness, to that of the Masters of Light, and receive healing vibrations. From my own experience with my guides, Rose, Joseph, and the Three Bishops, I knew that what he was saying was accurate because I had already experienced healing vibrations from light beings.

He talked about how the earth's vibration was in flux as it shifted toward the new age, how each of us must attune our bodies to channel more light, and how we must balance the sound vibration in our energy field so that we can better co-create with the Divine. *Yes,* I thought. This is what I'd already been feeling with my clients naturally. He was just putting words to it.

Dr. Tully talked of the difference between the *neophyte* and the *chela* in occult and mystical studies. He explained that the neophyte is a beginner and has lost touch with his Divinity and must work to regain it. Neophytes have little to no creative power because of this ignorance, and life for them is a series of disappointments. The *chela* (a Hindu word for "student") are those people who are becoming aware of their Divinity, their energy and vibration, and who are reclaiming their power to create their lives.

"The difference between a neophyte and a chela," Dr. Tully said, "is their point of view. A neophyte does not question anything or change anything. A chela questions and studies everything and seeks to change in all areas where he has made errors. This difference creates two ways of being in this world, one of harmony and creative manifestation and one of dissonance and creative frustration."

Yes! I thought. *He's talking about those who get what they want and those who don't, depending on their vibration and point of view.*

Dr. Tully continued, referring to the great avatars of the past—Buddha, Jesus, and Mohammed. He repeatedly referred to the Bible; and to astrology and numerology, as well as sound and color and their hidden meanings. He was focused and specific and offered a wealth of secret mystical information, some of which he said derived from the Gnostic texts, some from the Essene tradition, and some from ancient astrology. He said so much in those two hours that my brain hurt from being so full. I'd never met anyone so knowledgeable in all the things I craved to know.

I could feel my heart rejoicing and my guides singing. I knew that they had brought me here to learn from Dr. Tully. I realized that so much of what I was hearing was what they'd been transmitting to me all along. It was becoming very clear that my mission was to learn and then to teach what Dr. Tully was sharing—that we are here to learn to create by raising our vibration and becoming a clear channel of focus and intention. He said several times, "If you don't want something in your life, then don't think it in your mind." Like his voice, his message was powerful and clear. And so was his vibration.

Dr. Tully emphasized that every cell in the body—every thought, every belief, every choice, every emotion—vibrates at some level, either working consciously in harmony to create one's goals, or unconsciously in dissonance to tear one's goals apart.

"The greater our clarity and intention," he said, "the higher our ability to attune to Divine guidance and those Divine forces that are seeking to help us on our Earthly journey. We carry our intentions from lifetime to lifetime as we continue to grow as students of the Light."

I grasped that I was to use my psychic abilities to help people focus and learn how to create what they wanted, not just on a mental level, but also on an soul level. I could hear my guides cheer as this realization filled my awareness. As my mind was off and running, full of inspiration and direction from what I was hearing, the lecture stopped.

"Let us finish for the day," he said. "Let us close our eyes and bring these teachings into our bodies, into our cells, into our deepest consciousness with this next meditation."

I closed my eyes again, and for two minutes we all quietly breathed. I was grateful for the silence. Like a battery charged to maximum, I couldn't absorb any more. And I didn't want even one word of what I'd heard to leak out.

Then just as he'd begun the class, Dr. Tully started to sound a mantra—quietly at first, then gradually louder and louder, to the point that I felt as if I would levitate off my chair. My cells individually charged at full voltage from the inside out. I wondered if my hair was standing on end from the surging current in his voice.

Suddenly he stopped and said, "Light Is Eternal, O Soul of the Cosmos. Fill us and Light the Darkness of Night . . . go with us through all of life's journeys, Help us to Be One with the Light. So mote it be."

After another long pause he said, "Thank you."

When I opened my eyes, he was gone. The stage was empty. The classical music began to sweetly filter back into the room. I felt like I'd awakened from a dream. I sat there, unable to move. Slowly, the other chelas were getting up and leaving. Pat shook his head and said, "Pretty interesting, huh?"

"That was . . . was . . . was *something*," I said, searching for the right word and deciding none would do Dr. Tully justice. I didn't even want to talk about it for fear that inadequate words would somehow dilute the impact he'd had on me.

We were the last ones to leave the room. As we entered the foyer, we saw "Aunt Bea" whispering good-bye to everyone. Dr. Tully was nowhere to be seen.

I bought some incense for a dollar. I wanted to take something home to help re-create the experience in my mind.

Walking to the car, still not wanting to dilute my experience by talking about it, I asked Pat, "Can I come back here again? Or do I have to be with you?"

"You can come anytime you want now that you've been introduced. He teaches on Tuesdays and Sundays."

"Do I have to be a member or pay anything?"

"No, it's all run on donations. Give what you can. There's a collection box in the back. They don't even pass it around. It's up to you." That, too, was amazing to me, because Dr. Tully was giving out such gold that I wished I'd left a donation to repay him for it.

I didn't feel like driving home. My body was vibrating too much from Dr. Tully's voice and the mantras to sit still. Not knowing what to do with this heightened energy, I looked to my guides for direction. They said, "Walk home." *That's perfect,* I thought. *Great idea.*

"Pat, do you mind if I walk? I think it will help me absorb everything I just heard."

"After a class with Tully," he said, "it's probably a good idea."

We said good-bye, and I thanked him again for bringing me there. Then I turned east and started for home.

❈

Chapter 25

CREATING A PRINCE

Becoming Dr. Tully's student opened up a whole new world of psychic understanding and possibility for me. Charlie had trained me in the psychic arts, and now Dr. Tully was training me in spiritual law. His lessons filled in the holes in my understanding and addressed all my unanswered questions. He was a formidable and demanding teacher who taught me to be more objective and far less emotional and sentimental when interpreting what I saw, not only in my readings, but also in life. That alone afforded me deeper insight into the world around me and sharpened my psychic antennae.

Dr. Tully himself was extremely impersonal. Unlike Charlie, who was very personable and connective, Dr. Tully was distant and detached—not cold, just crystal clear.

Going to the mansion was intimidating at first, but in time, it came to be the most sacred and beloved place in my life. In the beginning, I was quite shy, still wondering how I got so lucky as to be able to sit in Dr. Tully's classroom. Feeling insecure and intimidated by the sophistication I found there, I came and left quickly and silently, unwilling to attract any attention for fear someone would tell me I didn't belong. I never greeted anyone with other than a shy smile or a whispered hello. Everyone was very formal and made little or no eye contact, so neither did I.

I didn't stay after class to chat with the other students, partly because I got so much from Dr. Tully's lectures that I didn't dream of asking for anything more, and partly because I had to hurry home to do homework. Dr. Tully rarely appeared in the foyer to shake hands and say good-bye after a lecture, so when he did, I felt triply blessed.

Not wanting to miss a single word of the lectures, I managed to overcome my shyness, especially after the other students got used to seeing me. I began arriving early enough to take the first seat in the very first row. The lectures began promptly at 7:30, but the Temple opened at 6:45. If I arrived just as the doors opened, I almost always got to claim my favorite seat in front of the podium and meditate in the quiet calm before class began.

After getting the seat consistently over a period of several months, I came to regard it as mine. One time I showed up at 7:15 to find an elderly man, who usually sat in the third row, sitting in "my" seat, and I was indignant. How dare he presume to take my chair? I walked right up and fixed him with an accusing eye, as if to say, "Surely you jest by sitting here," hoping he'd get the hint and move. He didn't. He stared straight ahead and refused to look at me, pretending not to notice. I let out a loud sigh and voiced a typical teenage "Tsk," before reluctantly sitting one seat over.

Using what Dr. Tully taught me, I directed all my power of focus to push him off my chair and send him back to where he belonged, three rows back. He didn't budge. I dug in and turned on all the juice I could muster. *Move,* I thought. Still, he didn't. Then at 7:24, six minutes before show time, he suddenly shifted as if he'd lost his balance. He shot me a hostile glance, which I pretended not to notice as I fixed my gaze on the 12-pointed star at the back of the stage. The next thing I knew, the man stood up and marched back to his regular spot. *Hooray!* I thought as I slid back to my original seat.

"Thought does create," I said, half aloud, glad I'd made him move. The music stopped, the gong sounded, and I was ready to listen.

I started bringing a notebook to the classes like the other students, but when Dr. Tully spoke, I was too mesmerized to write. Soaking up every word he said like a sponge, I committed everything to memory. I felt that on some cellular level, I already knew, or at least understood, what Dr. Tully was talking about, especially the parts about Jesus and the ancient secrets surrounding his life.

I loved it most when Dr. Tully told stories. He was a great storyteller and world traveler and shared fascinating tales about Jesus and Buddha, the Brotherhood of the White Light, and the mystery schools around the world. For example, I loved how he said that Christ, or Yeshua the Essene, as he called him, was a wealthy man, and the reason Pontius Pilate's soldiers cast lots for his garment just before he was crucified was because it was a seamless garment of India and was priceless.

Listening to Dr. Tully engaged my imagination. After only a few months, I decided that I wanted to start using Dr. Tully's principles to create what I wanted in life. According to him, creativity was our nature and our gift from God, and we created everything in our lives, like it or not. He said that the goal of life is to learn to create what we really want, from our heart, because that's where our soul lives and expresses itself, and not settle for poor creations and unfulfilled dreams.

"If we listen to our heart," he said, "and follow the laws of creativity, we can attract what we really desire." This was the point of our Earthly journey, to create and express our loving spirit.

No longer content to sit quietly on the sidelines, I felt inspired to use what I was learning and was determined to create what I truly wanted— something until then I wouldn't dare admit to myself, let alone anyone else—a date to the junior-senior prom only three weeks away.

Everyone at school had been excitedly talking about the prom for weeks. Since I wasn't popular—partly because rumor had it that I was psychic and therefore weird, and partly because I towered over (especially in this era of platform shoes) a school full of shorter boys who were too intimidated by my height and reputation to ever consider asking me out—I never once thought I'd be asked to go.

Then it dawned on me that by focusing on being left behind, I was actually creating it, according to Universal law. So, having had enough, thank you, of that creation, I reversed my course and began creating something much more exciting—a prince to take me to the ball.

Once I set about my task, the sky was the limit. Following Dr. Tully's instructions, I remembered that imagination was the substance that created my life, so I set mine free. If he was going to be my prince, I reasoned, then I could create him to be anything I wanted.

Being practical, the first task was to make my prince tall enough. I put on my best shoes and with a pencil in hand, I backed against the bedroom wall and marked it just above my head.

"There," I said to myself, looking up at the wall. "This is how tall he'll be." Once I made that mark, my imagination took off. I wanted my prince to be handsome and exciting, just like my new favorite singer, David Bowie. Inspired by that thought, I cut David's face out of the cover of the album

I had just purchased and taped it on the wall at the exact spot where I'd made the mark.

If I'm to create my prince, I want him to dress like one as well. I imagined him having big bell-bottom pants with cut-out inserts along the sides, like the ones a rock star would wear.

Becoming more and more inspired, I imagined my hero with every detail I could imagine. Why not? If I was going to create, I was going to create *big*. Feeling bold, I envisioned him with thick muttonchop sideburns, wearing aviator sunglasses and a long scarf around his neck, looking like he'd stepped out of a London nightclub. And while I was at it, I also imagined him driving a Rolls-Royce, or some other cool car.

170

Using everything I'd learned at the Temple the past year, I affectionately named my prince "My Guy" and joyfully embellished him a little more every day, adding another detail, another idea, another whim. There was no doubt about it; I was creating Mr. Cool and loving it. I not only focused on creating "My Guy" with every cell in my body, I *believed* it.

Days passed into weeks as I pursued my mission. Not only did I focus and imagine that my prince would come, I *expected* him to arrive at any moment. As I drove to school, I looked into every guy's eyes along the way, wondering if he was "My Guy." I was so positive that what Dr. Tully had taught me was true, that in my mind it wasn't a matter of *if* I'd meet him, it was a matter of *when* I'd meet my prince face-to-face. I was so sure that I even leaked it to my school friends. "You bet," I said, when asked if I was going to the dance. "I'm going with the coolest guy in the world." When pressed for details, I smiled vaguely and said, "It's a surprise."

Soon the word was out that the strange, tall psychic girl had a secret date to the prom, and everyone started teasing me, wanting to know more about him. I was the pillar of confidence, unwavering in my conviction that I would create a star.

But the days passed quickly, and before I knew it, three weeks had dwindled to three days before the prom. Despite my best efforts, and to my horror, there was no My Guy in sight. I panicked and was angry. "Where is he? Why isn't he here?" I argued to the heavens, questioning myself, questioning Dr. Tully, even questioning God. I'd followed the instructions to the letter of the law. I'd focused; I'd imagined; I'd used my full intention and attention, and indeed, every cell in my body, to create my heart's desire. I was absolutely certain I'd succeed. Why hadn't he arrived?

It was Thursday before the dance. Feeling utterly defeated, I lost faith. Embarrassed and disappointed, I announced to anyone who asked that I'd changed my mind and decided that going to the prom was childish, pathetic, and definitely not cool. I couldn't be bothered.

Needless to say, I became the laughingstock of the school. Bitter with disappointment and frustration, and wanting to disappear, I decided I'd console myself by buying a new pair of shoes and going to the movies instead.

The next afternoon after school, I walked to my favorite shoe store to check out what was new. Upon entering, right before my eyes on full display was the most exquisite pair of white, rhinestone platform shoes with silver shoelaces and six-inch, acrylic, see-through turquoise soles. They were incredible. Prom or no prom, I had to have them. As I picked them up for a closer look, my heart sank, thinking how perfect they would have been for the prom if only my creative experiment had worked.

As I turned one shoe over to look at the price tag, out from behind a curtain emerged the salesman, by far the cutest guy I'd ever seen. Long blond hair to his shoulders, 6'5", very skinny, with mutton-chop sideburns and wearing a very cool pair of plaid platform shoes himself, he looked like, oh my God, David Bowie! I was so surprised I couldn't speak.

Whisking the shoe out of my hand and thankfully ignoring my dumbfounded expression, he said, "Isn't this the coolest shoe you've every seen?"

"Yes," I admitted, regaining composure, "it is."

"Go on, try them on," he insisted. "They're just too cool for words."

I had to agree. I tried them on, and just like Cinderella's glass slippers, they were absolutely magical, fitting as though they'd been made especially for me.

"Get them, they're great," he insisted. "They're too good to pass up. In fact, if you buy them, I'll take you out," he said, inspired by the moment.

"No way," I said, overwhelmed. "I don't believe you."

"No, really, I'm serious." he said. "The minute I saw those shoes come into the store, I said to myself, 'I'm taking those shoes out.' So if you buy them, we have a date. Where do you want to go?"

Caught completely off guard, I hesitated. I looked at the shoes, then at him. I couldn't believe my luck. I was looking at The Prince. My Guy. My creation. "There is only one place to go with these shoes," I said, laughing. "To the ball."

"You're on. When? You tell me."

Summoning up my courage, I said, "Tomorrow night? If you don't have plans, that is."

"Perfect. As a matter of fact, I don't have any plans. Just give me the details, and I'll be there." I couldn't believe it. My heart's desire was unfolding before my eyes. Just as Dr. Tully had promised, the prince had shown up to take me to the ball, and as Divine humor would have it, I'd even be wearing (very clunky) glass slippers to the event.

On prom night, My Guy arrived right on time. This was my first date—ever. He didn't drive a Rolls-Royce, but he did drive up in his father's yellow 1968 Cadillac, which was cool enough for me. The best part was that he wore a red satin suit, complete with hip-hugger bell-bottoms, aviator glasses, a scarf around his neck, and to top it all off, red, rhinestone platform shoes to match mine.

172

Together we floated off to the ball and had a fabulous evening. He wasn't the love of my life, but he did become one of my dearest friends and best buddies. I don't know what made me happier: my new buddy, or the fact that I'd created him. I think it was the latter.

The more I practiced combining what Charlie taught me with what I learned from Dr. Tully, the more I understood the soul in action. It was an awesome and humbling experience to see how magnificent all people really are, even if we're in the process of creating a big mess of things. All of us, me included, created our lives, and that was the point. The fact that we could create was incredible. Now all I had to do was teach people how to do it a little better and keep learning better myself.

Perhaps I was imagining things, but I couldn't help but feel that Dr. Tully was talking to me personally as I sat right in front of him when he lectured—about reincarnation, karma, past lives, soul plans, vibration, energy, and working with the Higher Power and the Ascended Masters in creating our lives. I was sure he was speaking directly to me when he occasionally asked, "Do you understand?"

"Yes, yes!" I wanted to shout. I did say softly a few times, "Absolutely, yes."

Just as Charlie told me over and over again to observe and be detached, Dr. Tully emphasized relentlessly to study and question, but not judge. Ever. He said 10,000 times if he said it once, "Nothing is good or bad; only thinking makes it so."

Dr. Tully inspired me to use my psychic facilities to understand, learn, question, and help people grow—not just to see what was unfolding in lives but to understand why. Before his teachings, I never thought to ask why about anything, and neither did my clients. It was as though we collectively and unconsciously agreed that we got what we got and accepted it. I was coming to understand that this wasn't true. What *was* true was that we got what we focused on, and the better we focused, the better we got.

Week after week, I thought of all the clients I was reading for, and how much they wanted from life, and how little, if any, thought or discussion they put into realizing their dreams. At best, I saw their wishes and dreams as a lot of crossed fingers and hopes that it would "all work out." What they didn't know was that we all have a choice. I knew in my heart that to teach them that was my mission.

I'd do it by using all my psychic skills and metaphysical training. I'd leave no stone unturned in seeking out whatever hidden elements prevented my clients from creating what they really wanted. I wanted happy endings for everyone. I was going to be a profound guide, teacher, and healer as well as a psychic. I was going to show people *how* to create the future they desired by learning how to make honest and correct choices instead of being careless and sloppy. I would do it by using my psychic gifts and sharing my own mistakes. We'd learn together.

173

During this time, I was given another gift. I met and became girlfriends with two young women, Luann Glatzmaier and Joan Smith, who were also psychic. I met Luann when she'd gone to Mom for a reading, and Joan was her best friend. Only three years older than I, Luann read tarot cards for clients, and Joan was a professional astrologer.

Having them come into my life was a godsend. I no longer had to keep my interests to myself. We met regularly, practiced our skills on each other, and talked about our clients. Our souls feasted on tea, cigarettes (we all succumbed), and psychic readings. We spent hours in deep conversation about the psychic arts and bemoaned the trials and tribulations of our chosen vocation. We were devoted to creating our own reality and perfecting our psychic skills and spiritual understanding of the Universe. By our peers' standards, we were all eccentric. It didn't matter. We were on a mission from God, and it felt good to have company.

Little did I know as I sat in the front row at the temple trying to take notes and practicing my skills, that five short years later I'd be teaching these same lessons to my clients and students in Chicago. And in 20 years, I'd teach them worldwide through my books.

Nor could I have guessed that there would come a day, 30 years later, when I'd be invited back to stand in Dr. Tully's spot at the podium in the temple, as he once stood in front of me, and pass his lessons on to the next generation of students at the M.R.S.

And I never dreamed that I'd still be close with Luann and Joan, and we'd still be championing each other in our mission.

All I knew at the time was that my guides had led me here to the temple, this beautiful, sacred place of learning where the esoteric teachings were unsurpassed, and the standards for personal growth and spiritual integrity were impeccable . . . the temple, where I was introduced to kindred spirits to further support my soul's growth and this lifetime's mission.

Without this training, my readings could even mislead and set people back, especially those who were inclined to believe they had no influence over the present and future. My work with Dr. Tully transformed me from a psychic reader into a psychic guide, healer, teacher, and creator. And it prepared me to do my life's work properly and feel peace in my heart.

❖

❧ PART III ❧

My Own Future

(1977–2003)

Chapter 26

INTO THE WORLD

After my training with Dr. Tully, my guides directed me to venture farther out into the world. I enrolled at the University of Denver, and from there I was guided to move to France, where I lived for several years. I moved there through the help of the study-abroad program at school, first to Aix-en-Provence, and then to Paris, where I studied language, religion, and right-brain learning, as well as the human heart at large.

Although I was far away from Denver and my clients back home, the distance didn't stop people from contacting me for readings. I was surprised by how many clients wrote or called me wanting psychic readings by mail or over the phone and would do anything to have one, including flying to France, which one client named Cathy actually did.

Much to my surprise, distance made no difference in my ability to read for my clients. Using psychometry and listening to my guides, I found that I could do readings easily—maybe even more so than when a client was right in front of me because their emotional energy wasn't there to distract me. All I needed was their photo, a piece of jewelry, or a metal object, and I could psychically feel everything going on with a person at the time and where they were headed. I actually enjoyed doing long-distance psychic readings, because in some strange way it was grounding for me while living in this strange land. Doing readings helped me feel more at home.

The funny part is that some of my clients started being psychic with me, too. One client in particular from Denver named Jesse was going through a terrible time in her marriage and was certain that it would soon end. She called me several times in a panic for readings while I lived in Aix-en-Provence. Working from a photo of her and her husband that she'd sent me, my psychic sense assured me that their difficulties would pass and that they wouldn't split, no matter what. I told her to just hang in there and trust, and their differences would resolve. She listened to me, although she kept insisting that I was afraid to tell her the truth, that her husband was having an affair and didn't love her anymore. I assured her that although their relationship was navigating some extremely rough seas, he wasn't actually having an affair, and their marriage would survive.

This seemed to calm her down quite a bit and keep her grounded. I thought it was extreme for her to call me from so far away and talk for such a long time because it was really expensive, but she said that I was her only source of hope because everyone else in her life was urging her to get a divorce—and fast—which she didn't want to do.

In the meanwhile, being a somewhat stressed-out, sensitive student living on a very limited budget and eating a diet exclusively of baguettes and cheese for many months, I suddenly and surprisingly fell seriously ill just before the holidays. I was stricken with acute appendicitis and a severe kidney infection three days before Christmas.

Just as I was being rushed to the hospital in a feverish delirium, the phone rang. It was Jesse calling to say Merry Christmas. She was told I was very sick and on my way to the hospital. Her phone call couldn't have been better timed, though, because she was the only client I had who spoke French and could understand what was going on. She promptly told my parents about my predicament, and thank goodness she did, because not only was I gravely ill, I'd only paid my school health insurance up to the end of the month, and it was due to expire in 12 days. My parents renewed my insurance premiums in time, and I didn't end up paying myself for my operation.

I was in the hospital 19 days. It was quite an ordeal, and I was grateful that my parents came over and helped me. After I went back home, I called Jesse to thank her for finding me in trouble and letting my parents know.

"It was the strangest thing that made me call," she said. "I was at work that day when suddenly I was overwhelmed by the scent of roses, even though there weren't any around. I immediately thought of you and couldn't stop. I had to call. It was almost as if my fingers were dialing your phone number while my brain was asking why. I didn't have any questions for you. Instead, I had to know how you were. I felt as though some higher force had made me do it. Like one of those guides you talk about."

She was absolutely right. Once again, my guide Rose had taken care of me.

Back in Denver after my French experience and acting on a powerful instruction from my guides, I spontaneously followed Cuky's and now Neil's example and became a flight attendant, even though I'd never planned on doing that before. Open to whatever the experience would bring, and ready to see even more of the world right out of training, I was luckily based in Chicago and living with Neil, who was also based there. It was as if I'd been led there to meet my future husband, settle down, have a family, and continue my mission as a psychic and spiritual teacher—none of which would have happened in Denver.

Only a few weeks after settling in Chicago, the phone began to ring off the hook with requests for readings, not from Denver, but from Chicago, although I'd never once advertised or promoted my psychic work and barely knew anyone. The clients came mostly at Neil's urging. I realized then that he was as enthusiastic as my mother in spreading the word about my abilities. In no time, I was "back home" when it came to readings.

Word traveled so fast that between previous clients and new ones that I barely had time to take off my uniform between flights before I was back in my reading room. As a result, I only worked one or two months of the year as a flight attendant, mostly during the summer high season, taking long leaves of absence whenever I could. After five years, my psychic practice became so demanding that I quit flying altogether. Doing readings was now my main job.

Seeing how quickly my work had grown and expanded to the entire Midwest, I knew that it was my destiny to be here. I also knew from my astrological studies that Chicago was a very positive place to begin my life's work because of its high energy as part of America's heartland. Like everything else in my life, it was clear that my Higher Self was ahead of me and had placed me in Chicago for my higher purpose. Things had fallen so easily into place that I knew it was part of my soul plan. Later, I had an astrocartography chart done, which is an astrological analysis of the best locations in which to live, prepared for me by my friend Joan Smith, who said that Chicago was one of the best places in the world to begin my public career. It didn't surprise me.

During my early years in Chicago, The Three Bishops constantly guided me. They came into my dream state nightly to reveal more and more of my soul's history and plan. It was a difficult time in my life because I didn't have psychic friends or family in Chicago, and my love life was not (and never had been) the best. Even though I was professionally so busy that I could barely keep up, personally I was lonely and felt like a fish out of water. I'd long ago left Denver and knew that my time there was complete, but I missed my psychic friends and felt more than ever like the ugly duckling.

180

I also missed the elegance and sophistication of France, but that, too, was no longer the place for me to grow. Also, as a Libra, I was a lover of beauty and style and had assumed quite an international flair from living in Paris. I now looked more like Audrey Hepburn in *Sabrina* than the overgrown hippie of my earlier years. Between my French taste, my world travels, and my psychic profession, I was quite intimidating to most men my age (I was now 23). Older men were far too conservative for me, so I worried that I was doomed to being the odd woman out, never fitting in socially anywhere.

Rose assured me that in time this would all change and that I just had to be patient. She reminded me that I was on the right path being of service to others, and the Universe knew what was in alignment with my heart. I wasn't supposed to date just anyone, she said. It would be too disturbing to my vibration to spend time with the wrong man. *At least that's an excuse for sitting home on Friday nights,* I thought. Not a comforting one, but better than thinking it was just because I was so unlovable.

My guide Dot, who I always felt was my Higher Self, agreed with Rose, but my ego wasn't faring too well with it all. The only consolation was that I was so busy doing readings and guiding people to their heart's desire that on a deeper soul level I knew I was on the right path.

The Three Bishops told me that psychic work and teaching were to be my full-time profession in this lifetime, and I was to pursue no other job. They said that I'd chosen this path before I was born, and that I'd been a spiritual teacher and guide for many lifetimes, my soul originating in Egypt, following the tradition of Hermes Trismegistus, an ancient Egyptian philosopher who came to help elevate the human race.

The guides said that my soul then followed the path of the ancient Essene tribes of Israel, and I was a student of Christ. That explained my deep interest in religion and my love of the teachings of Jesus, as well as my ease with being a Catholic and a psychic. There was no conflict because it was Jesus himself who taught me to be psychic.

My guides said that my soul operated from a deep and ancient tradition of love, and that working through the principle of love was my highest mission. From there, they said, I went to France and became a worshipper of the Black Madonna or Mother Mary. Metaphysical history speculates that she went to France after the crucifixion of Christ and died in France near Aix, where I'd lived. It also theorizes that Christ had brothers and sisters, and they, too, went to France and had children.

This shed light on my obsession with France. I'd lived in France for many incarnations and was part of the tradition that designed the tarot as a means of retaining the secret wisdom of Hermes Trismegistus, especially during the Crusades and the Middle Ages, when esoteric and metaphysical teachings were at risk of being lost to the world forever.

Hearing this from my guides, especially The Three Bishops, helped make sense out of my life as it was unfolding. Even the airline deviation was necessary, they said, because it was a means of getting to the spiritual places I needed to go, including Rheims, France, where I had spent time in past lives; Delphi in Greece; and even the countryside of England— all places where I had soul history.

From these insights, I began to recognize my psychic practice as part of a larger mission to serve as a healer and guide to the soul. My guides said that I was a keeper of soul wisdom and told me that I was here to reignite and preserve this wisdom in other souls, first in one-on-one readings, then in classes, and later in books that would travel around the world.

Without our soul spark, our Divine sense, we harm and destroy one another and ourselves, the guides said, and people are doing so at an exponential rate. I was here as part of a great force of lightworkers, reincarnated specifically to help reverse this trend. I'd dedicated myself to this path because so many people were at severe risk of losing permanent touch with their Divine spark, which is felt through the sixth sense, the psychic sense. When we lose this spark, we enter into the dark night of the soul and lose our way in life.

My guides said I was right on schedule when I came to Chicago, that I'd lived a very hermetic existence, and I had to energetically adjust to being public about my psychic work in phases. I'd even been killed in past lives for sharing my message, which explained why I was so reluctant to talk about my psychic practice publicly with people who didn't understand.

As it was, I'd felt a significant sting from time to time, even from people who were close and knew who I was and the work I did. It always felt risky at best.

For now, the guides said, the flow of clients in the Midwest was just enough to adjust my energy until my core vibration was strong enough to move farther into the world. They also said I had endless help from them and from light beings on the other side. Looking at the past and seeing the continuing stream of mentors, teachers, and guides I'd been graced with every step of the way since birth, I knew this was true. I only wished that I'd meet some of those lightworkers in Chicago to make my life easier. So far I'd had no luck.

Soon I was receiving up to 30 calls a week for readings, sometimes more, a backbreaking demand. I said yes to nearly every one and felt that I was working in an emergency room for the soul.

Working out of the kitchen in my four-story walk-up apartment on the north side of Chicago, I saw a steady stream of clients. They came from different backgrounds and levels—from unhappy housewives to budding entrepreneurs, students and doctors, service people and politicians. No matter whom I read for, my goal was always the same: to guide people to their true path and connect them to their purpose, as well as reignite the spark in their soul.

It was a daunting task, as most people had no clue they had a path, a sixth sense, or even a soul, let alone that these things had anything to do with their present life or their future. Most were ignorant of how their life worked, believing that if they paid me enough money, I could make life better for them.

I tried to take the mystery out of the process of psychic awareness by teaching them spiritual law and how the psychic arts worked, which I hoped would give them a glimpse of their potential power. But that was easier said than done—not because they couldn't understand, but rather because they didn't want to.

I could see how unscrupulous storefront psychics could take advantage of these naïve and hurting people. They practically begged to be ripped off in their desperation for instant emotional relief. Many preferred to write a check and escape the painful ordeal of looking in the mirror. They often came to me in desperation after giving huge sums of money to these phonies, who told them that their lives would be cursed if they didn't continue to pay.

Repulsed by the emotional blackmail of these charlatans, and frustrated that people were willing to be duped, I became a crusader for enlightenment of the psychically uninformed. I couldn't allow a single client to leave without making them aware that with some effort they could open their own psychic channel and connect the hidden dots in their lives like I did. It was no grand secret. It just took awareness, attention, and honesty.

The psychic world is the unseen world, but it's not illogical. It follows a set of laws, just like the physical plane. There's no magic. It's not weird or bizarre. With attention and effort, the connection between thoughts, beliefs, and actions can be revealed, and you can create life exactly as you want. Granted, due to my soul history, my level of psychic insight is deeper and more sophisticated than most. But the sixth sense, necessary for a person to be truly happy or successful, is available to all.

With patience and persistence, I gradually succeeded in conveying my message. Clients listened, and their lives improved. Every person I helped sent ten more.

The challenges were many and varied. I read for the lovelorn, the poverty stricken, the lost, the addicted, the sick, and the up-and-coming. I helped them to refine their focus, correctly identify their desires, and reconnect to their soul. My guides worked overtime—offering insight, solutions, and details to hold my clients' attention.

A woman named Erica called in desperation because Bill, her fiancé of five years, abruptly broke off their engagement and moved out in the middle of the night as she was in the process of planning their wedding. Devastated, she came to see me with the sole intention of getting him back. Short, perky, and full of energy, she felt like fireworks standing at my door. I had to settle her down before I could even begin to tune in to her vibration. Once I did, my guides showed me that her fiancé had done her a favor by leaving because she didn't really love him. She was only engaged to him because she was afraid that true love wasn't in her future. My guides said her deepest desire, however, was nothing less than true love even though she was willing to marry the wrong guy. Her soul pushed Bill out the door because her real life partner was moving in. I could feel his vibration, and my guides said that he was literally next door.

When I told Erica that she didn't love her fiancé, she skidded to a halt, as though a bucket of ice water had been thrown in her face. She became perfectly quiet, started to protest, then took a deep breath and said, "It's absolutely true. I don't."

When I told her that true and genuine love was very near, her eyes widened.

"When?"

My guide Rose answered, "This year, and as soon as you release Bill completely."

"To think I might marry someone I really love sounds too good to be true," she said, shaking her head in disbelief as she put on her coat to leave.

"Believe it," I said. "He's right next door."

"Where? At home? At work?"

"I don't know," I said. "The guides just say 'next door.'"

To help regain her balance, I told Erica to be honest, let go of Bill, and, above all, open her heart to what she truly desired. I also suggested that she wish Bill well in the process.

Six months later, Erica called. "Guess what? I just got engaged to a man named Richard who works next door to my job, just as you predicted. I can't believe this happened," she gushed. "I've never been so crazy about someone in my life! I thought I loved Bill, but he never made me feel as passionate or excited about life as Richard does. I can't tell you how happy I am."

She continued. "Thank you for persuading me to let go of Bill, or I wouldn't have met my soul mate. I would have pursued Bill as a matter of pride until he came back. He even called a month after he left me saying that he'd made a mistake and could we get back together. Before your reading I would have said yes in a minute. Instead, I said I didn't think so, but I loved him as a friend. We both cried. Would you believe that I met Richard the next day?"

I also read for a beautiful woman named Kate. She was tall and slender, with light red hair, delicate features, and a sprinkling of freckles across her nose. She had clear green eyes, a gorgeous smile, and a gray aura about her. She had a 12-year-old daughter from a previous marriage and two stepsons from her present husband. She was bored and angry at being a stay-at-home mother and the neglected wife of a husband who traveled constantly.

Her solution was to have a loveless, unsatisfactory sexual affair with her next-door neighbor. "More smoke than fire," she said.

My guides said that her real problem wasn't her husband, but her failure to take any creative risks, and because of that she fell out of touch with her creativity and purpose. They said she was to go back to the theater, a love she had acted on from childhood through her teen years, but had abandoned in college at her practical mother's urging.

My guides said she had a real talent, and even if it wouldn't pay much, it would fulfill her need and contribute something uplifting to the planet. She didn't have to make a lot of money; she had the good fortune of being loved by a man who was more than willing to financially support her acting. This was a gift, they said, and would allow her to pursue her love without struggle.

I saw that Kate really loved her husband, but blamed him for her unhappiness just as she'd blamed her first two. She wanted to be closer to him, but felt so bad about herself that she pushed him away by saying he wasn't sexy or appealing. They said she criticized him so much about his inadequate (to her) income that he worked harder and was away from home more. As for the affair, they said it was a colossal and stupid mistake on both Kate and the neighbor's parts, neither willing to take responsibility for their unhappiness and harming themselves even further.

Kate resisted what the guides had to say and told me she was ready for a divorce. She did agree that she always regretted giving up acting, and in that, my guides were right. She resented her family, including her mother, husband, and kids for ruining her career, and having an affair was her way of getting back at them.

The next thing my guides said was very difficult to tell Kate, but I had to. I said that all the hurt and resentment she held all those years was now manifesting in a serious physical problem—a dark mass in her breasts. She should check this out right away.

"You mean cancer?" she said, unbelieving.

"Hopefully not. But you should see a doctor to be sure." Then I said that whatever the mass was, it offered a turning point and an opportunity to open up to what she really wanted—to be loved and supported as her true self, an artist.

Kate left feeling disturbed and cynical. "Are you sure you aren't just guilt-tripping me with that breast stuff because I'm having an affair?"

"I'm sure," I said, "but I wonder if part of the congestion in your breasts isn't maybe your own guilt trip."

She slammed the door and left. Seven weeks later she told me that after her reading she'd had a mammogram to be on the safe side and, sure enough, some cysts showed up. The doctor said they were nothing to worry about, but fearful because of the reading, she insisted on having a biopsy on two of the cysts. Upon further examination, it was discovered that she had cancerous tumors in both breasts and had to have an immediate double mastectomy.

"You may have saved my life, Sonia," she admitted, "because I would never have had a mammogram. I don't even believe in them. Or I didn't, anyway. After the mastectomy, my husband changed jobs to be home more, and now we're in counseling. I also signed up for an acting class and called it off with the neighbor. I don't know quite how I feel about all of this, but at least I'm not dead."

I know this was a hard road for Kate to travel, as she had a lot of learning ahead of her. But it was truly what she wanted and far better than the dead end she was headed for, and I told her so.

"You're right," she said. "I just didn't think it was worth the effort to pursue anything I wanted. Without your help, God knows what might have happened to me."

I was grateful that Kate took the reading I gave her to heart. I never knew if a client would or not. A few weeks later, I read for a young guy named Scott who worked as a line cook at the restaurant at the top of the John Hancock building in downtown Chicago. He was 6'3", about 250 pounds, and looked like he could be an NFL linebacker. He had blond hair, a boyish smile, and the warmest, most sincere heart of anyone I'd run into in a while.

In spite of his loving and generous energy, Scott felt insecure and frustrated, saying he wanted to quit his job and move to an island in the Caribbean to work at a resort. I told him it was a very positive step in his life and would build his confidence. With more self-esteem, I saw that he would one day fulfill his dream of creating his own successful restaurant in Chicago.

"No way," he said, finding that too hard to believe. "I would love that more than anything, but you've got to have money to do that. I'm not a businessman, and I don't think I'd ever find anyone to back me, without a degree or something."

I told Scott that my guides said it was his purpose and path to be a great success in the restaurant business, and he'd grow in leaps and bounds. "I see people lining up for blocks to get into your restaurant. My guides say that you're like a benevolent king, and one day you'll provide many people with food, support, money, and even safe haven. And you will prosper in the process."

"You really think so?" he asked in a moment of genuine receptivity.

"Absolutely," I said. "I'm sure of it."

Scott nearly skipped out of my office and on to the Caribbean, buoyant, but still disbelieving.

He worked at a resort in St. Thomas for a year and then returned, feeling confident and worldly, his horizons now broadened way beyond the southwest side of Chicago where he grew up. Trusting in the reading I gave him, he decided to take a risk and set about making his dream of owning a restaurant a reality. To his amazement, he found investors with little effort. Using that money along with his savings, he rented a small storefront on Clark Street and opened his first restaurant. He named it Mia Francesca after his wife, and true to my reading, people lined up for blocks to get in.

Scott was so successful that in the next five years he opened eight more restaurants. His empire is still growing. He's been able to employ dozens of people and provide great jobs and security for them and their families. This was his soul plan, and he's living up to it very well.

As much as I enjoyed helping other people create the lives they desired, I had yet to create my *own* heart's desire, which was to have a soul mate and life partner. I decided that enough was enough, and I finally asked the Universe to bring me my partner—*now*. I had a long heart-to-heart with God. I said, "Okay, God. Here's my proposal. I'll work for you if you'll work for me. We can be a team. I'll continue to guide and heal people through my readings. I'll even start teaching classes if you'd like, if you bring me my life partner. I can't give my heart and soul to others and not feel love in my own life."

In my heart, I felt that God heard.

After that conversation, I set about working my end of the bargain and began teaching classes on a regular basis in addition to readings. After each reading I invited my clients to attend group sessions in my living room where I began passing along the same wisdom that Charlie and Dr. Tully had taught me. My first class consisted of eight students, and we met on six consecutive Sundays, for three hours each time.

I taught my students both the psychic arts, which I'd learned from Charlie, and spiritual law, which I'd learned from Dr. Tully. I showed my students how to meditate, how to see auras, how to do psychometry and open their clairvoyant eye, and even meet their guides. I showed them, step-by-step, how thoughts create. Much to their surprise (and I confess, to mine, also), by the end of the six-week classes, every student managed to do at least one psychic reading, and some were very accurate. Several had created new and exciting situations in their lives, in love, and in work. One even recovered from serious long-term back pain. It was thrilling for all of us.

As much as I loved doing readings, I loved teaching my clients how to do them even more. To see the joy on their faces when they activated their own Divine spark was the best feeling in the world. It was like giving a blind man sight or a deaf man hearing. The students said they felt as though they were healed from some unnamed unhappiness as they got their own vibes working again. It was such a sweet feeling to put the fire back into their soul and the light in their heart, that I now understood why Charlie and Dr. Tully had been so devoted to teaching me. The difference between a psychic reading and a psychic class was the difference between giving a client a fish versus a fishing pole.

With the advent of my classes, my path deepened. I knew I was being true to my commitment to the Universe, so I began to prepare for meeting the love of my life.

Chapter 27

MEETING MY
SOUL MATE

To help the Universe along, I began to apply what I'd learned from Dr. Tully in the art of manifestation. Following the principles of spiritual law, I focused on exactly what I wanted in a mate. Dr. Tully taught me that the Universe creates what you focus on.

"Focus that is connected to the heart is the most powerful force," he said. "People don't realize that we do not create in the head, or what we think about. We create in the heart, the emotional center, because desire is the engine and spark of creativity. We create what we desire with our whole heart and soul and what we give our undivided attention to."

Therefore, if I wanted a mate, I had to *visualize* him coming into my life, and I had to do it with nonstop feeling and enthusiasm. That wasn't difficult, because it was what I desired more than anything in the world. According to Dr. Tully, imagination is a psychic magnet that attracts everything to us. We cannot create what we cannot imagine. Conversely, we always create what we do imagine. If our lives contain less-than-desirable conditions, we have to face the fact that we're imagining less than desirable conditions.

Imagining my soul mate the way I wanted to experience him became my full-time hobby. I saw him as tall, slim, and, of course, handsome. He could sing. He could dance. He was romantic. He liked to ski. He came from a large family. He loved to travel. He was single, had never been married, and was ready for commitment. He knew a lot about spiritual and psychic awareness and was comfortable with it. He was artistic. He could cook. And of course, he was looking for *me*.

Then one night I had a dream. I was making very intricate calculations on a large sheet of paper. I kept walking over to a large window and looking at the sky. Then I returned to the table to write some more. Standing across the table from me was a man, his back to me. We were both wearing gold and green robes. We didn't speak, but we were aware of each other.

Then my window disappeared. I still hadn't completed my calculations, so I needed to look out of the man's window. The man's hand touched my shoulder. I turned to look at him. His face was very beautiful. He put his finger to his lips to silence me. "Shh. Come here," he said. Then I woke up.

I lay there a long while thinking about that dream. It was more like a memory of a past life than a dream. I could almost feel the vibration from that other place and time. By morning it began to fade, and the image slipped away as the day wore on.

Weeks passed. I was busy with readings during the day, but my nights were quiet and lonely. One evening, my guides told me to call my old friend, Jimmy, and invite him to dinner. He said that he and his roommate had been painting their apartment all day, and they were both starving. Did I mind if this guy joined us? Actually, I did mind. I'd been looking forward to having a heart-to-heart talk with Jimmy, which wouldn't be possible with a stranger joining us. But I didn't want to be rude, so I agreed.

Moments later, another friend, Terry, called, and asked if I had any plans for dinner. Since three of us were already getting together, I invited him as well. Terry lived a few blocks away, so he said he'd walk right over. No sooner had I hung up then it started to rain, hard. Twenty minutes later, Terry buzzed the intercom. He was caught in the downpour and came in soaking wet. I told him not to worry. I had him remove his wet shirt, pants, and even his socks and threw them in the dryer. I gave him my robe.

A few minutes later the doorbell rang again. Jimmy and his roommate had arrived. "Come on up," I said, "I'll leave the door open. I'm still getting ready." Terry was in my bedroom waiting for his clothes. I was in the bathroom combing my hair and putting on my lipstick. Jimmy walked in. Terry and I came out at the same time, and we walked into the living room together to greet Jimmy and his roommate. To my complete shock, there stood the guy who was in my dream—the one I had been visualizing for months.

He looked a little embarrassed seeing Terry in my robe. I explained that Terry was my *friend* and that his wet clothes were in the dryer, hoping he wouldn't jump to the wrong conclusion. All the while I couldn't take my eyes off of him. This was *my guy,* the one I'd visualized, the one I was waiting for.

"Hi!" he said. "My name is Patrick Tully."

Patrick Tully. I couldn't believe that his last name was the same as my great teacher, and his first name was the same as the old friend who'd taken me to *meet* Dr. Tully. It was almost too much for me. I'd visualized lots of things in my life and had learned how to manifest quite well from Dr. Tully, but still it was hard to believe that the man I'd visualized was now standing in my apartment. I wasn't quite sure about the exact psychic dynamic that had brought him there, but something did. Did he pick up on my vibes, did we know each other in a past life, or what?

As I stood there gawking at Patrick, I wanted to laugh out loud because of my secret. But I couldn't tell him what I thought was so funny, or that I'd been expecting him. He'd think I was a nut.

Terry got dressed, and we all went to dinner. Throughout the entire meal, I completely ignored Jimmy and Terry. All I did was talk to Patrick. He told me all about himself. He'd just returned from traveling around the world for a year and had worked with the mentally ill for more than ten years. He was spiritually conscious and had devoted his life to helping the extremely sick. Needless to say, I was impressed.

Patrick was exactly as I'd envisioned him. He was 6'3", with thick, wavy, dark brown hair and a dimple in his chin. He had an impish, crooked smile; a boyish laugh; and deep blue piercing eyes that twinkled when he spoke. He was sinewy and very athletic. He loved to ski, sing, dance, and travel—all the things I loved. He really enjoyed playing, which was the perfect balance for my all-too-intense and serious life. He was from a large family like mine and had the good-sport energy that only comes from being raised in a group. The more he talked, the more I felt like I'd always known him.

The best part of our conversation was that it didn't focus on my profession. Usually, when someone found out I was a psychic, I spent the whole time explaining what that meant, and *then* they ran the other way. Patrick seemed interested, but unfazed, other than to ask me if it was draining. It was the first time someone acknowledged the *work* part and not the *weird* part of doing readings. I appreciated that.

The rest of the evening we laughed and told travel tales and had a great time. When it was time to leave, the four of us stood outside the restaurant making small talk. We weren't far from their loft apartment, so Jimmy said, "Let's walk home, Patrick." Patrick agreed, turned to me, and said, "Good night." And that was that.

I was so disappointed I could have cried, and I did a poor job of hiding my feelings.

Terry noticed right away. "You like him, don't you?"

"Of course I like him," I said, nonchalantly, "didn't you?" I would have gladly admitted I was crazy about Patrick if he'd so much as said, "Nice meeting you." But he didn't. My dream person, my soul mate, and he didn't show a flicker of interest in me. How could my vibes have been so wrong? What a letdown.

One surefire way to knock your intuition out of operation is to get your emotions stirred up. I discovered that it was nearly impossible to be psychic and be so invested in the outcome. Every time I tried to psychically tune in to Patrick, I hit a brick wall. I was left to merely guess what was up with him. *So this is what it must feel like not to be psychic,* I thought. *How awful.*

Days passed and I didn't hear a thing from him. Absolutely *nothing.* I knew that this was the guy I'd visualized, but just to be sure I went back to my journals and reread my entries.

> **Tall:** Patrick was 6'3".
> **Good-looking:** I know it's subjective, but he was subjectively good-looking to me.
> **Single:** Yes.
> **Never married:** He'd never been.
> **Large family:** Nine children.
> **Caring:** Took care of very sick people.
> **Traveler:** Just returned from around the world.
> **Could sing:** He sang with a chorus that went to India with President Carter.
> **Understood my vocation:** I don't know if he *understood* it, but he did seem comfortable with it.
> And I *had* dreamed about him: It was *his* face.

I was completely befuddled. I tried to use every psychic skill I possessed to influence Patrick to contact me, but I had no luck whatsoever. Finally, I decided to take a drastic step and do something I'd never done before in my life—I called him to ask him out. So much for my psychic ability helping me. This time I had to use the direct approach.

As I was dialing, I realized that this was the way my life had always worked in every step of my growth—from classes with Charlie to learning with Dr. Tully to going to France to moving to Chicago. It was all the result of following my inner voice and going after my dream with my whole heart and soul. It made sense that this would be no different. I had to summon the courage to pursue what I wanted, what I dreamed of, and what my soul told me, instead of waiting for it to come to me.

I felt strong and full of conviction as I dialed. This, too, would be right. I felt it. The phone was ringing. Once. Twice. Three times.

"Hello." It was Patrick! My heart stopped.

"Hello," I said, my voice barely audible. "Is Jimmy there?" I couldn't believe I'd just asked for Jimmy. What a wimp.

"Jimmy?" he said. "No. He's at work. Who's this?"

"Uh, Sonia. Remember me?"

"Of course I do. How are you?"

"Fine," I said trying to sound cool, calm, and collected. "I was calling to invite Jimmy out for a bite to eat. Too bad he's not home. [Pause.] How about you? Are you doing anything?" I was so scared, but I had to do this.

"No, I'm free. I'd love to go out to dinner with you. When? Now?"

"Sure," I said, ecstatic that it was so easy.

"I thought about calling you this week," he said, "but I've been so darn busy between painting the apartment and going to work that I haven't stopped for a minute. Where should we meet?"

I told him I'd pick him up in my little Renault Le Car and we'd decide from there. I hung up and screamed. We had a date! And he *had* thought of me. I was so excited I nearly jumped for joy. It was clear I didn't get out much.

We had another great time, and from this first date on, we became inseparable.

After a year of constant togetherness, I asked Patrick one night as we drove home in a snowstorm, what kind of future he envisioned. I meant for him, more than for us. His job was unfulfilling, and he was frustrated and unhappy.

It must have been a sore point, because he said point blank, "I don't know, but I don't plan on any big commitments with you if that's what you mean." It wasn't, but I *had* been planning on big commitments at some point. His saying he wasn't moving in that direction really hurt. Until then, I believed that we had a future together. When he emphatically told me we didn't, it threw me totally off balance. That's not what my vibes said. That's not what my guides said either. Could we all be this wrong? I studied

Patrick to uncover the truth of his statement. He looked cold, detached, and withdrawn.

"How presumptuous," I said, angrily. "I was talking about what you at 30 want to be when you grow up because you seem so miserable. I was just exploring how you could change that."

"Oh, I don't know," he said. "I don't want to discuss it."

We didn't speak for an hour, and the tension was high. Patrick turned on the radio. When we arrived at his loft, Patrick asked me if I wanted to come up. "No," I said, and sped off.

His snide remark threw me for a loop. I thought we were setting up a life together. Apparently, he didn't. "What should I do?" I asked my guides.

"Let go," they said. I knew they were right. I'd observed enough love affairs while doing readings to know that if someone wanted space, there was no way another person could change that. But space or not, *I* was ready to move on and make a commitment. If it wasn't what Patrick wanted, then it didn't take a psychic to know I was wasting my time. I had to accept that and pull the plug. I couldn't bear the thought of hanging around him like some lovesick puppy, hoping he'd take me in. I had too much pride for that.

The sad part was that during the time I was with Patrick, my psychic ability soared. Feeling so peaceful and loved expanded my awareness and ability many times over to tune in to others. With him in my life as an emotional anchor, I discovered that I could really open up my higher channels. My readings were better than ever. And the number of clients I had quadrupled since I'd started dating him.

My psychic gift had begun to bloom with my mom's love and support and continued to evolve with the love and guidance I received from Charlie and Dr. Tully. But with Patrick, my sixth sense burst wide open. I could see places, name names, give very specific details that shocked and surprised my clients, and really help them grow in very concrete ways. Would ending my relationship with Patrick diminish my psychic ability? Or worse, would I lose it altogether? I was so depressed that I cried myself to sleep.

The next day Patrick called and asked if I wanted to get together after he got off work. I said yes, although I wasn't sure why, maybe to tell him good-bye. I met him at his apartment, and he acted as if the episode in the car never happened. But it did.

"Patrick, I really love you," I told him, "but obviously you and I are not heading in the same direction. I've decided to move on."

He looked genuinely surprised. "What? Like date other men?"

"Exactly."

Of course, the idea of dating was the furthest thing from my mind, but I didn't want him to know that. He was silent for a moment, then he said, "Want to take a trip together before you move on?"

His question threw me completely off guard. This was definitely not the response I'd expected. But then again, he was the most unpredictable guy I'd ever met. "To where?"

"To Cairo."

"Cairo? You're kidding."

"No, I'm not," he said with a perfectly straight face. "I've never been to Africa, and neither have you, so let's go together. One last adventure before we go our separate ways."

It was such a crazy idea I didn't know what to say. "When?" was all I could muster.

"In two weeks. That's when my vacation starts. Let's do it."

"Okay," I said. "Why not end our great love affair in Cairo. But you plan it. And I don't want to see you before we go. I've got to make plans to get along without you."

I left, totally puzzled. I wondered if Patrick had been working in a mental hospital too long, because he was acting a little wiggy. Who breaks up by planning a trip to Egypt?

Two weeks later we boarded the plane at O'Hare, first to JFK, then on to Cairo. In both locations, the plane was so full that we didn't get seats together. But I was grateful for the distance. It gave me time to think. This whole adventure was ridiculous. Why was I going to Cairo with someone who basically blew me off? I had no idea. Curiosity, maybe? Denial? Not intuition, that was for sure. Or was it?

Arriving in Egypt was like stepping into a different world. There was a mob scene at the airport, and the crowds were intense. I'd never seen any place as exotic as this. It was pungent, dense, loud, and overwhelming. A man rushed up and took my suitcase out of my hand and started walking away with it.

Patrick screamed, "Stop!" at him, and "What are you doing?" at me. He pursued the man and grabbed my suitcase back. "Sonia, never give someone your suitcase unless you know who it is." I tried to tell him the man just took it, but he'd turned a deaf ear.

Patrick led me through a sea of beggars to an ancient Datsun taxicab, and off we went to the hotel. As we drove through the streets, I fell in love with the place. It was filthy, run-down, and a cacophony of sound and color, but it was by far the most romantic place I'd ever seen. Our hotel was luxurious and elegant, and our room overlooked the Nile. From the window I could see the Pyramids in the distance. It felt like déjà vu. I knew this place somewhere in my bones, in my soul.

I looked at Patrick, and his face looked different. At first I thought it was jet lag, but then I realized it was the old, wise face I'd seen in my dream. I gazed at the setting sun and listened to the Muslim call to evening prayers from the loudspeakers all over the city. It was eerie and soulful. I was hypnotized. Finally, jet lag kicked in. I couldn't stay conscious. I fell asleep.

Patrick woke me in the middle of the night. "What? Are you all right?" I mumbled. It was pitch black outside, and I was still so tired that I felt like I was on drugs.

"Get up, Sonia. We're going to the Pyramids."

"Now? Are you crazy?"

"Yes, I am. Come on."

I forced my eyes open. There was a knock at the door. "Room service," a voice said. An arm shoved a cup of coffee through the opened door. I poured it down my semiconscious throat while still in bed.

"Why are you doing this to me? First you blow me off, then you drag me to Cairo to torture me. What's wrong with you?"

"It's a full moon, and I want to watch the sun rise at the pyramids. We can sleep later."

"Go alone and take pictures. I'm tired." I buried my head back in my pillow.

He pulled me to my feet. "Let's go! We'll be late."

I gave up, convinced that Patrick was crazy. I resentfully pulled on my clothes, including a hat, scarf, and gloves because it was January and even in the desert it was cold. We found a taxi and climbed in.

Patrick looked as happy as I'd ever seen him. "This is exciting!" he exclaimed as we barreled into a pitch-dark night across the city toward Giza.

I couldn't argue—it was. Ten minutes later we were at the Pyramids. The taxi parked a half mile away, and the driver agreed to wait for us as we bailed out into the crisp, ebony night. We walked. I was freezing. And complaining. Patrick was unfazed. He put his arm around me and said, "Isn't this amazing?" as we approached the huge black shape of the Great Pyramid. I had to agree.

We walked slowly, taking it all in. The night sky lightened moment by moment. By the time we reached the base of the Pyramid, the first sun-rays of the day broke through like a song across the sky.

"Patrick," I gasped, "look at the sunrise against these pyramids." I swung around to grab him, but he wasn't there. Then I found him—on bended knee!

Before I could say anything, he said, "Sonia, will you be my wife?"

The light of dawn burst into the sky as if on cue. Stunned, all I could manage was, "What?"

"Will you marry me? I mean, what better place to ask a psychic to get married?"

"Of course I will, you nut! And by the way, you're the most outrageous romantic in the world."

We kissed until the sun rose high. We were back to our beginnings.

Patrick and I were married in Chicago in June. I was 25. Twenty years and two daughters later, I'm still crazy about him.

God and I had carried out our agreement. I continue to work for God doing readings and teaching classes and have taken my work around the world, both in person doing workshops and through my books, which are published worldwide. And Patrick and I still love each other, which is God working for me.

Divine law combined with Divine spark has far more than fulfilled my heart's desire. It has allowed my heart to touch the world.

✳

Chapter 28

KARMA AND PURPOSE

As much as I'd like to say that Patrick and I lived happily ever after once we got married, it wasn't quite that simple. In the beginning we were very much in love and got along beautifully, spending time going on picnics and taking lakefront bike rides, visiting art galleries and museums, and undertaking other little adventures. But then real life happened.

We purchased our first house—a 100-year-old, two-story home—and naively undertook a major renovation on our own with no experience and even less money. At the same time we had two daughters, one right after the other. All of this took a severe toll on our marital nerves and our ongoing romance. We were so overwhelmed by the cost and effort of the project and the demands of caring for two infants that we found all our physical, financial, and emotional reserves completely depleted. Needless to say, this succeeded in putting out the fires of romance and left each of us wondering why the other had become so crabby and unavailable.

We went from being two free-spirited lovebirds to feeling trapped by too much work and no play. Sadly, we'd left the soft-focus, slow-motion world of romance and had entered the more difficult waters of a real-life relationship. The honeymoon was definitely over. To add to our difficulties, our youngest daughter, Sabrina, didn't sleep at night, and woke up many times traumatized by nocturnal terrors. It all added up to Patrick and me becoming so exhausted and demoralized that it was torturous. I felt as though my spirit and our love had all but lost their life. It was all either of us could do to struggle through the day without snapping at each other or breaking into petty arguments before collapsing in bed at night for what little rest we could grab before starting all over again.

One November afternoon, Patrick took the girls outside to wash the car with him, leaving me a few moments to myself. I decided to take advantage of being alone and rest. It was an especially warm day for November, so I left the window open. As I closed my eyes, I could hear all three laughing and playing in the water, having great fun.

I was just beginning to drift into a deeply needed sleep when suddenly I found myself on the ceiling looking down at my body on the bed below. I saw what looked like a counsel of Native American medicine men and women kneeling and praying over me. I was in a completely altered yet perfectly alert state, aware of everything that was going on, but I couldn't move. I heard the counsel speaking softly to each other about me, and even though I couldn't understand their language, I knew they were discussing my distressed spirit and were about to perform some sort of healing ritual on me.

There were six of them: two on each side of me, one at my feet, and one behind my head, who felt like the leader. He was dressed in a huge headdress of white and blue-green feathers and white animal skins. They were all shaking rattles made of gourds over my body while chanting and praying to restore my soul to wholeness. Even though I observed all of this from the ceiling, it was so real that I could even smell the scent of leather from the leader's skins. His eyes were closed as he chanted special prayers over me, placing his warm hands on my eyes and mouth, while the others murmured to each other as if I weren't there. I could feel my spirit reviving.

Then the leader placed his hands over my heart and blew into my nose, sharply nodding to the others as if to indicate that my healing was complete. The next thing I knew, I snapped back into my body, now looking at the ceiling from the bed. I could still feel their presence and smell the animal skins as I lay there, but they drifted away and disappeared.

Something incredible had just taken place—my body was tingling from head to toe. I was almost afraid to move because I felt so peaceful and didn't want to lose the feeling of their presence. I felt as though a parasite on my life force had been removed, and new life had been breathed into me.

I put my hand on the place where the leader had touched me and could still feel the warm pressure he made on it. Tears streamed down my cheeks, only this time not in despair as they had so many times in the past few months, but in relief and gratitude. I wasn't sure what had just taken place, but somehow I knew it happened because my soul was in trouble.

Listening to Patrick playing with the girls outside, I felt the same deep love and affection for him as when we'd first met, which seemed like a long time ago. It felt so good to have that sweetness return to my heart that it gave me hope that our marriage would survive these demanding times. I hadn't admitted to myself how hard it had been during this period, but this surge of appreciation for Patrick left me with a deep sense of relief, and I wanted to feel more of it. I said a prayer of thanksgiving to the healers.

For the next few nights, Sabrina had fitful nightmares as usual, so I went to her room to try to rock her to sleep. One night just as we were both finally dozing in the rocker after a long effort to quiet her, I had another incredible experience. I entered another reality as I had several days before, only this time at the foot of the rocker appeared two of the most luminescent, beautiful, feminine beings I had ever seen.

Both had pale electric-blue skin with a radiant glow to their faces, and eyes of pure white iridescent light. They had thick, wavy cascading hair in a rainbow of light colors that changed moment to moment and fell nearly to the floor. They wore floor-length white gossamer brocaded cloaks with shimmering gold-and-turquoise silklike trim along the edges, and heavy gold sandals over bare feet. They were so incandescent that it was hard to look at them.

I stopped rocking, mesmerized by their beauty. One of these angelic beings put her hand out, touched my face, and said, "Please continue," nodding at Sabrina, meaning to rock her. I looked at Sabrina, but she was fast asleep.

I started to rock slowly, and as I did, the frayed edges of my nerves and the shattered, sleep-deprived feeling in my body gave way to a calm and rested feeling.

They began to speak. "We are the Pleiadean Sisters," they said, "and we bring you blessings and light. We are your spiritual teachers and guides called here by your soul, and we have come to assist you in your lessons and in your life purpose."

Their presence was so intense that it fully changed my vibration, and I found myself oblivious to my body, feeling only my spirit. Stepping out of my exhausted physical self felt so liberating that I didn't want to ever return.

The guides continued to speak. "We have come to restore your vibration to balance with love and light. You have shut your spirit away from love, and you are dying. We are here to help you recover your Divine spark and recommit to your path."

As I listened, I knew that I needed them because I was really floundering. Even though I had Rose and Joseph and my other guides, I still didn't fully understand why my life had taken such a sharp turn from the joy and lightness of being and had detoured into such despair.

"Why did everything become so difficult?" I asked. "Did I make a mistake in marrying Patrick and having these children and creating this home? Is that why I'm so unhappy now?"

"You haven't made any mistakes," they assured me. "You're only this unhappy because you're entering your karma and beginning to learn your deepest soul lessons, and it is not easy to do."

"What does that mean?" I said. "Did I do something horrible that I must pay for?"—which is what many people believe karma to be.

"No, of course not," they said. "Karma simply means those lessons a soul chooses to learn in any given incarnation. All humans have karma, or lessons, and you are beginning yours."

"What lesson must I learn that I'm not learning?" I said.

"Your personal karma is to learn to love in partnership," they said, "and to create and experience a family of your own. These are new experiences for your soul, which is why they've been so challenging. In past incarnations, you have not experienced personal or family love, focusing instead on learning spiritual law.

"You have learned many of the principles of Universal Love and unconditional love in theory. With marriage, partnership, and family, one puts these theories into practice, which is very difficult to do, as you are discovering. However, this is the lesson chosen by you to learn in this lifetime.

"You began to address your karma by reincarnating in a large family. You continued by meeting and marrying Patrick and having two daughters. Your lessons continue. You must remember to attend to and nurture yourself and your partnership just as you attend to and nurture your children and the house you are building. It is easy to forget.

"You need to connect to your partner and keep your love and affection alive in all circumstances. That is the lesson of love you seek to learn in relationship and family. It is very difficult, but it is what your soul desires. Have the fun you used to have with each other, and life will return to the state of joy and balance you once knew."

The Pleiadean Sisters' advice made sense and brought me a great sense of relief and enlightened understanding. As much as I loved Patrick and my children, life with them was difficult right now, for which I blamed myself. I had admitted to close friends that I didn't know what I was doing. It was true; I didn't. But at least now I knew I was learning and making progress and wasn't a hopeless failure. My heart lifted with relief, because now I had direction. I could accept my challenges with grace, knowing what I had to do.

Fascinated, my questions continued. "Is karma the same as purpose?"

"No, they're different. One's purpose comprises those spiritual lessons a soul has already learned and now wants to share with others. Karma is those spiritual lessons a soul has *yet* to learn and desires to do so. Karma varies from soul to soul, but all souls have karma, and the root of all karmic lessons is to arrive at unconditional love for self and others."

"What if someone resists their karma?" I asked, thinking of all the clients I had who had great struggles in life and relationships. They thought that it was caused by being with the wrong person, and never that it might mean *they* had something to learn.

"Then one suffers," the angels said, "to remind one of the need to learn, not to serve as punishment. A person will be given the opportunity to learn these lessons over and over again in this life and the next until they succeed, but the lessons will never go away."

"Then what is a soul mate?" I asked, still wanting in my heart to feel, despite all our challenges, that Patrick was *my* soul mate.

"A true soul mate," they said, "is one who grows your capacity to love."

Knowing how much I had grown in my ability to love ever since Patrick had entered my life confirmed that he really was my soul mate.

"Does everyone have karma or soul lessons as well as purpose?" I asked.

"Every soul has both."

"And is everyone's karma centered in their love life?"

"Not everyone's. But many. It is always found in those areas where one experiences the most painful conditions. It carries over from lifetime to lifetime, just as purpose does. In that manner, every soul struggles in certain areas and shines in others."

Hearing this from the angels helped me see myself in a new light. I'd been feeling guilty that I was having difficulty at home, while at the same time was able to help so many in my work. Now I knew that was unrealistic. I could be strong in one, and need to learn in another, and they were both valid parts of me.

My heart eased, and my perspective broadened. I knew that the angels had come to help me relieve even more of the psychic pain people carried in their hearts, myself included. At this realization, their presence faded. They had accomplished their mission.

"Now rest," I heard. The earliest morning rays peeked through the window, bringing the dawn. I looked at Sabrina, who was sleeping deeply. I gently put her back in her crib and placed my hand lightly on her back, waiting to see if she would wake up as usual the minute she felt alone in her crib. She didn't move, her slumber deepening even more. I waited to make sure, then went back to bed.

Patrick was just waking up. "Thanks for sitting with her," he said. "I really got some great sleep. Now you rest and I'll get up and take over." He gave me a hug. It felt good. I slept until noon. When I woke up, I had a new lease on life—because now I had a plan.

The first thing I did was slow down and cut back on all the things pressuring me and keeping me from feeling good. I cut the number of clients in half, reduced my workshops to only one every other month, took the mornings off, and convinced Patrick to slow the renovation on the house way down for a while so we could start enjoying ourselves again.

I asked him to take me out once a week just for fun, and made the rule that we couldn't talk about our problems that night. It was our night off from real life and a date with romance. We went to the theater, to art galleries, and to ethnic restaurants, which had been one of our favorite pre-responsibility things to do.

We began to talk in the evening after dinner, took rides with baby seats on the back of our bikes, and alternated museums trips with and without the girls. In the face of pressing demands like fixing the plumbing, rewiring the electrical circuits, and repairing the leaky roof, we decided to make having fun together our top priority. At times this felt impossible to do. But we did it.

Life didn't turn around overnight, but it *did* start to turn around. Slowly, laughter replaced arguments, hugs replaced cold shoulders, peace replaced anxiety, and joy replaced the sorrow I'd carried in my heart. I was learning the art of relationship and family, along with true intimacy with my husband. What a challenge it was for me.

Although it wasn't easy, the effort was well worth it. I no longer felt my life was as lopsided, shining like a star in my work, but suffering deeply at home. I began to enjoy and feel good about both, and frankly, without both I knew I could never be truly happy.

Seeing what understanding my karma and purpose did for my peace of mind, I asked my Pleiadean angels to help me bring this insight to my clients. I asked them to join my other guides and help me with my readings. They agreed, and soon they began showing up in the reading room. When they did, the focus of my readings changed entirely and took on a whole new depth and direction.

Chapter 29

PAST LIVES,
PRESENT HEALING

After the Pleaidean angels arrived, my readings shifted again. With their help, I began to see past lives and how each person's karma and purpose carried over from lifetime to lifetime. The new information helped my clients transform their lives from pain and frustration to healthier, happier ones. Readings became more than just a tour of upcoming events, or even a lesson in creativity and intention. They evolved into a profound and immediate means to help heal a person's soul.

I was so grateful to be able to provide this kind of service that I knew I was beginning to express the central purpose of my own life, my soul's desire to bring about healing and joy.

The first opportunity to share this level of psychic insight occurred when a long-term client named Ruth called me for an emergency reading. She was a world-class screenwriter and movie producer and enjoyed great success. But while her professional life was progressing fabulously, her love life was a complete mess. She had one disastrous liaison after another and was miserable.

She arrived weepy and blue as always, convinced that she'd never find her true love. She looked beautiful in her vintage silk suit, but it didn't cover up the pain and humiliation she was feeling over yet another cad loving and then leaving her, minus a few thousand dollars she'd lent him "temporarily."

I seated her in my reading room and told her that I was ready to get to the bottom of the problem, if she was. I asked my guides for help, and a tremendous light filled the room. I felt the presence of the Pleiadean angels.

I looked at Ruth. Suddenly she wasn't the prim and proper woman I knew, but a lusty, busty prostitute in a king's court. She was gorgeous and sexy, the king's favorite—he spoiled her, and she enjoyed all the pleasures her position afforded. But all the while, I felt that she had no self-esteem, no self-esteem or respect from others, and worst of all, no love from anyone. What she wanted most in that life was to find true love and self-respect, but the way she went about it had to change. This was her karma and soul lesson. Feeling a little embarrassed at what I had to tell her, I took a deep breath and shared it anyway.

"Ruth, guess what? My guides show me that in many past lives you were a prostitute, and you're here now to move past that emotionally debilitating pattern and begin to experience love and intimacy in a healthier way. Back then you were sexy and gorgeous, but manipulated and lonely. Your karma is to go beyond the soul-wounding and low self-esteem of past-life behaviors and learn to value and love yourself first and foremost. This must occur before anyone else can love you the way you want."

Ruth blushed, but she wasn't taken aback. In fact, she surprised me by saying, "I knew it. What you're saying doesn't shock me at all. If you look at my movies, you'll see that most of them center on that very theme." When she pointed that out, I could see it was true. We marveled at how obvious it was now that we saw it.

"I guess you can use your own movies for inspiration and guidance," I said. "Apparently you must know what to do on some level, or you wouldn't have written them as you did. Apply what you feel to your life and not just to the screen. And like your movie heroines, you don't have to be disrespected. It's an inside job."

"I know you're right," she said. "I've felt this myself, even though we've never talked about it. It all makes perfect sense." She laughed, which was a good sign. It showed that she was healing, considering that only ten minutes ago she was in tears.

During the reading, I was also shown past lives where Ruth was a teacher, only this time she was a man, celibate and pious to balance the sexual indulgences of the other pattern. I saw that her purpose in her current life was to share what she learned and inspire the people of the world to reflect on their spiritual connection to one another—and to do it through her movies.

Ruth was achieving her purpose quite well, but she was stuck in her karma. When she no longer saw herself through men's eyes, or permitted them to use her for their own ends, her pain and loneliness would cease.

I also saw that once Ruth began to address her karma, she'd attract a soul mate, but there would be little sexual energy between them at first to avoid confusion.

"What? No sex?" she asked. "What good is that?"

"I didn't say no sex. True love will come before sex. That's all."

"Will there be any sex?"

"Eventually. But don't hold your breath, because it will take time. Just remember, you need the time to learn the difference between sex and love and to change your past habits. And another thing, don't give any man any more money."

After the reading, Ruth's love life improved dramatically. She got rid of all the "user-loser" men, as she called them, and two years later she met a renowned musician who had as much acclaim in his profession as she had in hers. Slowly, over time, their affection deepened. So slowly, in fact, that she didn't know if it was a blossoming love affair or just a great platonic friendship. It didn't matter. It felt real, true, and good and made her happy. Their love grew, and their romance is now budding. And her career keeps expanding at light speed as she continues to fulfill her purpose.

Shortly after, I read for another regular client, Mary Ann, a high school principal in a western suburb of Chicago, who had won several awards for her school's record of excellence. Mary Ann was married to a very loving man named Bruce, who worked at Sears as a salesman in the auto department.

Her deepest desire and the only thing missing in her life was a baby. She and her husband had failed to conceive, even after trying every fertility means possible for the past five years.

At the reading, Mary Ann bombarded me with a half dozen questions all at once. "Sonia, we've given up on fertility. We've decided to adopt, if it's right. What do you think? Is this the right decision for us? And will we succeed in getting the baby we want? And since I'm asking a million questions, why do you think I could never get pregnant in the first place?"

My guides filled my room and showed me that Mary Ann had many past lives assisting people who were dying. These were extremely debilitating lifetimes, and as a result she'd become weak and sick and even at times died of the very illnesses she was trying to help others endure. In this lifetime, her karma was to stop rescuing others and allow them to love and give back to her. This is why she was to get her baby from another, an incredible gift of life. Learning this from the reading, an adoption made perfect sense to her as part of her karma.

Mary Ann had been a powerful leader in past lives as well, and her purpose now was to bring her gift of leadership to others. Being an educator served her purpose perfectly, which is why she did so well in her leadership role in school.

I told Mary Ann that she was furthering both her karma and purpose by allowing herself to adopt a baby and by being an advocate for high educational standards.

She was ecstatic. "I'm so excited to think we'll be given a baby. I can hardly believe it."

"Remember," I said, "trust and let go. Allow the Universe to handle the details, and don't force anything."

"I understand," she assured me. "After all, what a great lesson to learn, to let myself accept gifts. How hard can that be, right?"

In less than a month, she and her husband made contact with a pregnant teen in Indiana who agreed to adoption just as Mary Ann had envisioned, and an agreement was made.

She called month after month to tell me about their progress and that everything was going perfectly. Then one night, everything changed. My phone rang frantically off the hook at midnight—it was Mary Ann calling, and she was hysterical. "She changed her mind!" Mary Ann screamed. "She changed her mind!"

I was shaken to hear her sounding so out of control.

"Call her and tell her it's my baby, Sonia," Mary Ann insisted. "You have to tell her because you told me it would work out."

"I can't, Mary Ann," I replied quietly, my heart pounding as I witnessed her pain.

"What do I do?" she cried in anguish. "What do I do?"

"Let go, Mary Ann," I said quietly. "You have to let go."

"No! It's my baby!"

Again I said softly, "Let go for now. I don't know how or why, but my guides tell me you must let go and trust. This is your lesson."

"I hate you. I believed you," she hissed and slammed down the phone.

All I could do was pray. I still knew that somehow this wasn't the end. Mary Ann would have her baby, just not the way she wanted it to happen.

A month passed. One morning Mary Ann called. She asked if she could come over right away. She had to see me now. She arrived, eyes shining with tears, carrying a gorgeous baby girl no more than ten days old.

When I saw her with that beautiful baby, I burst into tears of joy myself.

"Mary Ann," I asked, "who is this?"

"My baby."

"But how?"

"A week ago I got a call," she said. "It was the young woman who was pregnant. She said she fled from me when she did because I was so needy and pushy that she couldn't stand it. She said she wanted to do the right thing, but neither her parents nor I had shown any concern about her feelings. She'd spent the last month only with her boyfriend. Together they decided that in spite of my pushiness, it was still the best thing for both her and the baby to go through with the adoption. So they called me.

"Sonia," Mary Ann said, "when you told me that my karma was to let go of control and learn to receive and allow the Universe to give back to me, I thought it would be easy. But I was only kidding myself. I was still trying to control everything. It was only when that beautiful young girl kicked me out and made me let go that I began to learn what that really meant."

After she left, I said a rosary in gratitude for how it had all worked out. I especially thanked God and my guides that I didn't lose faith even when Mary Ann had.

A month later, Mark, also a long-term client and student of mine, contacted me for a reading. An accomplished architect and considered one of Chicago's most eligible bachelors, Mark was also gay.

Raised in a very strict fundamental Christian background in Omaha, Mark hid his sexuality from everyone—especially his parents, who Mark felt would disown him if they knew. Consequently, he felt that being gay was inherently wrong, and he hated himself for it. In spite of his self-loathing, Mark was a very generous and loving man who devoted time to raising large sums of money for many charities, particularly those that focused on world hunger.

Although Mark worked tirelessly at his job and his philanthropic endeavors, he was tormented by his sexuality and his need for love. He was a saint by day, a sinner by night. He was a model figure at the top of Chicago's social and financial ladder, but behind closed doors he was sexually promiscuous and irresponsible, engaging the sexual favors of prostitutes and one-night stands. And so he contracted HIV.

Mark's spirit weakened, and so did his body. In the fall of 1996, when he was 43 and in a state of self-imposed isolation, he developed a full-blown case of AIDS. He came back for another reading as he began to seriously

211

deteriorate, tortured by his illness as well as his intense emptiness. To make matters worse, he finally told his parents the truth about being gay, and they *did* turn their backs on him, just as he'd predicted.

If there was ever a reason to uncover a person's karma and purpose, it was to help bring some psychic healing to Mark. As I lit the candles in preparation for his arrival, I asked all my guides and angels to come to the rescue so he wouldn't have to spend another minute in such misery.

When I opened the door, I was shocked to see him looking so wasted and frail. He looked like the incredible shrinking man inside his beautiful suit. He moved very slowly and had trouble breathing. I patiently watched him take three minutes to walk the 20 feet from the door to the reading room. I wondered how he'd managed to get here in a taxi.

Taking his seat, too weak to hold in his pent-up and gnarled emotions anymore, all Mark could do was break down and cry. Filled with love and compassion for his soul, I prayed for light and love to surround us before I began.

The Pleiadean angels arrived, filling the room with brilliant light. They showed me that in a past life, Mark was a Spartan warrior and athlete who had mastered physical excellence. He was an object of admiration and sexual desire, but he was never viewed or treated as a person with a heart or soul, nor did he view or treat others in a loving light.

They said that his karma in this lifetime was to break this pattern of isolation and superficiality and learn to connect with his and others' spirits in a heart-based and loving way. This is why he was so torn about his sexuality—not because he was gay, but because his past sexual experiences were devoid of love, which was destructive to his soul. A further karmic lesson was to accept that he *was* a soul, and a loving and beautiful one at that, and to take the risk of being vulnerable and human with others. When he understood that he was a soul, his spirit would heal, and he'd be free from his pain.

The angels said that Mark had also spent lifetimes as an agricultural expert and a structural engineer. Again he focused exclusively on the physical plane, but to far greater ends. His purpose in this life was to share his talent for creating beautiful public spaces that improved the quality of life for everyone. He was fulfilling his purpose very well through his work, which his success reflected.

He was struggling, however, with his karma, and had made only modest progress up till now. "It is not too late to make strides," the angels said. "The minute you begin to accept the truth that you are a loving spirit and allow others to love and support you as a vulnerable and valuable human being, your karma will be lightened."

Mark responded, "That Spartan stuff sounds right. I've always been obsessed with physical perfection. I guess I should have learned to let that go by now before I die." He sobbed uncontrollably.

"You can start with me," I offered. "I see you for who you are, and I love and accept you completely. I can be loving and supportive now if you let me."

"You don't find the idea of being near me repulsive?' he asked through his tears.

"Not at all," I said. "It would be my privilege to be with you and help you during this time. And if you let me, I'll hold your hand and walk you to Heaven when it's time to go there."

"What do you mean?" he asked. "Me? To Heaven? That's a laugh!"

"No, it's not. As children of God, we all go to Heaven eventually, after as many lifetimes as it takes to learn that it's our home. When it's your time to cross over, I'm going to hold your hand and walk you in, and I'm not going to let go until you get there."

He closed his eyes and quietly said, "Thank you."

Two months later, Mark's nurse called and told me he was near the end. I rushed to his condo where I found him barely breathing. I held his hand as he drifted in and out of consciousness. We sat like that for the next three hours. Then he shuddered, his eyes still closed, and he faintly whispered to me, "I see the angels, Sonia. Just as you said I would. I see them." He exhaled and breathed his spirit into their loving embrace.

For a brief moment, the room filled with a twinkling radiance. I knew it was the angels waving to let me know that he was now in their care.

Then all went dark, save for the soft light by the bed, and I understood that his spirit had departed. I breathed a sigh of relief. Mark was safely home. I got up, called the nurse, and went home.

Chapter 30

PASSING THE TORCH

After three years, Patrick and I finally finished the renovation of our home, and slowly but surely, life eased into a calmer, less stressful day-to-day existence. The girls continued to grow, and Sabrina's nocturnal struggles subsided, especially after my guide Rose advised me to place her in the same bed as her sister, Sonia. Giving away their two cribs and replacing them with a double bed did the trick. Sonia's calm, grounded vibration had a tremendous healing effect on Sabrina's more hypersensitive energy, and the two of them giggled themselves to sleep every night, leaving us all more rested and peaceful in the morning.

Patrick took a new job at the Chicago Merchandise Mart that same year, selling gifts and Christmas ornaments, which suited him well. I settled into a routine of doing two or three readings every morning while our daughters were in preschool and kindergarten, followed by afternoons running errands, going to the park with the girls, or occasionally visiting friends. I still taught psychic classes every other month and even invited Patrick to teach my students how to meditate as a way to stay connected with him, while staying on track with my purpose and love.

It was a constant struggle to juggle all the pieces of my life—keeping both my karma and purpose in balance and my life more or less working. All the while, I freely shared my psychic world with my daughters. I told them about our guides and angels and the world of spirit and vibes, and how loved they were. It was as much a part of their lives as their dolls and their Play-Doh.

My greatest challenge was not to overwork, because the demand for readings and classes increased over the years, as did my passion for my soul's assignment. My work was never done, and I never tired of it. In addition, I was given a new directive from my guides: to write books based on my training and experience to further help others connect to their psychic sense. It was both a provocative assignment and a new creative outlet, and I loved it more than any other.

Thus, with my all-consuming purpose, the challenging karma of mothering my two small daughters, keeping my romance with Patrick alive and healthy, and writing in my free moments, my life was filled to over-flowing. The only piece still left to address was finding an occasional moment or two of privacy, just for me.

One morning I was standing at the kitchen stove cooking CoCo Wheats for the girls' breakfast. They sat several feet away at the breakfast table stacking LEGOs and playing with naked Barbie dolls, and I felt an overwhelming need to be alone and get away from everything and every-one for a while. I'd reached a psychic saturation point, and as Charlie had warned me could happen from time to time, my nerves were overloaded. I needed a rest.

I wanted nothing more than to turn off my radar for the day and take a psychic breather. I didn't want to think about readings. I didn't want to plan my classes. I didn't want to converse with my guides or write another sentence about connecting to the other side. And I didn't want to be around anyone. Not even my family.

As I watched Sonia poke Sabrina in the eye with her Barbie's foot, I had an intense urge to cancel everything on today's to-do list and play hooky. I just wanted to go shopping by myself for new sheets and towels. My energy buoyed by the thought, I decided to do just that. Continuing to stir the CoCo Wheats and pouring a huge glob of Hershey's chocolate syrup into the mix to sweeten it out of guilt for wanting to ditch the kids, I secretly plotted my escape.

Mentally scanning my roster of teenage baby-sitters, wondering who would be available on such short notice on a Saturday morning, I shot a glance the girls' way and smiled, trying to hide my intentions. No sooner did I catch Sabrina's eye than she looked straight at me and said decisively, "Mom, I'm going shopping with you. I'm not staying home." Then Sonia piped up. "Me, too! I need new sheets for my bed, too. I want Little Mermaid sheets."

Busted, all I could do was laugh. Who was I kidding to think they weren't as psychic as I was? Why wouldn't they be? We finished breakfast and headed for the mall. Given how impressed I was with their tuning in to my vibes, they deserved to come along.

The girls' psychic antics continued. The following year, Patrick and I were getting ready for Christmas when a friend from the Mart called him excitedly saying they were getting rid of samples from their showrooms the last two days before Christmas. He said that he needed to unload a life-size Italian harlequin doll priced at over $500 wholesale and was practically giving it away at minimal cost. Months earlier, Patrick had seen the doll and had mentioned how beautiful it was and how much he thought little Sonia would love it. It was true, she would. She had two small harlequin dolls already and treasured them. The big doll was out of our budget then, but with the showroom clearance, it was a steal.

We quickly agreed to buy it and surprise Sonia for Christmas. We hatched a plan to hide it in Patrick's car trunk until Christmas Eve and then sneak it under the tree after the girls were asleep.

Patrick brought it home and stashed it in the trunk. Delighting by Sonia's upcoming surprise, I entered the house and started to make dinner, when I noticed the girls whispering to each other and laughing.

"What's up with you two? What's so funny?"

Looking as though they'd just got caught with their hands in the cookie jar, they squealed uproariously but refused to let me in on the joke. An hour later, after their bath, as I was tucking them in bed, Sonia pointed to her harlequin dolls and blurted out, "Mom, I want a doll just like that, only as big as me, for Christmas!"

My eyes popped wide open at this, not believing she was tuning in to her big surprise hiding in the car.

Stifling a smile so as not to give it away, even though her vibes were exactly right on target, Sabrina piped in, "Yeah, just like the one in Dad's trunk!" And they both fell over each other laughing as they let the psychic cat out of the bag. I burst out laughing, too. Playing Santa with these two was like hiding a rhinoceros in the living room.

"Good night, girls," I said, regaining my composure, hopelessly trying to keep up a front. "You never know what Santa will bring. It's a surprise."

"And what Daddy will bring, too," they said in unison.

It was a very merry, if not surprising, Christmas that year.

217

And so our spirit-full life continues. Today we live in a beautiful, old renovated three-story Victorian house on Chicago's north side in a quiet, friendly neighborhood where everyone knows everyone else. In that house lives Patrick; the girls; Miss T, our dog; and me . . . and, of course, angels, saints, guides, dead Romanians and now Irish relatives (from Patrick's side) who are just passing through.

My parents are alive and well in Denver, enjoying good health, peace of mind, and the ease and flow of life without seven kids underfoot. My siblings are scattered about the country, each trusting their vibes and following their heart's desire by working for themselves. Neil, Bruce, Noelle, and Soraya are designers and artists. Stefan is an engineer and consultant, and Cuky is now a clairvoyant and healer. She and I even work together from time to time, offering healing workshops in Kauai, Hawaii, and having great fun in the process.

As for life in Chicago, we're busy with our lives. The girls are 13 and 14 and just entering high school. I still do readings and workshops, and continue to write books about spirit. Patrick, our grounded protector, watchdog, and all-around resident, artist, painter, and landscaper, keeps us safe and well fed and surrounded by beauty. Our black miniature poodle, Miss T, "the wonder dog," as we call her, entertains us all, even my clients.

Christmas remains my favorite holiday, and Patrick and I both love to make a big event of it. As we were getting ready for Christmas this year, I asked the girls what they wanted, not even trusting my vibes when it comes to their tastes and interests. Much to my surprise and delight, they both said they wanted only one thing.

"Will you teach us to do readings?"

Afterword

After having served as a professional psychic for more than 35 years, I'm convinced that although my psychic journey is unique, my psychic sense is not. Working as closely as I have with people, I absolutely believe that until the age of ten, all children are psychic and are in touch with the world of spirit. Then the outside world begins to interfere and they forget.

Unfortunately, being out of touch with your psychic sense is like being a cut flower in a vase. Although still beautiful, you're separated from your source of soul support and nurturing and become seriously weakened by the fact. The good news is that with a little attention and a lot of imagination and awareness, your psychic sense can spring back to life. This is because it's a natural and basic part of your spiritual makeup. Not only can your psychic sense wake up, it can even once again become the major source of guidance and direction it's intended to be.

Therefore, let my story serve to remind you of your own. You, too, have an important psychic life waiting to reawaken, and an exciting story waiting to unfold!

About the Author

Sonia Choquette is a world-renowned author, storyteller, spiritual teacher, and psychic in international demand for her guidance, wisdom, and capacity to heal the soul. She is the author of 11 best-selling books and numerous audio editions. Sonia was educated at the University of Denver and the Sorbonne in Paris, and holds a Ph.D. in metaphysics from the American Institute of Holistic Theology. She resides with her family in Chicago. Website: **www.SoniaChoquette.com**

Hay House Titles
of Related Interest

Books

Adventures of a Psychic:
The Fascinating and Inspiring True-Life Story of One of
America's Most Successful Clairvoyants, by Sylvia Browne

Born Knowing: *A Medium's Journey—*
Accepting and Embracing My Spiritual Gifts,
by John Holland, with Cindy Pearlman

*****Crossing Over:** *The Stories Behind the Stories,* by John Edward

The Lightworker's Way: *Awakening Your*
Spiritual Power to Know and Heal,
by Doreen Virtue, Ph.D.

Power vs. Force: *The Hidden Determinants of Human Behavior,*
by David R. Hawkins, M.D., Ph.D.

Spellbinding: *Spells and Rituals That Will*
Empower Your Life, by Claudia Blaxell

Card Decks

Healing with the Angels Oracle Cards, by Doreen Virtue, Ph.D.
Magical Spell Cards, by Lucy Cavendish
The Oracle Tarot, by Lucy Cavendish
Power Thought Cards, by Louise L. Hay

All of the above are available at your local bookstore, or may be
ordered through Hay House (see contact information on next page).

* Published by Princess Books; distributed by Hay House

We hope you enjoyed this Hay House book.
If you would like to receive a free catalog featuring additional
Hay House books and products, or if you would like information about the
Hay Foundation, please contact:

Hay House, Inc.
P.O. Box 5100
Carlsbad, CA 92018-5100

(760) 431-7695 or **(800) 654-5126**
(760) 431-6948 (fax) or **(800) 650-5115 (fax)**
www.hayhouse.com®

Published and distributed in Australia by: Hay House Australia Pty. Ltd., 18/36 Ralph St.,
Alexandria NSW 2015 • *Phone:* 612-9669-4299 • *Fax:* 612-9669-4144 • www.hayhouse.com.au

Published and distributed in the United Kingdom by: Hay House UK, Ltd., 292B Kensal Rd.,
London W10 5BE • *Phone:* 44-20-8962-1230 • *Fax:* 44-20-8962-1239 • www.hayhouse.co.uk

Published and distributed in the Republic of South Africa by: Hay House SA (Pty), Ltd., P.O.
Box 990, Witkoppen 2068 • *Phone/Fax:* 27-11-706-6612 • orders@psdprom.co.za

Published in India by: Hay House Publications (India) Pvt. Ltd. • www.hayhouseindia.co.in

Distributed in India by: Media Star, 7 Vaswani Mansion, 120 Dinshaw Vachha Rd., Churchgate,
Mumbai 400020 • *Phone:* 91 (22) 22815538-39-40 • *Fax:* 91 (22) 22839619 •
booksdivision@mediastar.co.in

Distributed in Canada by: Raincoast , 9050 Shaughnessy St., Vancouver, B.C. V6P 6E5 •
Phone: (604) 323-7100 • *Fax:* (604) 323-2600 • www.raincoast.com

Tune in to **HayHouseRadio.com®** for the best in inspirational talk radio featuring
top Hay House authors! And, sign up via the Hay House USA Website to receive the
Hay House online newsletter and stay informed about what's going on with your
favorite authors. You'll receive bimonthly announcements about: Discounts and
Offers, Special Events, Product Highlights, Free Excerpts, Giveaways, and more!
www.hayhouse.com®